Sperekas

Rorschach's Test
I. BASIC PROCESSES

Rorschach's Test

I. BASIC PROCESSES

SAMUEL J. BECK
University of Chicago

ANNE G. BECK

EUGENE E. LEVITT
School of Medicine
Indiana University

HERMAN B. MOLISH
United States Navy

THIRD EDITION
FULLY REVISED

GRUNE & STRATTON

NEW YORK AND LONDON

1961

Library of Congress Catalog Card No. 60-15724

First printing, January 1961
Second printing, August 1964
Third printing, September 1966

Printed in the U.S.A.   (E-B)

In Memoriam
Emil Oberholzer

CONTENTS

PREFACE

The laying of the foundations for sound, normative method in using the Rorschach test for the study of personality continues to be the purpose in this, the most extensive revision of the present volume. Recourse to the test has been spreading during the years, over ever widening areas, both as research tool and in clinical practice. It is standard equipment in many hospitals, children's clinics, and university training centers. Description of the procedures that enable the valid application of this instrument, with exemplifying samples, should therefore provide an indispensable aid to the student entering the field. It is, in fact, for the initiate in the Rorschach test—and he is also likely to be in his early growth years as clinical psychologist—that this revision is intended.

In inscribing this book to Doctor Emil Oberholzer, the writers are striking what may be called its mood chord. Oberholzer was Rorschach's closest colleague in Zürich. On Rorschach's untimely death, Oberholzer carried on the essential work of solidifying the test's psychological foundations. He tried out Rorschach's assumptions in ever more psycho-pathologic conditions, always strengthening his statistical base by enlarging the number of patients in the several conditions. It was a compulsivity that one could not but admire wherewith he always had to have his theoretic hunches confirmed by new patients and their clinical behaviors. These are the habits which, as I worked with Oberholzer, he impressed on me and which I hope to transmit to the new student.

My own experience has fully justified this disciplining in fundamentals. It is the essential *sine qua non* toward setting the test on a quantitative, and so an experimentally verifiable, basis. True, the ten ink blots are being employed in ways that deviate far from the Rorschach-Oberholzer discipline. True too that some valid results are so obtained. But these uses are not the Rorschach test. They are in many instances the examiner's qualitative judgments. At times they are the examiner's intuitive free associations to the patient's free associations to the ten ink blots. Many of these qualitative or intuitive interpretations are good, clinically accurate. But they are not the test as quantitative, statistically based instrument. This, as Rorschach explicitly states, is what he wanted to achieve. He envisaged nothing less than a truly scientific tool that reached into depth layers of the human personality.

In describing our technics, those being tried out within this orientation, a first aim has been for unequivocal clarity in presentation. With this purpose in mind, numerous examples are being offered for each kind of response and scoring principle. The worker with some experience will find new light and fresh samples of the more problematical among the Rorschach test variables. Such are DW; the variety of white space responses; and my organization activity (Z). Two of Rorschach's important concepts that have been largely neglected in American use of his test are Approach and Sequence, both of which are important diagnostically. In instances Sequence has a differentiating value. The chapter on that most important of Rorschach's discoveries, the fantasy association (M), window that it is onto the unconscious, in the main is rewritten. Exposition of the other emotion-probing variables—color, shading, vista, texture—should smooth the paths toward identifying these important test data.

The older student of the test may here twit—especially if he is familiar with the *Psychodiagnostik*—that I have myself altered Rorschach's test. I have done so, in some details. In so doing I have, I think, been more loyal to Rorschach's central intent than are those adherents who want to retain the test in the exact format published by him. To do so is to glaciate both the instrument and the principles which vitalize it. Rorschach would not have been content to freeze it in its pristine purity. He speaks at more than one point of the need for research and further testing out of his assumptions. Such changes as I have introduced have grown out of clinical-experimental testing out of his ideas. They have not deviated critically from Rorschach's original structural processing of the associational material, and they have served to confirm his own interpretive principles.

The most important new assist in this volume, we hope, will be the list of good and poor forms, F+, F−. Lead that Rorschach's *"gute Formen"* are to ego functions, this concept is a corner-stone in his test. It follows that a stable guide list of F+, F−, is critically essential. The responses that now make up Chapter xii are the latest compilation of such guide lines. To construct it, a representative sample of American psychologists actually collaborated. We wrote to over 1800 members then in the clinical division of the American Psychological Association, requesting them to send us responses that were presenting difficulties in scoring F+ or F−. About two hundred replied, with associations cumulative for the ten test cards. These we absorbed into our own already revised scorings. The associations in Chapter xii are thus a broad sample, well representative of experience for the entire United States. An advance though this is for this very important technic, it is not final. Such a list can never be all inclusive. However many and different the persons on whom an examiner has used the test, the probability is always high that his next subject will produce a totally new association, one for which there is no exact precedent. Any F+, F− list is therefore always tentative. In this it accurately reflects the fluidity of this instrument, as fluid as the variability of human mentalities which it probes.

A great amount of labor was requisite in carrying on the correspondence with our fellow psychologists and organizing their answers so that they could be studied in relation to our known norms. For taking on and successfully completing this assignment, I am indebted to our colleague author, Dr. Eugene E. Levitt, Chief of the Section of Psychology, in the Department of Psychiatry, Indiana University School of Medicine. He enlisted, too, the support of his department for the administrative help that this task required, thus facilitating it immeasurably. We acknowledge our debt to the Department of Psychiatry, Indiana University School of Medicine for this invaluable aid.

Essential as is the benign attitude of the higher echelon, it is the effective cooperation at grass roots that is decisive in perfecting the final product, a typescript precise in content and pleasing to the eye. For this achievement—and I speak here for the four collaborating authors—I express our praise and thanks to two secretaries: Mrs. Bonnie L. Dorner at Indiana University, and Mrs. Marcia Cowing in the Department of Psychology in the University of Chicago.

Most gratitude of all is owing meanwhile to the 200 or so psychologists who replied to our request for their unscorable associations. Theirs has been a gracious help. They had to take time and energy out of busy days. They could look to little immediate profit for their help to us. To name them would of course go far beyond the scope of this acknowledgment. I can only express this appreciation to them in their anonymity. They know who they are. Such knowledge can itself be a compensation.

S.J.B.

Chapter I

TESTING PROCEDURE

The Test

The ten ink blot figures that constitute Rorschach's test need by now no introduction in clinical psychology. All responses reported in the present text were obtained with the figures as published by Rorschach in 1921.[27] All responses or scorings here treated were obtained with the test as an individual (not group) technic.

Preparing the Subject

It is important to have the subject, S,* in a condition that represents his usual state of relaxation. On his entering the office of the examiner, E, the latter, with all informality, asks him whether he knows anything about the Rorschach test. The answer is still almost invariably in the negative, notwithstanding the few notices that have appeared in public print. Assuming that S's age is in a range anywhere from midadolescence up, and that his intelligence is average or higher, and assuming too that the relation is a clinical one—i.e., the test findings are to be used for diagnostic purposes—E's preliminary chat is to the effect that the test is just one of many gadgets being used nowadays to understand people. By the time a person reaches the Rorschach procedure, he has already been subjected to multiple examinations and accepts this as one more. He can usually be told too that the test is more especially useful in getting at some interests that he may not realize he has, and that knowing them, E will better understand him and so be in better position to help him.

Usually S accepts the situation at this level. He may become curious about what the test will elicit, and it is essential not to use any provocative term—such as "intelligence," or even "thoughts." The term "imagination" I have, however, found innocuous. Should S ask whether the test will aid in uncovering vocational potentialities, he may be told that it sometimes does. He may be reassured as to its not being an "IQ test," though only if he asks. E never volunteers information beyond that required in S's own questioning. Should S's questions become specific, or pertinent as to critical test factors, E promises to answer them at the conclusion of the session. He may take S into his confidence to the extent of

---

* The letters S and E are used throughout this text as conventional designations respectively for subject, or person taking the test, or examiner. The relation may of course be that of patient and physician, of two colleagues, or some other.

1

explaining that it is best not to know much about the procedure until one has gone through it. S is usually ready to proceed. It helps too, for establishing the atmosphere, to have the test cards lying on the table, with stop watch, paper, and fountain pen all as part of the scene when S enters. The process of bringing these out one by one in S's presence can create tension and apprehension, with a resulting unsatisfactory atmosphere sometimes unfavorable to normal productivity in S.

INSTRUCTIONS TO S

No formula is used verbatim. The following instructions are the essence of what is said:

You will be given a series of ten cards, one by one. The cards have on them designs made up out of ink blots. Look at each card, and tell the examiner what you see on each card, or anything that might be represented there. Look at each card as long as you like; only be sure to tell the examiner everything that you see on the card as you look at it. When you have finished with a card, give it to the examiner as a sign that you are through with it.

Paraphrasing of this language may be very liberal—e.g., "The test consists of a series" instead of "You will be given" and the like. But I make no departure in essence from these directions as a standard.

It must be emphasized that the essence of Rorschach test procedure is to leave S entirely free. He makes his own selection, in each test figure, of the portion to which he reacts; any of a number of factors may determine what he sees; the content may be anything. In his test Rorschach has thus combined two sets of conditions, (a) fixed objective stimulus with (b) freedom of S.

SEATING ARRANGEMENT

Rorschach's original technic is followed. S sits in front of and with his back to E. This is told to S at the point when he is ready to begin looking at the test figures. The explanation is twofold: (a) the lighting arrangement requires it; (b) it is always done in this way. The first reason is accepted as a matter of necessity, the second as a matter of good grace. It is essential, incidentally, that the lighting should be so arranged that it does strike the test cards more directly when S sits with his back to E. Whether the lighting is daylight or artificial does not appear to have any observable effect on the results.

TIMING

A silent stop watch—accent on *silent*—is necessary. It should be graduated to one-fifth second. To measure time per response: E starts the watch when figure I is exposed to the S; he turns it off when S returns figure X, following his final free association. The record of the elapsed time in minutes and seconds is the total time, or T. Divide T by the number of scored responses, R. This is the time per response.

To measure the time per first response the examiner records the stop watch reading as he hands S each test card. When S produces his first association with scorable content, E again records the stop watch position. For example, S receives figure IV at 12' 47". He begins to say, "It looks like a gorilla" at 13' 18" and this time is noted. The time for the first response in figure IV is then 31". The time is reckoned from the point at which S begins to verbalize his associations, even though he may preface the actual content with qualifications lasting some seconds. In some instances, however, S begins to report an association, e.g., "Well, that could be"—then stops, and as much as half a minute or even more will pass before he tells what he sees. In these cases, the time is reckoned from the point when the response content was actually produced.

The Free Association Period

This is the test proper. In it, S looks at the cards and associates to them. As indicated under the instructions to be given to S, he looks at each card, one at a time. The cards are always first presented to S in the same orientation. In the cards now supplied, top and bottom are indicated on the back.

E's Role in the Free Association

S now has the first card, and begins to associate. Some subjects are so freely productive that E is hard put to it to get the record. However, many subjects will begin by asking questions, some of which may touch on critical points—e.g., "Am I supposed to look at all of it or just parts?"

The answer must be nonleading: "Anywhere at all; no matter what you see, be sure to tell me."

Less significant questions run about as follows: "Am I supposed to use my imagination, or to tell you what they remind me of?"

The answer may be, "It doesn't matter, so long as you tell me whatever they bring to your mind."

The essential need is to get S started in producing associations. The test itself takes hold from then on. S's question is not concerned with *imagination* in any technical sense. He is simply at a slight loss as to what to do and needs a push.

While E keeps himself unobtrusive, he should be ready with the next card, in order to give it to S as soon as the latter has exhausted his associations for the one he has. After S has given two or more associations for a figure, any declaration that he is through with it is accepted. But E should not hurry to remove a card and offer the next. Occasionally S will say, "That's all, I guess," but will continue looking and will produce one or more additional responses. S, to repeat and emphasize, remains free. The experienced examiner soon learns to achieve smoothness of transition from card to card.

If S returns the test card after only a single response, it is E's task to encourage him. The common formula is, "But most people see more than one thing. Look at it a bit longer." And even the incentive in a phrase such as, "Give yourself plenty of opportunity," is permissible. But under no circumstance may S be aided by any suggestion, such as mention of cloud pictures, and much less by having attention called to any factor of critical significance, e.g., whole or part, color or shape, people or animals.

Encouragement is progressively reduced as the test proceeds and is entirely discontinued after figure V. If S, in figures VI to X, still "sees nothing," E simply waits in silence. Eventually, responses usually emerge.

Card Turning

Nothing is said in the instructions about turning the card. If S asks about turning, he is of course informed at once that he is free to do so. Some subjects do not ask but start to turn, or do so and then return the card to the original position. In these instances it is permissible to encourage: "It is all right to turn the card if you want to." E must be alert as to S's behavior in this respect. He may encourage any real trend to turn, however slight the actual motion. But he must not originate the suggestion as to turning.

Rejections

In a small percentage of subjects, there are full rejections of one, but seldom more, of the figures. Any tendency to reject is countered by E with the encouragement indicated for underproductive subjects. The encouragement is necessarily stronger. I try to make S hold the test figure for a minimum of two minutes before permitting rejection.

Withdrawing Test Cards

A few subjects will continue free association without let-up. Barring extraordinary clinical circumstances, such as require full communication from S, I now remove a test card from S after ten minutes. This must of course be done unobtrusively, diplomatically, so as not to prejudice freedom of productivity in the figures following.

The Inquiry

This is as important a procedure as the free association itself. Without the information obtained in the inquiry, E cannot know how to process the responses and is not in a position to pattern out the personality structure. The inquiry commences immediately after S has given his final association in figure X. Each card is returned to S singly, and he is asked about each response in order. This is time-consuming, especially in a lengthy record; but the Rorschach is a time-consuming instrument. The task in the inquiry is to ascertain (a) what S selected to react to, and (b) what determined his percept—i.e., form, color, movement, light values, or a combination of these—and frequently to clarify the content itself.

E's language in starting the inquiry continues to be informal, although following a standard pattern: thus, "Now I have a question or two to ask concerning some of the things you saw."

S is usually relieved on realizing that the figure he has been looking at is the final one. He may of course light a cigarette or otherwise relax. Usually, too, it is well to suggest to S that he turn his chair around. The face to face situation facilitates confidence and the easy conversation necessary toward eliciting the needed information. But standard procedure is not essential, and with some subjects, i.e., suspicious or resistive patients, it is advisable to proceed with the inquiry at once. Any break may set the resistiveness going again.

In regard to the portion selected, the first question is, "Where is the butterfly?" or whatever it may be. If S's indication leaves E in doubt, S is asked to trace with his finger or with any pointer other than pencil or pen. In figure III it is best to ask S at once to trace the *human figure* (assuming that he has seen it), in order to establish his inclusion of D 5. In figure VI, if the *animal skin* has been seen, the tracing technic most satisfactorily clears up whether the whole or D 1 was intended. In figure VII, the *two women*, as D 1, D 2, or W, are best clarified by tracing. In regard to some very fine or unusual Dd, the problem is as likely to be that of S himself finding it again as of E's identifying it. In general, identification of the stimulus selected, whether the whole, a D, or the more common Dd, does not offer serious difficulty.

The problem is a harder one in respect to the determinants, most especially in the color and movement responses. In regard to color, it is necessary to know (a) whether color entered into the response at all, and (b) if it did, to what extent form participated, if at all. The first question here is, "What about this [e.g., figure VIII, D 2] reminded you of a butterfly?" or, "In what way does this look like a butterfly?"

The answer we want may be forthcoming: e.g., "because of the shape" or "the color and the shape."

E then asks, "What first made you think of the butterfly?"

This line of inquiry will elicit the desired information in many subjects. But in a considerable number of instances S is not informative. Whatever the form of the question, the reply is some variation of the first response: "It looks like it." As a last resort, in order to rule color out, or in, Rorschach advises the critical question, "Suppose this were exactly the same shape as now, but gray or black; would you still think it a butterfly?"

The usually instant and emphatic replies, either affirmative or negative, are evidence that the testimony is dependable. As will be seen (chap. x), we are at the mercy of S's introspective evidence. Hence, skill in questioning is critical. The importance of remaining nonleading cannot be overaccented.

The light response is quickly cleared up in the case of most subjects. "It's an x-ray" because "it's black," or "clouds" because "gray," or "snow" because "white." A little more questioning is required in vista, but there too the answer is usually definite: the "mountain" is "far up" or the "lake" and "hills" are seen "way down below." General experience is also more definitive here, as will be seen in the chapter on light-determined reactions including vista; and the *texture* determinant, which I am now scoring.

Movement in most instances is obvious, but in some a very deceptive problem. S's language may be, "The men are pulling; the girls are dancing; the priest is kneeling." But in the Rorschach test not everything that moves is movement; this topic is more fully discussed in chapter VIII. Within the range of the principles there stated, the movement response may be clear. But the few instances in which it is not certain prove very hard to establish as M or F. The response in figure II may be "two men" (either lateral half).

E asks, "In what way are they like men?"

S replies, "They look like it."

E asks, "In any special way?"

S says, "They're shaped like men."

E asks, "Anything else about them that recalls men?"

The reply is still indecisive, and E now tries the question, "Are they any particular kind of men?"

Any specific vocation, e.g., "clown," immediately opens an avenue for further inquiry. It should be added that the more that questioning is needed, the less is the likelihood of M. The individual with M potentiality is mentally energetic and brings it to the surface quickly. In some instances in which I have elicited M only after much extended questioning in this way, I have scored F.

The position response, Po, is fully described in chapter XVI.

The content is usually sharpened by the time E has inquired concerning the area selected and the determinant. In talking about these, S has embellished his original response as much as he is likely to.

New Responses in the Inquiry

Some subjects will give totally new associations in the inquiry: "I see something now I did not before." These are recorded but not scored. New embellishments of the free associations are not scored, although they may influence the scoring. The "butterfly" of figure V may become "black and glossy." E here must question as to whether it was so seen in the free association. The purpose of the inquiry is, primarily, to make possible the accurate scoring of the free associations. New material is welcome but it is not the primary objective. It adds highlights to the personality picture but it is not part of the pattern.

Inadequate Response Totals

Rorschach holds that an average of less than one response per card is inadequate for diagnostic purposes. While it is possible to etch out a personality picture from some records of only ten responses, the result is likely to be incomplete. I prefer fifteen or more scorable associations. The effort to obtain more responses by stimulating *ad hoc*, after the standard test procedure, is a legitimate one. The method, in these new efforts, being no longer controlled, ranges from (*a*) simply showing the cards anew with more strenuous encouragement, to (*b*) pointing out some details, with a question as to whether they resemble anything and implicit suggestion that they do, and (*c*) actual suggestion of content, with a view to striking a responsive chord. Klopfer[16, 17] has gone further than other workers in formalizing this approach; he designates it "testing the limits."

Recording

Ordinary sheets of blank paper and a well-filled fountain pen are the only tools necessary for recording the free associations. Responses should be taken verbatim, and most examiners develop some system of shorthand. Certain abbreviations are soon acquired.

Turning of the card is indicated by the signs $\wedge$, $>$, $\vee$, $<$, the peak of the angle in each case indicating the position of the top of the card. For this suggestion we are indebted to Loosli-Usteri.[19]

Edging is behavior in which S studies the card edgewise, usually with eyes narrowed. It is an odd manner of inspecting the figure, observed frequently enough to warrant the term. Not quite so common are occurrences of other peculiar angles at which subjects will manipulate the cards or twist their heads in getting some special perspective. Holding the card at arm's length belongs here, also studying the obverse of the card, which should, however, be discouraged.

The record for the free association period would normally include also any positive behavior notes that are of interest in a psychologic test situation. One behavior manifestation which is of especial Rorschach test significance is the acting out of responses. It is likely to occur during apparent movement responses but has been observed in others. Among other behaviors are odd positions by S in his chair; obvious wanderings of the attention to objects in the room; mouth noises; and, in instances, abdominal rumblings. The specific cards at which S so behaves may be significant diagnostically and must be recorded.

For purposes of recording which blot element is selected, two methods have proved practical. The first is that of using reproductions of the ten test figures. These are available in printed form on a single sheet and are entirely workable. E needs only to mark off on the reproduction the area selected. The second is that of using numerals to identify the more common details and the rare details.* This method is faster than use of the reproductions, especially when S happens to be one of those who point to what they see. E thus may complete in the free association record some of the work belonging to the inquiry. For example, in figure II, his record might run: "two men clapping hands [W]; and down here is a butterfly [D 3]; and these two are chickens [D 2]; this [Ds 5] is a body of water with mountain masses on the side [D 1]."

For the determinants, it is best to record S's language. Without it, E will in many instances find himself at sea or at least in some doubt when he scores. For example, his record may show—e.g., figure IX— > "a landscape at twilight, on the edge of a lake reflected" (FC). As this stands, he has to score Ds FC+ Ls. But often E will be troubled by the question whether another factor, such as light variations or vista (chap. x), may not have entered in, and whether he is not scoring inaccurately. S's actual language would be a big help, and E usually wishes he had it. When the question is one of form or movement, E is even more grateful at having this verbatim testimony at hand. These considerations hold for all the response determinants; in fact, S's actual language is useful in all formal treatment of the responses.

Such uncertainties as those just cited demonstrate how important the inquiry is in obtaining a scorable test record. Hence, what the examiner does in the inquiry—i.e., *his* behavior, verbal and other—is a large factor in eliciting that behavior which we identify as S's and from which we develop out S's personality. The examiner's technics, both as he administers the test and as he conducts the inquiry, are critical for attaining the twin objectives: (a) that the associations are truly S's free ones; and (b) that

---

* The list of numerals used in this text, will be found in chapter III. Hertz[15] has published another set of identifying numerals.

the information about the associations is such that the scorings—which structuralize the whole reaction pattern—truly refer to S's mental processes.

Assuming that an examiner has trained himself to follow the same technic from patient to patient, his method is to that extent constant. His scorings of, for example, the color responses for any one person, and the differential color patterns he so obtains, have been elicited under comparable conditions by exactly the same set of stimuli. Two or more examiners who have trained themselves to follow the same technic, in the inquiry as well as in the administration, will obtain Rorschach test records that are replicated experiments. Unless examiners are so trained, the records obtained by any one are not comparable to those of another. They are not the same operations.

Deviations from Standard Procedure

The foregoing exposition presupposes that S is an individual whose age is somewhere in the range from middle childhood through adult life, but this side of senility, whose intelligence is at a level anywhere from average through the highest ranges, and whose mental health is good as judged by the criterion that he carries on efficiently in his living generally.

However, these procedures can also be followed with most patients who are mentally disturbed or even disordered. The attempt should in any event always be made to use the standard methods. But deviations are necessary. These are followed, as clinical needs dictate, but such atypical records cannot serve for study as part of a group treated statistically.

Among conditions encountered are such as the following. An elderly person in senile deterioration stubbornly remains sitting in a chair in a manner incompatible with carrying out the usual arrangements. E's requests and coaxing are without avail. The cards are presented to him sitting where he is. A full set of responses under these conditions is a real triumph. A schizophrenic keeps staring into space, or looks vacuously at E as the latter begins the usual instructions. These are best discarded, and E forces each card before S, persisting in the effort to obtain associations. It is hard work. But, surprisingly, many such patients will give full, scorable records. A depressed person will stare at the card in long silence, sigh heavily, start to return the card. Encouraged, he retains it but complains, "I can't see anything, Doctor," and possibly weeps. In the case of some such patients, silence and patience are E's best technic. In some instances, encouragement, always kindly, is in order. Essentially, all depressed patients give complete records.

A feebleminded subject looks at figure I, says, "A tree," and turns to other environmental stimuli, possibly talking about them and other irrelevancies. His attention is forced to the test card with, "But look at this and tell me what you see."

If S repeats, "A tree," it is permissible to ask:

"What else do you see?"

Here is one group with whom a stern voice, and a strong attitude, are in order.

Similar distractibility is encountered in manic excitements and in many organic conditions. When these are acute, both the standard seating arrangement and the formal instructions are dispensed with. The job is to get the associations and it is "catch as catch can." The timing of first responses to the figures in these groups, as also in the feebleminded and in some schizophrenics, is not dependable and can be dispensed with.

Adult neurotics occasionally present serious difficulty in the inquiry. Often, these are persons who have been very productive. The test appears to stir up their tensions, and they show signs of exhaustion in that they are irritable, evasive, or overtly antagonistic. E has no choice but to persist, using all clinical diplomacy but firmly reaching for his information. No deviation from standard procedure is necessary.

A young child comes into the examining room bubbling over with the excitement and eagerness characteristic of his age. He wants to "play games." There is no point in running through the instructions. If the child is very young, the usual seating arrangement can be dispensed with. The procedure is to get the child comfortable, give him figure I, and ask him what he sees.

Judgments as to deviations in formal procedure will depend of course on the clinical situation. Necessarily, E's experience with the kind of personality to be tested will be a factor in the freedom or rigidity with which he adapts the test to the person.

AGE FACTOR

If a person can see and talk, he can take the Rorschach test. I have given it to children as young as two years of age and to adults in their late sixties. Rorschach reports tests of a woman of 80 and of a man of 78. In research in geriatrics at Michael Reese Hospital we have obtained adequate Rorschach tests from persons in their late eighties and nineties.

ABOUT TEXT FORMAT

For the sake of typographic relief, verbatim response material in the following chapters is shown within single quotation marks. On occasion, a verbatim response may appear italicized instead, for specific emphasis.

In regard to position of the card, $\wedge$ orientation is always implied when no other is indicated. In clarifying some selected responses, it has been necessary to use the designations "upper half" and "lower half," i.e., of the whole or of some detail. The terms "upper" and "lower" are always with reference to the card in the original or $\wedge$ position. S may actually be holding the card in another position at the time—thus the response record, figure IV ($\vee$) 'a castle between two crags,' entire lower half. It is lower half when the card is $\wedge$, though as S holds the card it is actually upper half. Communication is facilitated by having one fixed point of reference. The D and most Dd are identified by their appropriate numerals.* Since the figures are symmetric, there are two each of nearly all D and Dd. The text does not state whether the D in question is that on the right or on the left. An early effort to show this was abandoned, after it was found that it encumbered more than it clarified. The reader is advised to study both D of the same number; a response not clear in relation to one can be patterned out in the homologous configuration.

* The symbols D and Dd are used as both singular and plural. This usage has been found to serve better than would "D's" and "Dd's," since it avoids confusion with the symbols Ds and Dds representing white space reactions. Whether singular or plural is implied is clear from the context.

CHAPTER II

THE WHOLE RESPONSE: W

The first judgment in scoring an association refers to the blot area selected. Since S is free to select any portion of the test figure, the possible selections fall into two broad categories: wholes and parts. Concerning W, the rule is simple. W is whole. To score W, *all* portions of the blot figure must have been attended to by the S. A response is either W or not W. The different modes whereby S's arrive at their percepts of the W does not alter this rule. But there are differences. To paraphrase a well-known *bon mot*: some W are more W than others.

'Bat' or 'butterfly' for the entirety of figure V is the simplest and most common W. Among others are 'bat' or 'butterfly' for figure I; 'animal skin' or 'rug' for figure IV; and 'animal skin' or 'rug' for figure VI.

In each of these, S has reacted to the whole figure as an individual unit. This is Rorschach's *simultan Ganzantwort*—the instant whole. Usually, these responses are given quickly—seldom with much qualification, i.e., nothing more than 'it looks like' or 'it could be.' Also, S is in essentially no doubt concerning the parts (of whatever he happens to be seeing) as belonging to the entire percept. The form of the 'animal,' 'man,' or whatever it may be, is satisfying enough for him to find it unnecessary to criticize and to exclude component details. In evaluating the responses, E never finds himself uncertain about scoring these as W. This holds true even though in the inquiry S attempts to qualify or to reject some details. Examples follow:

Figure I

'Airplane'; ∨ 'crown'; ∧ 'child's glider'; 'coat of arms'; 'leaf'; 'map'; ∨ 'pagoda'; 'scarab'; ∧ 'United States seal'; 'vampire'.

Figure IV

'Ape'; 'Buddha'; 'bush': ∨ 'crest' (i.e., on official seal); 'fish'; ∨ 'flower'; 'head' (of one of the 'horned animals'); 'human' (any form, frequently in fur coat); 'insect'; 'lyre'; 'dancing phantom'; 'wineskin.'

Figure V

'Bird'; 'bridge'; 'flattened-out insect'; 'Chinese kite'.

Figure VI

'Airplane'; 'flying duck'; 'fan'; 'fish' (various forms of); 'melting ice sheet'; 'Japanese lantern'; 'shield'; 'star'; 'turtle'; 'wagon cart' (Louis XIV style).

The unequivocally simple or instant W is best found in figures I, IV, V, and VI. These are decidedly "easy" percepts, involving no synthesizing or analyzing effort on the part of S. They may well be termed the "lazy W." In diagnostic value, insofar as they reflect any capacity for complex achievement, they stand nearer to the more common unbroken D than to the more difficult W.

Qualitative differences in intellectual functioning inhere in these different modes, i.e., the instant and complex W, the additive W, the simple (lazy) W. But for purposes of scoring, and so for counting purposes in the structural summary, the W is a W. To be sure, the S has not read the textbook—thankfully—and it is not always clear whether he is including the entire test figure. This is a question to be handled at the time the test record is obtained; it should not still be one at the time of scoring. Experience eventually develops the skill by which the examiner reduces to a vanishing minimum the number of instances in which he cannot make this judgment with confidence.

Figure VII is of special interest in exemplifying both kinds of W. This figure consists of details connected at narrow junctions. It lends itself to a breaking-up and reorganizing activity. Examples of simple W in this figure are: 'bowl' (for flowers); 'cloud' (i.e., single cloud); 'coat of arms'; 'collar' (for woman's dress); 'fireplace'; 'sea growth'; 'mask'; 'dissected mouth of insect'; 'pie crust'; 'eroded rock'; 'earthenware vase.'

The organizing activity shows up in the following: 'isles of the sea, with all those little bays and inlets to explore.'

'Pieces of stone, grown together . . . touched together; nothing else could be like that.' Here is an association in which S presents evidence—evidence more valuable because he is scientifically naïve—of how the organized whole gives meaning to the part: 'nothing else could be like that,' i.e., they are stones because 'touched together.' Before this unity was grasped, the pieces were without identity, simply rounded pieces of something.

Of like character, although seen by a man anything but naïve, in fact an outstanding scientist, is 'formless pieces of modeling clay,' all taken as a unit. Still others, in all of which the W is instant, but with a spilling over of organizing activity, are: \/ 'like smoke coming from chimneys and meeting'; /\ 'a rock opening up'; /\ 'something torn in half . . . torn paper'; 'balls of cotton'; 'beads and a bracelet'; 'pieces of a puzzle.'

Figure VII illustrates thus a transition phase of the W process. It evokes (a) the simpler, instant wholes, resembling the lazy W of figures I, IV, V, and VI, and (b) that more complex organization process in which the larger whole contributes meaning to the part. This is the kind of W more characteristically evoked by figures II, III, VIII, IX, and X. These are internally well broken up, either by white spaces or by the contours of the component details. The W seen in them are therefore of the variety unloosing a more vigorous organizing energy. W resembling the instant species are produced in these figures, but they are less frequent, and question of organization can usually not be excluded. But this activity is not always as clear as in the true organized W (cf. chap. VI). For diagnostic purposes, all W in these figures are treated alike, i.e., as representing Rorschach's "achievement drive" (*Leistungswillen*). The examples following illustrate (*a*) W of the apparently instant kind and (*b*) those in which some organization process can be detected.

Figure II

"Sea animal'; "butterfly'; 'impressionistic drawing'; 'fire moth'; 'flowerpot'; 'primitive organism'; 'vertebra'; 'cross section of brain,' in which the white space is a factor.

Figure VIII

'Basket'; 'biology illustration'; 'coat of arms'; 'flower'; 'headdress'; 'brick of ice cream'; 'color print of the West'; 'coral reefs.'

Figure IX

Here the proportion of W's that are clearly instant is smaller than that of the W tending toward organization. Among the few observed are: 'crab shell'; 'wallpaper design'; 'dragonfly'; 'cross section of flower'; 'skull in wax'; 'x-ray.' It is easier to adduce W that contain in them the organization element: 'gladiolus'; 'islands connected'; 'map'; 'goblin mask'; 'palette'; 'marine plant'; 'scenery.'

Figures III and *X* are the least integrated and offer the greatest resistance to being perceived as wholes. In figure X a few W are found that group under this instant variety. Examples are: 'butterfly'; 'cobweb'; 'oriental design'; ∨ 'fan'; ∧ 'microscopic stain—or tissue'; 'stage decoration'; 'pliers.'

However, some organization process (chap. VI) is always implicit in the W in this figure. Most W in figure X are in fact very difficult achievements, as will be seen from the examples in chapter VI.

So far as figure III is concerned, every true W involves organization effort of a difficult order. That is, even the apparently instant W are organized ones.

It occasionally happens that an apparent W in the free association is cut down in the inquiry as the S critically alters his first percept.* However, I still score W, following the general rule for all scorings that what

* Klopfer[16] identifies this as a separate scoring category, the "cut-off W" (see below, p. 23).

S says in a free association, i.e., unconstrainedly, takes precedence over what he tells me in the inquiry. A change in the W percept is particularly noted in certain of the instant associations in figures I, IV, V, and VI. S's criticism in these cases, when given in the inquiry, appears to be retrospective or, better still, reactive—i.e., it is self-criticism in reaction to the questioning by E. This kind of rejection is usually found in the anxious; even the most impersonal inquiry puts them on the defensive. When, in the inquiry, S refers to a W that in the free association was an apparent D, the examiner's problem is to establish whether S is clarifying what indeed he had intended as W in the free association or whether his W is new in the inquiry. It takes skill on the part of the examiner, but again it is a skill which experience teaches.

Figure IV

'It looks like a bat,' excluding D 1 from W.

'Looks like a gorilla, doesn't it?' excluding D 1, stressing D 4 as hands, and scored W.

But compare this example with, 'These have got feet [D 2]; if it had a head it would look like a gorilla,' specifically excluding D 1, and scored D.

It may seem a contradiction to call the one W and the other D. But it will be noted that in the first of these instances S is reproducing one of the conventional wholes for this figure; in the second he is never identifying anything but details. A similar case in figure V was, 'That part looks like butterfly feelers,' D 2; and 'that part looks like his legs [D 3] and that part looks like his wings,' D 4; and S specifically denied reacting to the whole as butterfly. Scored D.

In this connection, responses such as the following are instructive:

Figure I

⋀ 'A butterfly . . . it has wings and a body; has two horns or claws, some kinds of hands or feet, or something. ⋀ I don't know what that thing [Dd 31] is . . . it must be his tail.' S himself verbalizes some dissatisfaction as to the whole, but spontaneously resolves his doubts in favor of W. Here is unsolicited evidence that criticism of details and exclusion of them is consistent with reaction to the whole.

Similar is, 'A butterfly . . . would be a perfect butterfly except for the holes in the wings . . . looks as if it's been dead, and crumbling away' (because of the 'breaks' in the wings). This criticism is directed toward elements not usually forming part of the association—the white spaces. S does not subtract but adds on. That is, the percept may be qualified in sundry ways, but it is still W.

In figure VI, some subjects respond to the whole, others to D 1, with essentially the same content. When S says that the upper section—D 8 or D 3—is not part of, e.g., 'the animal skin,' this is taken as evidence that the percept is D. The best technic for ascertaining S's selection is to have him trace his percept. The doubt is more common in the skin or rug association. But it develops in others, e.g., the 'sweater,' 'coat' or 'jacket.' Least doubt obtains in those associations that are statistically so frequent as to be unequivocal W. Thus, the 'bat' for figure V, even though in the inquiry the S finds fault with the lateral projections (D 1). For the 'butterfly of figure I, the S may try to correct himself by eliminating the outward extending wing detail (D 8). Or for the "fur rug" of figure IV, S may not like the upper lateral details (D 4). All these retrospective criticisms may, in view of the statistical frequencies of these W's, be taken with so many grains of salt. They can be scored W with the highest degree of confidence.

The Organized W

The organized W is distinguished from the simple, instant one by S's synthesizing activity. In the more obvious of these responses, this activity is clear—e.g., the common 'Peas porridge hot,' for figure II. Examples follow for each of the ten figures. More will be found in chapter VI (on organization).

Figure I

'Winged lion in a fountain group.'

Figure II

'Two grotesque figures in a tableau.'

Figure III

Rorschach, Oberholzer, and European workers generally, score W whenever the two *humans* are seen, with the leg detail (D 5) included. Usually these figures are organized in a relation to each other and in action. The practice of the writer is to score W only when all portions of the figure are included. Thus, 'two very playful figures on a stage, bent . . . they're revolving around a set piece on the stage [D 3] and there are decorations hanging from the ceiling [D 2], hanging down, swinging in the breeze, of colored paper'; D 3 is 'scenery; it is quite pleasant and cheerful to look at.'

Another kind of W in this figure, resembling the instant variety, is ∨ 'a bumblebee magnified.'

Figure IV

'Elephants back to back.'

Figure V

'Rams bucking each other.'

Figure VI

'Spire on a cathedral'; > 'whale lashing the water and his reflection.'

Figure VII

'Two dogs balanced on a crag.'

Figure VIII

'Christmas tree with presents.'

Figure IX

'Vase with workmanship and base'; > 'sunset scene with reflection.'

Figure X

'*Alice in Wonderland* figures.'

Rorschach distinguished two varieties among the organized W: (*a*) the instant organization, exemplified on p. 12f., and (*b*) what may best be termed the "additive" organization. Rorschach's term is *sukzessivkombinatorisch*. He illustrates (fig. I): 'two men [lateral details] and the figure of a woman [middle]; the men are in struggle over the woman.' In this response, S has perceived details separately; he adds them together piecemeal, and the sum is the W. It is unlike that rapid activity in the instant organized W by which S achieves a swift grasp of relations, and, with that vibrancy characteristic of the vigorous mind, quickly builds up his whole. In the additive organization, the process is much slower. The attention steps from detail to detail. The connections between them emerge and these connections happen to add up into W. Not S but the details of the stimulus control what is seen. S is not the master of his percept, or is so only to a minor degree.

Quantitatively the differentiation is immaterial, since all these responses are W and influence the configuration of the response summary as such. But qualitatively they are discriminating. The additive W takes less intellectual ability. No precise rule for discriminating the two kinds of W can be stated other than that in the additive variety the component details receive precedence over and more emphasis than the wholes.

Examples of the additive organized W are:

Figure I

∨ 'Like two dogs [D 2] leaning up against something,' D 4; S further reveals his D approach in indicating the 'dogs' snout, tail, one foot.' ∧

'Two people dancing [both D 2] and a third one in the middle is just standing up,' D 4.

Figure II

'Two people [D 1], they've got red hats [D 2], they're stooping and their knees are touching [at D 3], like they're playing paddy cake.' This is a good instance of how gradually the usual W in this figure may develop.

Figure III

True W in this figure are rare, and, as already noted, difficult feats of organization. I have not observed the additive W in this figure.

Figure IV

V 'Some sort of a tree [D 1] and the two objects on the side, the rest of the figure, are used as a temple.' Another example is: ∧ 'Like a fire [upper half and lateral details generally] coming down on a castle,' D 1.

Figure V

'He seems to have the devil in him'; looks like 'the devil' because D 2 are the 'horns: these seem to represent the wings that the devil is supposed to have, or something [D 4]; his legs [D 3] are rather peculiar; they are not strong enough or healthy enough to support the devil.' Every part of this figure is finally included; but the several details are added piecemeal to compose the devil figure. As another example: 'Looks like a man [D 7] carrying some bushes, and trees,' D 4.

Figure VI

> 'A rocky cliff [the now upper lateral half] and water [D 5] with reflection of the cliff in it,' the now lower half; V 'like two mountains [both D 4] and water coming down between them.' The flares, D 6, are not indicated by S; but inquiry in these responses usually shows that these details are included.

Figure VII

> 'Like here's a country [one lateral half] and here's another country [other lateral half] and here's the border line,' D 6.

Figure VIII

V 'A face with a big mustache [all D's except D 1, with D 6 as 'eyes' and the two D 5 together as 'mustache'; and 'he has hands [D 1] on the sides of his head.'

Figure IX

∨ 'Like a girl; this [the two D 3 as a unit] is a girl's dress; she has a big blouse [D 1, both] and has a big neck part,' D 6. In the inquiry S adds that D 5 is the 'bone through the girl.' The response is first given as a W, the 'girl'; but S's elaboration is of the variety seen in the additive W, an addition of detail percepts the sum of which is the 'girl.'

Figure X

Inspection of the W in this figure shows them to be either instant or of complex organization. The additive variety has not yet turned up. See above, this section, concerning this response in figure III.

The DW and DdW Response

Rorschach observed a group of W which he identified with the sign DW (his DG, i.e., *Detail-ganz*). They are responses for the determination of which no statistical criteria are available. We score DW when S associates to the entire test figure in accordance with a form suggested by one of the details. To recognize DW we must therefore know (a) that in the free association the S attended only to some one detail, and (b) that the content which this detail suggested is the one with which he associates to the entire test figure. Example: figure V, 'like the Elks' emblem,' in which the patient indicated the upper horn details (D 2), but it is 'the whole thing.'

DdW is a special case of DW; it is a Dd to which the S attends and which suggests the W response. Thus: figure II, 'a box of some kind,' because the outer corner Dd (Dd 23) are the 'legs.' The W association may also have its point of departure in a Ds or a Dds, and the scorings then are DsW and DdsW, respectively.

We must depend much on the patient's replies to our inquiry in ascertaining that the response is truly one of the DW group. But since these responses characterize patients having a mental disorder or defect we are dependent on introspection in minds that are inadequate. The subjective element in these scorings is large. Fortunately they are few. They are diagnostically very important, however, and in some instances are the first lead to the patient's failing mental status. The Rorschach test investigator has, therefore, no choice but to apply himself and learn to know them. Examples follow:

Figure I

'A good idea of a crab' [D 1, then W]. 'A false face' [W] because suggested by Dds 30 as 'eyes,' Dds 29 as 'teeth,' and Dd 27 as 'nose.' Scored DdsW F+ Hd.

'A butterfly, because it has wings [D 2] and antennae' [D 1].

∨ 'A rustic chair'; Dd 22 is part of the 'seat,' as though in a plane coming out from the test card and toward S; the rest of D 4 is the 'back of the chair'; DdW F− Hh.

∧ 'A map [W] because of the islands' [Dd 23].   DdW F+ Ge.

∨ 'An airplane'; D 5 would be the 'propeller' and Dd 31 the 'tail,' hence the entirety is an 'airplane.'

Figure II

∨ 'A spider' [W] because Dd 25 are 'stingers' and 'head' and D 1 would make it a 'winged spider.'

Figure III

'Like a cat's face': D 3 is the 'nose,' D 6 the 'eyes'; D 2 fills out the shape of the 'face,' hence the entirety is a 'cat's face' and the interior white space is also part of it.   Scored DsW F− Ad.

Figure IV

'The whole thing looks like the front of a dog with these as the ears.' Only because D 4 were 'ears' was the entirety taken as a 'dog's head.'

'Lobster'—entirety, because D 4 is a 'claw.'

A question of DdW scoring was raised by the response: 'like a walnut kernel, because it is dented,' i.e., the Dd within; 'where the light hits it makes a sort of valley.'

Figure V

'A flying devil' because D 2 are 'horns.'   'Meat' because D 2 are 'bones.'

Figure VI

'A system resembling the human body,' W, because D 5 is a 'purifier' going through the body.

∨ 'Some kind of fish'; the only explanation elicited was that D 10 is 'where the food reaches through' and 'this is like claws where he grabs his food; and here a membrane, like,' D 6, on the 'end of his tail; and here is where he excretes'—at the end of D 7. Yet the fish is the whole. This is another instance where room for error in scoring is wider than one would like. It was scored DW, because no evidence could be elicted that S was regarding portions of the figure other than those noted.

'They all look like creatures to me . . . that's the backbone,' D 5. The inquiry made clear that the figure as a whole was indefinitely taken as a 'creature' because of the 'backbone.'

'Something ghostly [W] because of its two eyes [D 7] and long nose [D 2, then D 5] and it has two hairs [Dd 26] sticking out from each side, at its neck,' D 2.

In *figures VII, VIII, IX,* and *X,* the DW is very rare. Rorschach, however, reports one for figure VII and also one for figure IX, both given by the same patient, in senile deterioration. Thus, figure VII, 'flowers,' scored by Rorschach DW F− Bt O−. He does not say which detail set off the response.

Figure VIII

'Iceland, isn't it . . . with the bears? Snow and ice. I can make a winter scene out of it.' Only D 1 as the 'bears' and D 4 and 5 as 'snow' and 'ice' were regarded; but the entirety was the 'winter scene.'

Figure IX

'Flowers, roses,' scored by Rorschach DW CF+ Bt.

The DdD Response

Responses are occasionally encountered that are the counterpart of the DW response, except that the Dd now plays the role of D, and the D that of W. That is, the meaning given to a Dd is the basis for the form ascribed to the larger D of which the Dd is a part. Examples are:

Figure I

'A cat.' Dd 31 is the 'cat's tail'; hence D 4 is the 'cat.'

Figure II

'Rabbits [D 1] because of the ears' [Dd 31].

Figure III

'A tree trunk with branches [D 8], hollowed out, because of the hole,' the inner Dds. Here it is white space that suggests an idea, and a larger detail is interpreted thereby. This was scored DdsD F− Bt.

Figure IV

∨ 'The engines of a four-motored bomber, if it were straightened out.' Dd 21 and the outer curve of D 5 suggested the 'engines' and D 5 was therefore the larger section of the 'bomber.'

Figure IX

∨ 'Like a bird [D 6], a fat bird, because he has feet [Dd 21] and an eye'— the usual "eye Dd" of D 4.

Figure X

'An animal [D 9], a monkey, because of its face,' i.e., Dd 25.

The Contaminated W

Rorschach also identified certain whole responses as "confabulated" and "contaminated." In the former, S seldom engages in any directed organizing activity. The details happen to be seen in relation and eventually all are included. The W is accidental, not intellectual work of S. In the contaminated wholes, as in all contaminations, the patient fuses two concepts that in normal thinking are distinct. The abnormality in these lies in the fact of the contamination; the W percept may be an instant, simple W. Such is Rorschach's example for figure IV (ref. 27; p. 38); 'liver of a respectable statesman,' in which 'liver' and 'man' are contaminated; either of these percepts would be scored W and the fusion of the two is also W. The lack of central control represented by these contaminations is seen in the fact that they occur exclusively in mental disorder—in schizophrenia, manic excitements, states incident to brain pathology or due to drugs, and occasionally in mental defect. They are not found in healthy children, even in those of the same mental age as feebleminded (chronologically older) subjects who do produce them.

DW and DdW may occur in any personality group, even in the healthy, superior type. But they are rare in the latter.

Examples of contaminations and confabulations are, naturally, few. Some specimens follow:

Figure I

'A condor [W] because [D 2] is like a mountain' and reminded S of the Condor mountains, where she had once been.

Figure II

'A space of some kind, I should say a physical part of nature'—indicating D 3, then the whole—'as if someone were drawing something physical in nature; and that [D 4] would give a different explanation.'

Figure V

'A scarab.' This was a condensation. When it was unraveled the ingredients turned out to be 'bat, vampire, mysterious Egypt, scarab.'

Figure VI

'This is way off in Egypt' because of the 'emblem' at the top, i.e., D 2; 'the Egyptians can see farther than any one else; it's from the Allah tribe, the Garden of Allah.'

'As a whole it might be a June bug when it hits my windshield on a hot summer's night, as it goes fifty miles an hour; the windshield is nonshatterable—the bug is shatterable; windshield's speed is eighty-eight feet per minute, and June bug's speed is thirty miles an hour.' S confabulates on: he has watched June bugs and has watched them break on his windshield. His final comment is that D 11 looks 'like the heart of a human, or the liver.'

Figure VIII

∧ 'It might be a man with his head chopped, legs cut off, and his body cut open for autopsy; we have a man's chest, his lungs, the red on each side might be the ribs laid open'—W. This is a good case of confabulation.

'Representing different shadings of colors . . . that's as much as it is . . . there is no species to explain . . . just colors . . . it represents some idea . . . some image someone has . . . but it's just colors . . . rather a difficult thing . . . its color space placed so as to coordinate with a visual purpose.' After seeing D 1 as the usual 'bears,' S continued: 'like some sort of astrological symbol; I don't know much about astrology.' Another condensation. The chain here was 'bears, constellation, astrology.' She topped the association off with 'and I was born under Aquarius.'

The "Cut-Off" W

In addition to these W, two others are identified by Klopfer[16]—*the incomplete whole* and the *cut-off whole*. Among the former he includes instances of W responses suggesting that "there may be certain minor areas in the card for which they [the subjects] have no use." When S criticizes some minor portion of the figure as discrepant from the entire percept, his response is a cut-off W. The problem in these responses, as this writer sees it, and as discussed below in chapter IV, is whether they are W or D. This is in some instances hard to determine, especially when S engages in petty criticism of one or more details, as previously shown. Frequently, S is not himself certain. Such criticisms, uncertainties, or partial rejections of one's own responses are among the very important qualitative factors that are part of Rorschach test procedure. Their value lies in filling in the picture structured out in the response summary.

Klopfer uses also the symbol D→W, to represent "a whole tendency." It is hard to see, however, how his two examples of D→W raise any scoring question not covered by Rorschach's original exposition of W and D. In figure I the 'two Santa Clauses with Christmas trees under their arms hanging up stockings' is a good W—just as in figure VIII, the 'animals stepping over something' is a D.

CHAPTER III

DETAIL AND RARE DETAIL: D and Dd

Of the responses in which S selects less than the whole figure, some are designated D, detail, while all others are Dd, rare details. These scorings can be unimpeachably normative. The very simple procedure of counting establishes the differentiation between D and Dd. This my co-workers and I have done in a population including representative samples of the mid-group of American life.[7]

The majority of the D responses are readily identified. They relate to certain portions in each ink blot figure that most prominently attract attention to themselves; in consequence, they are the most commonly selected. Not that the same conditions operate in the several figures to favor one or another detail. Size, position, and space rhythm play roles of varying importance. Rorschach apparently considered rhythm important, since he especially noted sensitivity to it (*individuelle Empfindlichkeit für Raumrhythmik*) as a research need, to clear up theoretic problems as to D and Dd (ref. 27; p. 39). The role of size is apparent in the fact that most D are larger than most Dd. A case of space rhythm overcoming the disadvantages of smallness is that of D 3 in figure IV. In each of the figures, while the choices of Dd can be endless, certain portions, not frequently enough selected to be D, are still attended to regularly in any considerable number of response records. These are the better known Dd, Rorschach's *Kleindetail*, in English commonly called the rare detail. In addition, meaning is found by some subjects in elements of the figures so tiny or obscure that they remain unnoticed by most other persons. Tiny dots or white flecks take on real form in these highly individualized responses. Shapes that have never before been perceived are torn out of the context of the entire figure, contours being sometimes patterned out where there are no lines at all. On having his attention called to them, E can usually recognize the indicated form, though in years of work with the test that shape may not have emerged out of that background. Among thousands of responses, this particular association may be the first evoked by the small detail in question, and it may be the only such association. All these are Dd. Together with the more frequent Dd, they are rare selections in relation to the others in the same figure. That is, each of the Rorschach test figures sets its own standards for D and Dd. The same percentage does not necessarily make for D or Dd in the several figures. This is as is to be expected, since each figure represents a different set of perceptual conditions.

TABLE 1.—*Most Frequent D and Dd Selections*

FIGURE I

D 1	hooks projecting from top of middle
D 2	entire lateral wing detail, including D 8
D 3	darker portion of lower middle, resembling human body from hips down
D 4	entire middle, including D 3
D 5	uppermost 'head' detail of lateral
D 6	projection from lateral, below middle, resembling inverted, poorly formed tree or shock of wheat (usually $\vee$)
D 7	D 5 and D 8 selected as a unit D
D 8	triangular portion projecting from upper edge of lateral
D 9	Dd 25 together with animal-like prognathic projection immediately below it. $\vee$ D 9 takes on form of larger human profile
Dd 22	rounded bulges at top of middle, between D 1
Dd 23	tiny flecks off lower lateral of main figure—any or all
Dd 24	bell-like lower half of D 4; may include D 3, which is, however, ignored in the response
Dd 25	edge of lateral, below D 8
Dds 26	all inner white spaces simultaneously
Dd 27	light gray oval detail in center of D 4
Dds 29	lower inner white spaces
Dds 30	upper inner white spaces
Dd 31	portion of D 3 projecting below figure as whole
Dds 32	white space above D 4 and between D 5

FIGURE II

D 1	lateral black figure, entire
D 2	upper red figure
D 3	lower red figure: 'butterfly'
D 4	conelike portion at upper middle: 'hands' of 'clowns'
Ds 5	inner white space
D 6	both D 1 as single D
D 7	approximate upper third of lateral black, but always including Dd 31— jowl-like outer corner
Dd 22	lower outer corner profile: $\vee$ 'old man of the mountain'
Dd 23	'profile' in lower edge of D 1, between D 3 and Dd 22
Dd 24	lighter pink section in middle part of D 3, whether or not tiny white spaces innermost to it are included
Dd 25	projections from D 3—any or all
Dd 26	red on 'shoulder' of D 1—weasel-form Dd
Dd 27	two light thin lines bridging upper small portion of Ds 5
Dd 28	rounded inner 'knee' portion of D 1
Dds 29	uppermost section of Ds 5, bounded by D 4 and Dd 27
Dds 30	white area between D 1, D 2, and D 4
Dd 31	outer upper corner 'jowl' only of D 7

FIGURE III

D 1	both human figures, with leg details, when seen in relationship to each other, with large black details of lower middle usually fitted into response; always M

TABLE 1.—*Continued*

FIGURE III—*Concluded*

D 2	upper lateral red
D 3	middle red
D 4	larger, black details of lower middle
D 5	lower lateral black—'leg' detail
D 6	'head' only of D 9
D 7	entire lower middle, including both D 4 and intervening gray, sometimes also intervening white, all seen as one
D 8	gray portions in lower middle, between D 4
D 9	each 'human' figure, with leg detail, with or without the detail of lower middle but without organization of relationship between figures. Material included may actually be same as in D 1; but in D 9 each lateral half is seen independently of the other; there is no larger unit. This may be M (chap. VIII) or F (chap. XIII)
D 10	lowermost gray of D 5: 'hoof'
D 11	body portion only (with head) of 'human' figure; i.e., D 4 and D 5 not included
D 12	both D 11 with D 7, all as continuous unit
Dd 21	'rump' portion only of D 11
Dd 22	D 11 exclusive of head and neck portions
Dds 23	white space between D 4, D 5, D 11
Dds 24	white space interior to two D 11
Dd 25	upward extending projection of D 2: 'tail'
Dd 26	projection inward of D 5
Dd 27	triangular projection inward from chest of 'human'
Dd 28	connecting Dd between halves of D 3
Dd 29	each half of D 3 seen separately
Dd 30	projection of D 11 to D 4: 'arms'

FIGURE IV

D 1	lower projecting half of D 5, beginning at upper limits of white spaces
D 2	lighter gray portion projecting at lower corners: 'vamp,' including toe and heel of 'boot' or 'shoe'
D 3	at top, 'flower'-form detail—approximately to line that would connect first larger indentations
D 4	slender projection hanging out from upper corner
D 5	darker middle column, entire
D 6	both D 2 and D 7 as one—entire 'boot'
D 7	darker portion of 'boot'—its 'upper.' Upper limits not exactly defined in most cases and not at same points in each case. Occasionally extended to top of middle. But D 4 is never included in this designation. Usually ∨.
D 8	about one inch of outermost projection of D 2: head and bust of 'old woman'
Dd 21	profile-like detail in upper edge, just interior to point where D 4 is attached to main figure
Dd 22	'face' in center of upper lateral portion

TABLE 1.—*Continued*

FIGURE IV—*Concluded*

Dd 23   lowermost 'head' and 'beak' portions of D 4
Dds 24   white spaces bounding D 1 when all are seen together. See Dds 29
Dd 25   'face' in upper central portion of D 5
Dd 26   projections at center of bottom of D 1
Dd 27   hooflike detail, upper of two Dd bridging D 7 and D 5
Dd 28   projections at corners of bottom of D 1
Dds 29   only upper Dds of Dds 24
Dd 30   the lighter gray in the upper center of D 3; the "core" of the "flower"

FIGURE V

D 1   upper and thicker of outer corner projections
D 2   upper 'horn' projections
D 3   projections at middle bottom
D 4   entire lateral, whether or not outer corner projections are included
D 5   profile-like bulge in upper edge of D 4: 'boy's face'
D 6   'head' at upper middle, whether or not D 2 are included
D 7   entire middle, including D 2 and D 3
D 8   both D 2 as unit, with or without Dds 28
D 9   both D 3 as unit, with or without Dds 27
D 10   D 1 with Dd 22 as unit, with or without Dds 29
D 11   noselike bulge in upper edge of D 4, beginning at 'chin' of D 5 and ex-
           tending to but not including D 1 and Dd 22
Dd 22   lower and thinner of outer corner projections
Dd 23   lower edge, beginning at D 3 and extending to Dd 22; usually >, <, or
           V and, in such position, 'profile'
Dd 24   tiny projection at top, about ¼ inch from D 6
Dd 25   projection in bottom edge, forming 'nose' when Dd 23 is seen as 'face'
Dd 26   twiglike projection in upper edge, at junction of D 1 and mass of blot
Dds 27   white space between D 3
Dds 28   white space between D 2
Dds 29   white space between D 1 and Dd 22
Dd 30   shadowy 'head' within D 6

FIGURE VI

D 1   entire lower large section, i.e., both D 4 as one
D 2   upper portion only of middle black column
D 3   upper flared details, inclusive of black portion between, i.e., entire
           detail upward of level of lower of flared details
D 4   either lateral half of large lower section; usually selected in V position,
           and as 'animal with outstretched paw'
D 5   entire middle black column, as one D
D 6   upper flared details, exclusive of black portion between
D 7   at top, portion above Dd 26: 'snake's head'
D 8   upper portion, i.e., all above D 1
D 9   portions projecting outward laterally from D 4

TABLE 1.—*Continued*

FIGURE VI—*Concluded*

D 10	two egg-shaped details at middle of bottom
D 11	two inner gray ovals
D 12	lower portion only of middle black column, i.e., portion downward from D 11
Dd 21	at bottom, larger, lowermost, beaklike details
Dd 25	small projections at upper corners of D 1
Dd 26	uppermost very thin projections: 'whiskers' or 'vibrissae'
Dd 28	at bottom, smaller, inner, beaklike details adjacent to D 10
Dd 29	profile formed by edge from Dd 25 to and including upper edge of D 10
Dds 30	white space at bottom between Dd 21 and D 10
Dd 31	sloping Dd on each side of lower half of D 2

FIGURE VII

D 1	upper profile detail, whether or not D 5 is included, though usually it is
D 2	D 1 and D 3 seen together as unit
D 3	second or middle of profile details
D 4	both D 10 as one, whether or not D 6 is included, though usually it is
D 5	projection upward from D 1
D 6	darker 'clasp' at middle bottom
Ds 7	white space within figure
D 8	on 'forehead' of D 1, lighter gray bulge, with tiny 'horns'
D 9	either lateral half entire, i.e., D 5, D 1, D 3, and D 10, all as continuous unit
D 10	lowermost section, beginning at D 3 and extending to darker 'clasp' detail at middle bottom
D 11	gray Dd below D 6
Dd 21	projection extending outward from D 3
Dd 24	'chin' of D 1, i.e., darker, lower corner portion of D 1
Dd 25	gray Dd just above D 6
Dd 26	gray Dd in middle of D 6
Dd 27	two dark streaks within D 11
Dd 28	used only to indicate junction point of D 3 and D 10

FIGURE VIII

D 1	'animal' at side
D 2	entire lower section, i.e., orange and pink, seen as one
D 3 or Ds 3	middle riblike portion, irrespective of whether attention is centered on 'ribs' or on these together with white spaces between and around them. Ds 3 designation is of course used when white spaces are included
D 4	upper grayish blue portion, whether or not interior green portion is included
D 5	middle blue: 'flags'
D 6	pink portion of lower section
D 7	orange portions of lower section

TABLE 1.—*Continued*

FIGURE VIII—*Concluded*

D 8	D 4 and D 5 seen as one
Dd 21	entirety of middle green stalk, i.e., both thicker, upper portion, Dd 30 and Dd 27
Dd 22	projection, like forearm and hand, from D 4 to D 1
Dd 23	at middle bottom, lighter orange-pinkish portions
Dd 24	two very small upward projections at very top
Dd 25	pink-purplish detail within D 5
Dd 26	small portion of orange projecting outward and laterally from D 7, directly below D 1
Dd 27	lower, thinner portion of middle green 'stalk'
Dds 28	space between D 1, D 2, and D 5; usually $\vee$
Dd 29	loop just below Dd 27
Dd 30	upper, thicker portion of middle stalk
Dd 31	either half of D 4 selected separately
Dds 32	white space between D 5 and D 6

FIGURE IX

D 1	lateral green
D 2	grayish elongated portion within green where it merges with orange: 'camel's' or 'alligator's' head
D 3	entire upper orange section
D 4	end section of lower pink: 'head,' > or <
D 5	middle 'stalk,' green fading into blue, including purple continuation lower down
D 6	entire lower pink section seen as unit
D 7	branching inward projections at top, sometimes but not always including Dd 26 and Dd 27; usually, but not always, including Dd 25
Ds 8	space between D 3; frequently including D 5, though reaction is primarily to space detail
D 9	D 5 and D 6 seen as one: $\vee$ 'tree'
D 10	either of inner two sections of pink
D 11	both D 1 seen as continuous unit
D 12	one of D 3 together with D 1 of same side, seen as unit
Dd 21	'fingers' at bottom of D 1 where it adjoins D 10
Dd 22 or Dds 22	in center, entire portion between D 1 and Dd 28—'bridge'—hence including Dds 23. But response does not always take white spaces of Dds 23 into account, and whether to score Dd 22 or Dds 22 will depend on this factor
Dds 23	in center of Dd 22, 'eyelike' portions consisting in part of white slits, in part of darker green slits
Dd 24	upper, outer 'head' portion only of D 1
Dd 25	very light orange projections inward from D 7
Dd 26	revolver-form detail just above D 7
Dd 27	small bulky or square portion just below and adjacent to D 7
Dd 28	'muzzle' portion only of D 3

TABLE 1.—*Concluded*

FIGURE IX—*Concluded*

Dds 29	small white space within D 1
Dd 30	lower, purple portion only of D 5
Dd 31	lower edge of D 1
Dds 32	space within both Dd 25

FIGURE X

D 1	lateral blue
D 2	inner yellow
D 3	in upper middle, triple-form orange detail
D 4	long green details at bottom: 'caterpillars'
D 5	'rabbit's head' between D 4
D 6	inner blue
D 7	gray 'beetle' between D 9 and outer yellow
D 8	gray 'animals' of upper portion
D 9	large pink mass, entire
D 10	D 4 and D 5 seen as one
D 11	D 8 and D 14 seen as one, i.e., entire gray cluster at top
D 12	upper green: 'fish' or 'cow'
D 13	outer corner brown at bottom
D 14	in upper gray figure, 'stalk' only, between two 'animal' figures
D 15	outer yellow
Dd 25	upper profile portion of D 9: 'head'
Dd 26	always ∨, in inner edge of D 9, profile of 'old man'
Dd 27	lighter outer half of D 1
Dd 28	darker inner half of D 1
Dds 29	portion of inner white space bounded by D 11, D 6, and Dd 25, irrespective of whether D 3 is included
Dds 30	entire white space between D 9, irrespective of whether any of inclosed details are included
Dd 31	lower end of D 9: ∨ 'animal's' or 'monster's' head
Dd 32	always ∨, profile in outer edge of D 9
Dd 33	'nucleus' in D 2
Dd 34	connecting portion of D 6
Dd 35	'branch' and 'group' of D 1

The list of D and Dd here published is as revised (1949) in accordance with statistical study of our group of normal adults. This formed part of the larger investigation of schizophrenia, under USPHS grant. Full statistical results for this normal group have been published.[7] An earlier statistical norm is that of Löpfe[21] (1925). In one of the earliest reported Rorschach test investigations, he offered 1:22 as the critical ratio. Anything selected less frequently than once in 22 times in a given figure would be Dd. This rule of thumb is open to the obvious objection that the given ratio does not apply equally in backgrounds offering such different perceptual conditions as do the ten Rorschach test figures.

Descriptions of all my own D and Dd are presented in Table 1. The details are numbered in the order of frequency with which each is selected. D 1 is always first in each figure. Dd are numbered from 21 and up, with Dd 21 as the most frequently observed. (All judgments are based on the percentages found in our normal controls.) However, in the present revision, Dd 21 will be seen as missing in figures I, II, V, X. The statistics have shown these to be D, and they have been numbered anew. But to prevent confusion incident to renumbering all other Dd in these figures, it was deemed best not to change numbers of the other Dd. For the same reason some Dd numbers will be found lacking in other of the test figures.

My own oldest D and Dd discriminations had been arrived at on an experiential basis following Rorschach's confidence that "after one has given the test to fifty persons of the normal average range, he knows most of the normal details" (ref. 27; p. 41). A comparison of the present designations with the older ones will show that changes have been made. But that earlier set of standards, empirically determined though it was, has in the light of the statistics turned out to be gratifyingly stable.

The table includes all Ds and Dds, fuller discussion of which will be found in chapter v. Rorschach looks on white spaces as a special case of Dd. Experience shows, however, that statistically some Ds are true D, although the majority are Dd. It seems entirely logical, therefore, to group all Ds as D, and the rarer white spaces, Dds, as Dd. Similarly, Rorschach calls his Do (my Hdx and Adx) a form of Dd. But since any, even major, D may be selected in the "Do" interpretation, it becomes clear that Rorschach was here mixing his categories. The "Do" may be D or Dd, depending on whether S is reacting to a D or Dd.

CHAPTER IV

SCORING PROBLEMS

Nature seldom follows the textbooks. The Rorschach test experimenter will rarely find an individual whose responses refer unequivocally to the formally identified details or rare details. The problems constantly posed are (a) whether to score W or D; (b) whether to score D or Dd; (c) how much of what has been selected is to be scored; (d) whether to score more than once; (e) whether to score at all. The problems vary again from figure to figure, owing to the differing configurations of the entirety, the inner contours, overlappings, white spaces, and the degree of clarity of outlines.

The sections that follow exemplify the scoring problems encountered in figure I, and their solutions. These are representative also of the problems met with in the other figures.

OVERLAPPING OF W AND D

'That looks like two Chinese [W] dressed up in fur coats and capes like Santa Claus; they seem to be talking to each other at a turnpike or post [D 4], or in a symbolic dance (because of its symmetry); they are bearded and suddenly for no reason at all they seem to be floating in space. They don't seem to be down on the ground.' The percept includes everything in the figure. Details are selected but find meaning only as determined by the meaning of the whole. Hence, W, and scored W M+ H.

'It might be a rack to hold something (each half is like a newspaper rack in the public library).' What looked like a W was shown by the inquiry to be D. Even then a question remained as to whether *two* racks were seen. The inquiry, however, showed that S was looking at each half as a separate rack without any connection. Only one D was attended to at any time. Scored D F− Object.

∧ 'Two birds fighting'—W excluding the middle; D 1 'is where their feet are together.' Almost a W. Yet the 'birds' embrace only D 2; of the middle portions only D 1 is included. Scored D F+ A.

A similar example is 'a couple of wolves dancing,' in which D 5 were the 'faces' of the wolves, and D 2 their 'wings'; they were 'all dressed up' and a moment later they were seen 'holding on to something,' i.e., to a Dd in D 4; but D 4 as a whole did not enter into the response. Hence, D.

Tracing whole outline with finger: 'Looks like a butterfly [D 4], only it would be just exactly with the wings'—indicating portions of lateral. Although only separate D are first indicated, there is no question about the entirety being intended. The behavior of S, in tracing the whole, is confirmatory evidence. Scored W F+ A P.

'It looks like a . . . bear [D 4; and D 1 are arms], the arms up. Men are taking the bear.' S continued: 'Those look like two men [D 2] as if they are going to walk with it,' i.e., with the bear. Here is unquestionable organizing activity, but with an open question as to whether this is W. All selection is of D. The two responses amount to an additive W, even if it is on the borderline. The safest scoring is as for two responses: D F− A; W M+ H, 3.5.

'This is a body, like from a bird on the side, like wings. . . . Fly. I made one.' The question is whether 'fly' is a development from 'wings,' thus requiring only one scoring, possibly DW. However, the 'wings' are a bird's and the emphasis is on D 2. In 'fly' the whole is seen. It is necessary to score one D and one W, especially since considerations relative to Adx and to F+ also dictate this. Scored D F+ Adx; W F− A.

Overlapping of D and Dd; Elaborations

'And suddenly I see something else, a female form [D 3], and it looks as though it is covered by a thin dress and the light is against it [Dd lateral to D 3, on each side]; it's just from the waist down—it has no connection with the rest of the picture.' The light gray Dd around D 3 has meaning value only by virtue of the meaning that S has already put into D 3. The 'dress' is seen only because the 'woman' is there. This is a very frequent elaboration, usually employing Dd, occasionally a D. The elaborated element is not scored. A marginal note needs, however, to be made to indicate S's trend to Dd. Scored D F+ H Cg P.

'And you can see two people that look like Spanish ladies up here—two of them are not Spanish, they are Arabians, they have veils on them—with their arms held akimbo': D 4 with Dd 22 as 'veiled' portions, 'arms akimbo' at the center. Dd 22 are occasionally seen as 'human heads' independently of the rest of the figure. Here all of D 4 is seen as 'women,' and the 'veiled' heads are an integral element of this percept; therefore, only the simple scoring D M+ H Cg. Another question: Are the 'veils' a separate Dd, i.e., does S perceive them as something aside from the head? The problem is similar to that of 'dress' in the example preceding, and of many *clothed human* responses, e.g., 'man with fur coat on' in figure IV—i.e., a simple form with an outer layer is seen. Therefore, it is scored only once. Still, S's special attention to this Dd, and the original content, 'veiled,' tell us something additional concerning her, which is used as an aid in understanding this personality.

'And a gnome [D 4] . . . is a playful little creature: he is whistling or laughing; has a slender body; his eyes are laughing; he is ready to move—waiting for you to play with him, as though he has just said "Oh."'   Here Dd 27 is 'mouth.'   This is first indicated in an elaboration, entirely in the inquiry; and these responses are never scored.

'An oriental priest . . . in an attitude of prayer or supplication, holding up his two hands, and head bowed in prayer . . . head down on chest,' D 4. *Hands* (D 1) is a common elaboration of the *human* (D 4).   Elaborations pure and simple are never scored.   D M+ H for 'priest' suffices.

∧ 'In this position it could look like two dancing women [D 4], one having one hand up in the air [D 1] and the other having the other hand up in the air.   Or like two nuns, sisters, standing in an abbey . . . with veils on; two women ending in one buttock; or the one figure becomes two.' D 4 is actually broken up into two.   Should this be scored one D, two D, or two Dd?   The reaction has been to D 4.   Even though S has broken it up, she has resynthesized it into a single percept.   In the one D she sees two women; hence, D M+ H.   Note the elaborations, 'veils,' 'buttocks,' unscored both because they are elaboration and because first given in the inquiry.

'It resembles a butterfly [W] with some sort of feelers on it, protruding eyes, and . . . a lizard's tail. . . . It has a double body.'   The elaboration 'lizard's tail' is one not inherent in the original percept; hence, it needs to be scored Dd F−Ad.   It will be noted that the contaminatory and confabulatory trend (S was a schizophrenic) continues, as in 'double body.' This is all elaboration of the butterfly.   Ws FY+ A P.

∨ 'Upside down it's nothing, although it might be a series of mountains' —each dark layer is the series of mountains—'a range of mountains surrounded by water . . . an island in the sea'—because of irregular outline, and the outer white is the sea.   Scored DdsW, for the following reasons. The 'water' fills out the scene initiated by the Dd in D 2 as 'mountains.' As a further elaboration the entirety—hence, W—becomes 'an island in the sea.'   But it was all based on Dd; hence, DdW.   Since one of the Dd is a white space, the designation becomes DdsW, and the whole formula thus DdsW FV−Ls.   The restriction to a single scoring emphasizes that 'water . . . sea' is elaboration rather than a new association.

'I see here an ink blot, and it's something like a wasp . . . because of the wings and claws; it looks as it it has two claws by which it can grab his food, and you can see its eyes.   The outspread part on each side looks to me as if it were wings.'   This example shows how much a response may be elaborated, utilizing D and Dd.   The single scoring, W F−A, tells what has been seen.   The trend to Dd and that to Ad are significant, and help to fill out the diagnostic picture by either stressing or lightening traits patterned out in the response summary.

'And part of it looks like a map'; the white space below D 8 is water and like a port, and the surrounding black suggests a map. Scored Dds FY+ Ge. The reaction was to the white space as 'water' of the 'port,' the black elements filling in. This is a reversal of the usual response mode. Also, not enough of any D was chosen to warrant scoring D. The Dds scoring—rare white space—most nearly represents S's percept here.

'That part looks as if that was a sky and as if there were dark clouds'— D 2, indicating sundry Dd as clouds. The sundry Dd, while more than elaboration of 'sky,' D 2, are still part of that reaction. It is possible that I am here too observant of the law of parsimony, but a certain amount of error is still inevitable in Rorschach experiment. One scoring is used, D FY+ Cl. A marginal note calls attention to the strong Dd interest.

D or Dd Not Clearly Defined

'And some thunderclouds looming up in the west, breaking off in little fleecy bits [D 2]; black clouds rolling up before thunder and lightning; it is a heavy mass.' Essentially all of D 2 is selected, although neither E nor S can know precisely where the 'cloud' ends. For purposes of identifying the mental activity in question, this vague boundary is no handicap. We have a clear D, and score D FY+ Cl.

'There are a series of hidden faces, grinning faces, as though angels in the clouds of the Italian painters . . . Really cats'—Dd in region of Dd 25. S is attending to several Dd, no one of which he precisely identifies. The reaction is Dd. So much is certain, and no more. Dd FY Hd Art.

'Monkey': upper portion of D 4; S then points to various details. This association was produced by a feebleminded subject, and enough D was identified to warrant the scoring D F— A. Exact location is frequently difficult with subjects of this group, this reflecting their inability to discriminate. E is likely to be more at the mercy of subjective judgment in his scoring of these records, and some of them cannot be used statistically.

'Like a bear or something': D 5 with adjacent Dd. S is encouraged but only repeats 'a bear or something.' Dd are sometimes vaguely indicated, elaborating a D that is otherwise clearly identified. The Dd are disregarded in the scoring, except that as Dd trend they help qualitatively in completing the diagnostic picture. D F+ A.

'And another face in here and here and another one in there.' Here the Dd just could not be fixed. It is better in such instances to leave the response unscored. Location is too indefinite.

'Couldn't be the lungs, could it?'—middle portion of D 2. An indefinite portion of D 2 is selected. Although not precisely outlined, the selection is clearly Dd. Scored Dd F— An. The association was expressed in question form. Such interrogatory responses are scored as though they were affirmative statements.

'It looks as though it were holding on to something [Dd in D 4], a rock or something; looks like there was a rock behind and a couple of rocks up here'. The 'something' is a Dd in D 4 not further defined, but clearly selected as an object to which a 'wolf,' a preceding response given by S, is clinging. It is necessary to score, and structurally there is no question but that the percept is Dd, even if its exact boundaries are not known. Scored Dd F Ls.

VERY RARE Dd

'You can make a funny-looking little dog there, the head of a dog'— edge Dd just below D 6. The unusual details that may rise out of the ink blot background are limitless in number. E's problem in relation to many extremely unusual ones is that of identification. He needs to see what S does. The shape, once perceived, may be as sharp and clear as any Rorschach response. The present 'dog's head' can easily be identified just below D 6. A half-turn of the card toward < will help.

'I should think on that right side you have dog and cat put together': Dd 25 together with adjacent Dd. The actual contours in the test figure are not very sharp but can be made out. The scorings are: Dd F+ Ad, for "dog", Dd 25; and Dd F− Ad for cat and dog put together.'

'I see a pig's head in there': Dd in upper part of D 2. Dd F Ad.

'And that's an animal too, like an elephant': Dd in middle of D 2, seen as tusks and eyes. Dd F+ A.

'I don't know, I see a man's face, one half man's face and mask, only the eyes and the nose': Dd group in upper part of D 4. This represents very fine details within the areas indicated; the reader can discover them by close scrutiny. Such percepts are always certain to be Dd.

'And then up here, there are two . . . you can see, like a person's face . . . on both sides'—very fine edge Dd just below D 8—'and the white space is a chasm.' The profile is readily identifiable, just below the point where D 8 junctions with the mass of D 2. Dd F Hd, and an additional scoring of Dds V for the 'chasm.'

'Another face here'—a barely identifiable profile on the lower edge of D 8. For permanent recording of these very rare as well as of the poorly outlined Dd, the best method is to use the reproductions now available of the Rorschach ink blot figures.

TO SCORE OR NOT TO SCORE

Every Rorschach student is familiar with instances in which S produces two or more associations for exactly the same portion of the figure, separated only by an 'or.' From the language alone, S is merely correcting a first impression: he is offering an alternative response, as though he considers it more precise than those that preceded. I designate all these as "precision alternatives." Most of them need not be scored. But some must be treated as new responses, on structural grounds usually, sometimes because of content. Thus, S produces the following responses in succession:

∨ ∧ 'At first it looks like a bat, when I first look at it' W F+ A P 1.0. 'Then it looks like a drawing of a skull, of a brain . . . a frog's skull; I suppose it looks like anybody's skull.' This is W: Dd 31 is the end of the spinal cord; the rest, including inner spaces, is the entire skull. Ws F+ An, Sk 1.0.

'And these two [D 2] might be winged figures attached around a central tablet . . . or bell; winged figures . . . they might be horses,' i.e., winged horses. Scored W F+ Art.

∨ 'That might look like a topographical map of some kind.' The dark midline is a river; D 2 is land; it is a physical map; the white all around might be the ocean; or someone might be riding in an airplane and 'this is what he'd see'; he would get outlines, not details. Scored W FV+ Ge.

Are all these precision alternatives, or new responses? In the drawing of the skull, S includes material—the spaces, i.e., ventricles, Dds 26—that is additive to that attended to in 'bat.' Also, the content is so different as to warrant the conclusion that this is a new perceptual act. Similarly, in 'winged figures' she has again done something new—broken up the entirety and rebuilt it. Finally, in 'map' she is concentrating again on new elements and utilizing hitherto disregarded qualities of the figures as determinants. It would be under-scoring to designate all these associations by one or two or even three scoring formulas.

Another S produced the following associations in sequence: 'A large beetle with two mandibles of some sort . . . like a flying beetle' (W). Scored W F+ A. 'Or two dancing girls swinging about some piece of gymnastic apparatus, with their draperies flying out, as they whirl around the center.' W M+ H. 'The first reaction I really got was a great big bat . . . an animal of course.' W F+ A P.

Turning the card in the ∨ orientation, S continued: 'Ah, now we have, instead of the priests, a Japanese decorative urn . . . the things Japanese have in formal gardens . . . carved in stone' (W). Ws F+ Art. 'Or it might be a man standing, his legs wide apart . . . the head has to be as of one hidden behind—and in—draperies': W, with D 8 especially as draperies. W M− H.

S went on, holding the card at arm's length: ∧ 'It looks like a skull of an animal would look to an individual who knew no osteology . . . the details are all wrong but the total configuration is that.' W; spaces are 'eye holes.' Scored Ws F+ An. Then (card held at angle): 'A conventionalized picture of two perching birds ... the wings upheld as in lighting, the two claws represented as a crest above the head and body, as though reaching toward the central line. . . . . You have to think of them as though spattered out': W, with D 1 as claws. W F+ A Art.

The 'dancing girls' are clearly distinct from either 'beetle' or 'bat.' There is legitimate question, however, whether 'beetle' and 'bat' are not precision alternatives. If so, practice now is to score only one.

For 'Japanese urn,' the card was $\vee$. A turn of the card provides a new stimulus; hence a new response, always. This was the stimulus also for 'man standing with legs apart'; but 'urn' took account of the white spaces, 'standing man' did not: the one is F, the other is M. For 'animal skull' the card had again been turned, a full 180 degrees; and this differed from 'perching birds' because the latter involved breaking-up and synthesizing activity, different from that of 'skull' and with different emphases on the several D selected, and with Ds.

After seeing the two dancing women, who were also 'like two nuns, sisters, standing in an abbey, with veils on; two women ending in one buttock' (the one figure becomes two), S continued: 'It looks like a person with a body up to the waist, and from the waist on it looks like two figures' —chiefly D 3. The material selected in 'dancing women' is not the same as in 'body up to the waist,' i.e., there have been reactions to two D, even though there is overlapping of them. Second, the determinants are different, F+, M, each very important in the entire psychogram. Scored respectively D M+ H; D F+ Hd.

$\vee$ 'Looks a bit like a turban, a hat of some sort ... it is a crown ... regal attire,' because it is rounded and has a peak at the top, and Dds 29 are jewels. S went on: 'That's about all I see—but first it looked like a bat [W] ... but it doesn't complete the silhouette.' Two wholes are reacted to, in succession, yet the percepts are quite different—in giving meaning to the white space, in the organization activity, and in originality of content as contrasted with the stereotyped *bat*. It would do no justice to S's perceptual activity to score only once, and it would be unrepresentative of what he did. Therefore, Ws F+ Ro; W F+ A P.

$\vee > \vee \wedge$ 'It looks something like a bat.' W F+ A P. 'And it looks something like a lobster': W, because D 1 is the pincer. DW F— A. 'And it might be a fly ... certain sorts of fly' (W). W F— A. $\vee$ 'Upside down it's nothing, although it might be a series of mountains ...': each dark layer one in the series of mountains. Dd W FV— Ls. 'Bat' differs from 'lobster' with respect to mode of approach, W, DW, determinant,

F+, F−, and the P element. 'Fly' differs from 'lobster' with respect to mode of approach, W, DW, from 'bat' in regard to the determinant, F+, F−, and in regard to P. All three responses differ from 'mountains' because the card was now $\vee$; a new determinant, $\vee$, entered. A simpler instance of this same response pattern was: 'Looks like a design of a beetle' (because of wing spread), followed by 'or a butterfly . . . ink spots are on it—light, shade; dark.' The 'or' shows that 'butterfly' is a precision alternative. But one response is DW, the other W; only one is P. It requires two sets of designations to record what S has been doing.

$\vee$ $\wedge$ 'Looks like two witches fighting over something, trying to get hold of this': D 2 are witches and D 4 is a person whom they are trying to seize. 'Like a design': an organized W followed by a simple W. More often the sequence is the other way. In either case there are two responses. As seen in chapter VI, the complex activity in the organized W is other than that in the simple W. In addition, one response is M, the other F. Scored W M + H and W F+ Art.

'Could be an emblem . . . a bird there [upper half]. Could be a sort of seal, like family seal.' *Bird* is an element in *seal* or *emblem*; it is an elaboration, just as, e.g., *animal's leg* would be, following an animal association. There has been no new D selection and no new determinant. This may be added into the simple scoring formula, thus: D F+ A Art.

'A beetle [W]. Can it remind you of more than one thing? $\vee$ That way it reminds me of a coat of arms' (W; does not know why). Two simple W, for the same figure, in immediate sequence, yet two responses. The second was produced with the figure in another position, changing the stimulus. Hence it is scored anew, even though the scoring is the same, the only difference being in content. Thus, W F+ A; W F+ Art.

However, not all instances of changed position of the card dictate a new scoring. In figure I and in figure V the *bat* or *butterfly* is seen with the card in any position, and repeated with the card completely reversed. This is scored only once. Or the *bear* of figure II may at first be seen standing up; with the card <, the bear is on all fours. This is likewise scored as one response.

The general rule for precision alternatives is to score only once when the following conditions are met by two or more responses:

(a) all responses are to the W, or to exactly the same D or Dd, with the position of the card unchanged;

(b) the determinant is exactly the same;

(c) the alternative responses are given with no or only one or two intervening responses.

The content may vary, even widely, in the alternative associations. Stated

differently, if the two or more successive associations can be designated by
exactly the same scoring symbols in respect to (a) the selected area and
(b) the determinant, then it is scored only once.

QUESTIONS AND DESCRIPTIONS

< ∨ 'I don't know what you'd call these—teeth, or what?' (D 1).
S puts his association in question form. It is always scored. The questioning is again a highlight of value in the personality picture. Self-
confident individuals do not ask; they tell you. The same practice is
followed in respect to negatively stated associations, or those instantly
denied. These also are important, qualitatively, in completing the personality picture.

'A picture'; 'a drawing'; 'ink'; 'some lines and dots.' These responses,
and variations of them, are problems because in some instances they are
S's association in a real sense; i.e., they evoke an older mental impression,
one that has had meaning to him at some time past. In many cases, S
is only describing the stimulus before him: the Rorschach figure is *ink*; or
it belongs to the general classification, *picture*. A white space is called a
hole; it may be simply an aperture in the larger figure, or recall a hole that
S has once seen. E's problem is to determine, in the inquiry, what is
intended in such a response. If he establishes that S is only describing, it
is not scored. If it is true associational content, it is scored. See also
examples of color description, and of reactions to light values, not scored,
in chapters IX and X.

CHAPTER V

THE WHITE SPACE: Ds and Dds

This term defines itself. The varieties of white space responses and some consequent perplexities inhere in the fact that, in associating to a white space, the patient usually attends also to a blot detail proper in the same percept. Usually, but not necessarily. Some associations have only a white space as their stimulus. The rule is as plain and as operational as the proverbial nose on the face. If the person perceives a white space as something with meaning, whether in connection with another detail or by itself, the scoring includes an s.

The white space was treated by Rorschach as always being a rare detail (ref. 27; p. 39). Our statistics show, however, that three of the white spaces are true D. These are the large inner areas of figures II, VII, and IX. Being the only space forms that are D, the vast majority of white space responses are thus Dd and confirm Rorschach's judgment that these percepts are a special case of Dd.

VARIETIES SELECTED

Reactions to the white space occur in four varieties: (a) S selects one of the major spaces (fig. II, Ds 5; fig. VII, Ds 7; fig. IX, Ds 8); this is scored Ds. (b) He selects a minor white space, a Dds. (c) He picks a major solid portion, D, with white space, major or minor, as a unit, 'a Halloween pumpkin'; this is scored Ds. (d) A minor solid portion is seen as a unit with inclusion of a minor white form, 'an open mouth'; this is scored Dds. Thus, identical symbols are used for responses that differ in one essential. Ds and Dds may indicate a white space alone or a space forming a unit with inclusion of solid details. The writer experimented for a time with separate symbols for each of these reactions. He found that he was heaping up complexity in the scoring armamentarium without adding to its diagnostic virtues. The importance of the white space percept lies in the opposition it reflects; that of D and Dd, in representing certain intellectual approaches. Use of Ds and Dds adequately indicates these mental activities.

When the white space is a statistically rare one but the selected part of the blot is D or W, the scoring records the Ds or Ws and a marginal note records that the space detail is a Dds.

The Ds and Dds referred to under c and d above and exemplified below are unitary reactions. 'A face' may be seen with white dots as 'eyes,' because the blot details and the white are a continuous percept. These differ from the responses in which the white space is organized with solid forms, with new meaning, e.g., 'a lamp, throwing shadows.' The scoring in these organizations too is Ds or Dds, as the case may be, with the organization value separately set down.

A difference of practice obtains with regard to some Dd and the one D that are distinguished from the rest of the blot figure in being much lighter gray, but not white. These are Dd 27 in figure I; the smaller gray portion in Dd 21 of figure III; and D 11 of figure VI. Some writers, Oberholzer for one, score responses to these three selections as space percepts. Since they are filled in, even if with notably lighter gray, I score Dd and D. To score s, the reaction must be to a totally empty space.

The following are examples of Ds associations in figures II, VII, and IX. These are all reactions to the major space forms as such. Special scoring problems that arise are also commented upon.

Figure II, Ds 5

'Vase'; 'hanging basket'; 'fish'; 'modern building with setbacks'; V 'ballet dancer'; ∧ 'entrance to grotto'; 'uterus'; 'turnip'; 'bat'; 'spinning top'; 'bird with spread wings'; 'expanse of snow.'

'The central space is something definite, and solid; something central around which everything seems to emanate.' This is a true reversal of figure and ground: the white has substance, and the black is the field. These reversals are found most frequently in two groups, healthy superior adults and schizophrenics.

It is frequently hard to decide whether the black, in these reactions, is simply the boundary for the white, giving the latter its form, or whether it is separately attended to and organized with the white. The inquiry must in these instances be more than usually meticulous, sometimes painfully so.

Figure VII, Ds 7

V 'Sphinx (head and neck)'; 'lamp (shade and base),' i.e., the upper section of Ds 7 is the 'shade' and the portion between the two D 5 is the 'base.'

V 'Ravine': S indicated only the large portion of Ds 7, i.e., the section between D 4 and the two D 3. Since not all of Ds 7 is included, the question of Dds is raised; but enough is included in the percept to score D; hence, Ds.

'A lake—outline of—seen from above in an airplane.' The question here again is whether any of the black is counted in or whether it is only a white space reaction. The mere fact that an outline is seen does not prove that S included any appreciable portion of the gray.

'The center space again seems like something safe, something that is solid.' Compare the very similar 'something solid,' by the same S, in figure II. Also, 'vase'; ∨ 'silhouette of Napoleon'; 'Hudson's bay'; 'tent'—with inner edges of black as 'sides of the tent.' 'Path, with shrubbery' (see chap. x); 'stomach cavity.'

Figure IX, Ds 8

'A picture under water . . . a well-defined vase . . . a fish globe, as you see the objects through the glass . . . not clearly but in a hazy way.'

'Vase'; 'cello'; 'bottle'; 'snow'; 'hole'; 'inlet from ocean'; 'bulb, tulip or onion'; 'sherbet glass'; 'mirror'; 'cow's face,' with Dds 23 as 'nostrils.' This Ds illustrates also how some percepts are an organization of a major white space with a blot Dd—e.g., with card held on the side, 'a lake on a hazy day,' in which the entire white space is the 'lake' and the gray-blue shadowy Dd is the 'haze.' The scoring is Ds, with a marginal note calling attention to the patient's having attended to the Dd. In fact, a number of responses to this Ds are on the borderline between Z (organization) and not Z. This is due to the presence of D 5 in Ds 8, and to Dds 22 or 23, any of which may be brought into the percept, although the original reaction is to Ds 8 as an individual unit. In this Ds, therefore, there is likely to be greater error as to whether we have a simple Ds or a Ds in organization with other elements. For examples of the latter, see chapter VI.

All Other Space Responses

The associations that follow illustrate all other varieties of Ds and Dds: i.e., solid D with Dds, Dds seen alone, and Dd seen with Dds.

Figure I

'A Halloween lamp . . . a grinning demon': Dds 30 as the 'eyes,' Dds 29 as the 'teeth,' and the black enclosed between the four white spaces filling in the 'lamp.' Enough of the figure is included to warrant scoring D; hence Ds, although the white space is Dds.

'A fox's head': lower half of D 4, with Dds 29 as 'eyes.' Scored Dds, since only Dd is involved. The solid is Dd, and so is the white space.

'Here's a little lake: two little lakes' (tiny Dds just under and interior to D 8).

'Remains of a snowstorm, when it begins to melt . . . the crevices': the edge of D 2, with the white indentations as 'snow' and 'ice crevices.' S first attended to the black edge itself and only secondarily gave meaning to the white. However, the percept is a single one and is labeled Dds, the same symbol that would be used if the space form alone were perceived.

'Moose's antlers,' Dds 30; ∨ 'tunnel,' Dds 32; ∧ 'geological map': the

white between D 8 and Dd 25—a complete reversal of figure and ground—
scored Dds.

Figure II

'A greyhound's face': Dd 24, with the long white inner space giving the
form of a greyhound.   Only Dd is seen; hence, Dds.

'Sexual organ . . . the vagina,' Dds 24.   A common response to this Dd,
with emphasis sometimes on the tiny inner space, sometimes on the filled-
in Dd, but including the space.   The scoring is the same, Dds.

$\vee$ 'Anus and buttocks': both Dd 28, with the space between, and with
Dds 24.   As in the preceding example, the present selection is a unit, even
though in the inquiry S breaks it up.

$\vee$ 'Immature birds, sticking up their heads,' Dds 30; $\wedge$ 'mountains,'
Dds 30—complete reversal of figure and ground.

Figure III

'Pumpkin cut open,' D 8, with emphasis on the white.   The white space
is Dd but the solid portion is D.   Scored Ds.

$\vee$ 'A conventional decorative flower; elongated petals,' Dds 24; $\wedge$
'country map,' Dds 24, complete reversal of figure and ground; 'face'—
what would be about the lower third of Dds 24 when the card is held in
the normal position; 'person's mouth,' Dds in center of D 8.

Figure IV

'Heads of dogs, two, shepherd or collie,' the lowermost Dds 24 on each
side of D 1; 'island,' Dds 24—reversal of figure and ground; 'map,' D 6,
outer edge only, at about the middle, with the adjacent white as 'shore.'
The space was attended to as a detail in the unit 'map.'   Dds.

Figure V

'Bird with beak open,' D 1, Dd 22, and Dds 29 seen as a unit.   The
white space is attended to, but only as an element of the larger percept.
A marginal note—Dds—is made, for aid in filling out the diagnostic picture.
The same considerations hold for the frequent response of: $<$'alligator's
mouth . . . or crocodile's,' both D 2 with Dds 28—scored Ds.

$<$ 'Mouth of queer bird,' D 3 with Dds 27 as the opening between the
jaws—scored Ds; 'vagina,' Dds 28; 'canal . . . inland bay . . . from ocean
to land,' Dds 29; 'arrow pointing to hell,' the tiny white notch at the extreme bottom of Dds 28; 'body of water'—space, generally, upward from
left lateral.   Dds.

Figure VI

'Section of spinal cord at fourth ventricle,' Dds 30; 'rectum,' tiny space between the two D 10; 'little lake,' Dds just interior to junction of D 9 with D 4.

Figure VII

'Open mouth,' Dds in inner edge of D 1, just below D 8.

Figure VIII

'Vertebrae.' The spaces between the rib details of D 3 were singled out. Scored Ds.

∨ 'Two people leaning against something . . . and the children leaning against each other.' In D 3, the separate portions of the white are each seen as the 'people leaning.' Scored Dds.

∨ 'Water,' Dds 28; > 'woman with white eyes,' contour of D 7, separating it from D 6, with tiny Dds as 'eye'—only Dd is involved, hence, Dds; 'island,' Dds interior to D 1, between one front and one rear leg—reversal of figure and ground.

Figure IX

'A piece that's torn out and folded back,' Dds 22. In giving meaning to Dds 23, some subjects embrace the larger area, i.e., Dd 22, some attend specifically only to Dds 23. In either instance, it is Dds.

Chapter VI

THE ORGANIZATION ACTIVITY: Z

A grasp of relationships is constantly going on as an individual associates to the Rorschach test ink blots.   This will be observed in any statistically appreciable number of test records, even in those of the feebleminded.   The relationships organized are of various degrees of complexity and may include all or only portions of the test figures, not only the gray or colored blot details but also the white spaces.[5]

The core criterion for Z is that S is building two or more percepts having no necessary relation to each other into a new unit percept, the meaning of which as a unit confers upon the organized details the meanings which the S sees in them.   Example: figure III, 'could be a garden . . . a pond of water,' in which all the black details are 'flowers, grass, shadow' while the inner white space is the 'water.'

The varieties of organization activity are:

(1) adjacent details,

(2) distant details,

(3) the inclusion of any space detail in the perceived relationship; and

(4) all W are Z.   These include the simple W of figures I, IV, V. But no form of DW is ever scored Z.

Rorschach does not identify the organization process as such.   But in his treatment of the whole response he is essentially describing this activity.   "The number of W," he says, "is, before all, index to the energy at one's disposal for the organization drive [*Assoziationsbetrieb*]" (ref. 27; p. 63).   It is an achievement, he notes, in the philosophically inclined and in the fantasy-endowed: "An optimum of these abilities is a further component of intelligence."   With apparent inaccuracy, however, he puts the label W on one response that does not include all elements of the figure. This is in figure III, when S sees the two humans in an active relation to each other, and irrespective of whether or not he attends to the red elements. Rorschach here recognizes that there can be organizing activity, *Assoziationsbetrieb*, without W.   His language is: "Even when the red details are not included, provided only the two human figures are seen, it is nevertheless denoted as a whole response" (ref. 27; p. 39).   He does not further elaborate at this point, but in another context he says: "The legs of the figures are separated off from the rump.   It requires, most likely, a primary movement experience to enable one to transcend this dividing point" (ref. 27; p. 26).   Granted that a movement experience, *kinästhetischer Moment*,

46

is involved, there is no reason why it should be designated W.   We have here what looks like a confusion of the two concepts, M and W.

The ongoing Z organization process that is present when S is associating to the Rorschach ink blots is obvious, but it was long missed.   One of the earlier commentators on it was Goldfarb.[14]   It is recognized by Ford[13] in her study of children; and by other writers.   In my basic study[5] of the organization activity, I discriminated between the degrees of difficulty in achieving each kind of organization in each of the ten test figures.   I used a statistical procedure in setting up the numerical values for all of these.*   These values are instrumental in differentiating the vigor and fluidity of intellectual processes that can go on in grasping meaningful relationships.   I find this table of values especially helpful in identifying the richer mentalities.

A short cut which makes possible very much the same over-all evaluation of organization activity as do my differentiating values is provided in a research study by Wilson and Blake.[34]   They correlated Z scores as obtained by my method with a simple count of *one* for each Z activity and found correlations of not less than .98.   In their report they publish a table showing the predictions to be made of Z score by my method from a simple count of the number of Z responses.   Since norms are available for Z activity at various mental growth levels as obtained by the weighted scores, the Wilson and Blake table enables us to convert these scores into the simple number of Z responses.   (See in this connection, appendix 5.)

To recapitulate the rules for Z, a response is scored *organization, or Z,* when two or more portions of the figure are seen in relation to one another, and when the meaning perceived in the combination, or in any of the component portions, obtains only from the fact of this organization.   Specifically:

(1) All W is Z.

(2) Any two or more component elements of a figure may be organized into relationship.   The unit may then consist of two or more D, D with Dd, Ds, or Dds, or any combination of these.

(3) The meaning reported by S must belong to the larger organized material.

(4) All Z must be in responses determined in part, at least, by form.   Responses determined entirely by color, C, or by light values, Y, therefore cannot be Z.

(5) The portions organized need not necessarily be external to each other, since subjects will sometimes analyze and resynthesize a figure or detail.

(6) Mere presence of contours between two details is not *ipso facto*

* My method has been criticized by Kropp.[18]

evidence of Z. Certain portions of the figures are broken up by contours but are frequently selected as units without any Z activity. Examples will be found among the responses listed as *not Z* below.

(7) When two or more kinds of Z occur in the same response, the one of higher value is credited.

(8) In those precision alternatives that need to be scored, Z is credited only once.

In those descriptive-art responses that are just sufficiently more than description to be scorable, Z is not scored. In all responses, the burden of proof is on the response before it can be scored Z.

Z IN FIGURE I

W, 1.0

All the examples of simple W in chapter II are instances of this Z process, with a value of 1.0. Z thus includes the common *bat* and *butterfly* and also the other instant W.

W with Adjacent Detail Z, 4.0

Two kinds of Z are used in each of the following responses, which are W and adjacent detail. The higher of the two values is scored, in this instance adjacent Z, or 4.0. Examples are:

'Arms in supplication,' D 1; 'in some fantastic costume,' D 2; 'the body is quite marked,' D 4.

'A central figure D 4 and two buttressing figures,' D 2.

Adjacent Detail Z, 4.0

'Looking down from an airplane ... water and mountains,' D 2. Portions of D 2 are the 'mountains' and other portions, differentiated because of varying depth of shading, are 'water.'

'Two wolves [D 2] and they have sticks [D 1] in their paws.'

'Two little children loving or kissing each other.' D 4 is broken up into the 'two children' and resynthesized into the 'kissing' relation.

Distant Detail Z, 6.0

'Islands and irregular coasts,' Dd 23, and the edge, nearest them, of the figure proper.

'A papa bird [D 5] perched on top and watching the baby birds' mouths open [D 1]; fledglings ready for the food which the mother bird will bring.'

White Space Organized with Filled-in Elements, 3.5

∨ 'A Japanese pagoda'; here is the entrance to it,' Dds 30; and 'two windows,' Dds 29; 'with various levels of rooms.' Ws F+ Ar, 3.5.

$\vee$ 'Those things [D 1] are fishes going through a bridge in a bowl.' Dds 30 are seen as the spaces through which the 'fish' swim.   The scoring is Ds FV+ Hh, 3.5.

$\wedge$ 'Like a map.'   The Dds below D 8 is the 'port' and the adjoining black is the 'land' of the 'map.'   Dds FY+ Ge Ls, 3.5.

$\vee$ 'A turban . . . a crown . . . regal attire': the entirety, with Dds 26 as the 'jewels.'   Scored Ws F+ Cg, 3.5.

Not Z

'What you see in dark field illumination; you get it in perspective.' The association was determined exclusively by the shading.

'Two faces of deer,' about the upper third of D 4.   The figure is broken up, but no meaningful relation between them is grasped.   No Z.

'A body,' D 4.   In the inquiry this response was elaborated into 'as though they [D 2] are ready to wrap around as if it is going to do a dance.' No Z, because the elaboration was entirely in the inquiry; it is a new idea, not an explanation of the response given in the free association.   The latent capacity for Z activity is here the important indication.   The S is capable of more intellectual grasp than he freely uses.   Any discrepancy between potential and achievement must arouse clinical curiosity.   What is preventing the exercise of this ability by the patient?   Inhibition? Blocking?   Disruption?

'A bear (D 4) and the arms (D 1) are up.'   D 1 is a continuous unit with D 4, and is frequently so interpreted.

'A sea animal . . . crab or lobster': D 1 with Dd 22.   The two details are frequently seen as a unit, each contributing toward the entire percept. This shows no new meaning attributable to a relation between the two details.

Z in Figure II

W, 4.5

'Modernistic painting'; 'section of medulla'; 'lovely sea animal . . . a sea anemone'; 'primitive, few-celled animal.'

W with Adjacent Detail Z, 4.0

'Peas porridge hot'; 'cartoons . . . as though doing a Russian dance'; 'a pair of clowns clinking glasses at a carnival,' 'clergymen going through rites.'

Adjacent Detail Z, 3.0

'Heads of queer animals [D 1], their topknots are fastened together,' D 4; 'a bridge, supported on rock formation,' D 4, with the lower portion of this D as the 'rock'; $\vee$ 'a profile [Dd 22], with the foot lost in the pre-cipice,' i.e., adjoining portions of D 1; $\wedge$ 'islands, united in some way . . . as if Malay Archipelago,' i.e., the two D 1 are the separated 'islands, united'; 'a sunset . . . with the sun [Dd 26] going over the mountains,' i.e., area of D 1 adjoining the 'sun.'

Distant Detail Z, 5.5

'Like two dancing hippopotami,' D 2; 'a duck with a fur coat on, looking at a mirror,' D 2; 'a spark gap,' Dd 27, with the intervening space as that across which the 'spark' would leap. The scoring formula would be Dds F Im. Z credit is 5.5.

'A fireplace,' D 3—because of its color, and including adjacent portions of D 1—'and two red stockings on top of it,' D 2. D 1, intervening be-tween D 3 and D 2, is disregarded, but the 'stockings' are nevertheless seen in relation to the 'fireplace'—'on top of it.'

White Space Organized with Filled-in Elements, 4.5

'A colored picture of the vocal cords, in the physiology of the larynx, as in books of singing': the entirety, with Ds 5 as 'orifice' (of singer). The scoring formula is Ws CF− An, 4.5. Regarding this response as a W, the organization value would be 4.0; regarding it as a white space response, 4.5. Since two kinds of Z are used, the higher value is credited.

$\vee$ 'A modern building [Ds 5], and it might be a red light on top of the building,' Dd 24; $\wedge$ 'a temple [D 4] in perspective or at a distance, a vista . . . and the white [Ds 5] is the approach'; < 'an animal, rhinoceros [D 1] close to the side of a lake,' Ds 5; $\vee$ 'entrance to a tunnel [Ds 5], like looking down from a side angle into the fire pit of Vesuvius,' D 4; $\wedge$ 'a lot of land [D 6] with a pond in it,' Ds 5; $\vee$ 'something sexual [Dd 24], the red seems to be shooting into the white,' i.e., the red Dd of Dd 24 is shooting into the inner white.

Not Z

'Like a pail of water has been spilled on all the place [D 1 and D 3] as if splashed.' Two D receive attention, but none of the meaning depends on the organization.

'As if someone had a cut here and the blood has been running a long time,' D 3. The 'someone' is not in the figure. The only D to which S attends is D 3; there is no Z based on two or more elements.

'Some part of the body,' D 1. The red Dd in D 1 could be 'blood.' Ds 5 could be the 'stomach.' Dds 29 could be the 'vaginal duct.' D 2 could be the 'ovaries.' This is indiscriminate naming of details bearing some relation to one another, but at no time is there an integration into a meaningful whole; it is chain association, without organization, seen in very low intelligence and in some mental disorders.

'Two ancient monsters,' D 2. Unlike the examples above of D 2 in distant Z, the figures here are not seen in relation. The mere attention to several details at once does not constitute Z.

'They look like two characters, like two clowns with their hands up [W]. Then they are apt to look like two dogs' heads facing each other,' D 1. There is Z in both responses; but the second is a precision alternative, even though the 'clowns' are W, and the 'dogs' are D. There has been only one Z activity. The respective scoring formulas are W M+ H P, 4.0; D F+ Ad.

Z IN FIGURE III

W, 5.5

This is the true W, i.e., all elements of the figure are included. Examples are:

Sketch done in shadows'; $\vee$ 'praying mantis'; $\vee$ 'cyclops'; 'heraldry symbol'; 'pelvis'; 'satyr from waist down.'

D 1, D 9

In D 1, we always have both of the human figures, leg details, D 5, included, and a relation expressed as between the two humans. In D 9, the humans are separately perceived; D 5 is always included, but a relation with the other D 9 is not seen. D 4 may or may not be included. In either D 1 or D 9, meaningful organization may be expressed with each D 4 separately, or with both together, i.e., D 7.

D 1, 4.0

'Distorted people, bending toward the front, and holding something between them'; 'games, as when you hold hands and swing around a circle'; 'a silly dance, two peculiar-looking gentlemen.' 'Dance' is what makes this a D 1, i.e., the two humans are a group.

D 9, 3.0

'Two women, bending forward'; 'kangaroos'; 'jumping jacks'; 'human beings, there's only one leg on each'; 'a crazy-looking man . . . bending over like that, holding on to something or lifting something up'; 'two men . . . the bodies in pieces'; 'monkeys'; 'there's a man . . . and there's a man.'

Adjacent Detail Z, 3.0

$\vee$ 'An evening landscape; trees [D 4] and a bluff [D 11]; a Japanese painting.'

$\wedge$ 'Skeleton of a woman's pelvis,' both D 11, with D 7, in a unit. Although no relation is seen here between the parts, this integration is infrequently achieved. It is a counterpart of the W in figures I, IV, V, and VI, i.e., a simple, instant organization. A similar response, for the same unit, is 'design on the wall'; also, $\vee$ 'like something carved out of the side of a mountain.'

'Vegetation [Dd 27] growing out of the chest'—i.e., of the usual human. That this was not a chance association but an organization is seen in this schizophrenic's fuller development of his premise: 'more like a tree that has human properties.'

Distant Detail Z, 4.0

D 9 is really a distant detail Z, since it includes D 5, which is separated off by white space. The statistical value of D 9 has, however, been found to be 3.0, as against 4.0 for all other distant Z in this figure. It is exemplified as follows:

$\vee$ 'Siamese twins; persons close together [each D 9]; each one seems to be raising his hands [D 5] in the air.' S is organizing meaningfully across intervening white space. But he engages in more of this, since the response continues: 'The red blot [D 3] now looks like some means of connecting the two.' Only a single Z is credited, however.

$\wedge$ 'Two little devils [D 2] are sticking out their tongues at each other.'

$\vee$ 'A sort of furred hat': all details except D 2; D 11 as the 'sides,' D 7 as the 'top,' and D 3 as a 'bow.'

'A crab,' both D 11 with D 7 as a unit, 'and there are his claws,' D 5.

$\vee$ 'A bird [D 11] is sitting on a tree', D 5. 'A face,' both D 11 forming its outline, and D 3 being the 'mustache.'

White Space Organized with Filled-in Elements, 4.5

'A landscape with inlets': Dds 24 is the 'water,' and D 11 the rest of the scene.

After having seen D 1 as two women, S indicates Dds 23, and elaborates: 'The dresses would have to be of the nineteenth century.'

$\vee$ 'Shrubbery,' D 4; 'water,' Dds in D 8; 'like a scene, and this is shadows,' i.e., D 8 forms 'shadows' of the 'trees' and the 'water.'

'As though an artist had drawn a picture of a man with a white collar, and a tie, but didn't complete it.' Both D 11 together form the 'face' outline of a 'man': the middle white space is a 'white collar,' D 3 is the 'tie.'

Responses with More than One Z, Requiring More than One Credit

'Two men getting ready for a boxing bout [D 1], putting on their gloves [D 4]; they're evidently fighting, because of the splashes of blood back of them,' D 2. Scored twice: D M+ H P, 4.0, for 'men about to box'; D CF+ Blood, 4.0, for 'splashes of blood,' distant Z.

'Two people warming themselves [D 1] over some fire; like in a house, a fireplace.' D 7 is a 'grate'; D 4, because of its position relative to the 'grate,' is a 'reflection.' Scored D M+ H P, 4.0, for the 'people' and, again, D Po Fi, 4.0, for the 'reflection.' A response determined by position (scored Po) without influence of form (F) is never scored Z. It refers to an accidental thought process and as such can not be the directed intellectual activity manifest in Z.

Not Z

'Embryonic chickens': seemingly a D 9, but in the inquiry it was found that D 5 was not included; the response is only to D 11 with Dd 30. Similar instances are: 'two men or skeletons'; 'a kind of bird'; 'like dogs'; 'two women with legs missing.' In other responses, D 4 also forms part of the percept, but as a unit D with D 11, without new meaningful Z. Thus, with card in ∨ position 'the way people protect their farms . . . scarecrows.'

Z in Figure IV

W, 2.0

Chapter ii provides samples of instant W. Each of those responses would be credited with a Z value of 2.0. Following are more examples:

'A design—some rough block in the form of an eagle'; 'one of the developmental forms in the starfish'; 'sloth'; 'dense forest'; 'like an overcoat, as if acid was on it, and it's in pieces'; 'undersea animal.'

Adjacent Detail Z, 4.0

'An animal [D 4] coming out of a rock,' i.e., main figure where it adjoins D 4.

'Shoals, as you look down on land, from a distance, the land [D 7] visible through the water [D 2], land covered by water.' The entire figure is included, hence W; but adjacent Z has higher value in this figure. W FV+ Ls, 4.0.

'A fountain, the water flowing up here [D 5] and falling off from each side,' i.e., lateral details, excluding D 4 and D 2.

'A huge ape, ambling forward, with long boots on; as a matter of fact, he seems to be sitting on top of a log, or some footstool, or seat.' Scored for adjacent Z.

'A man with his head cut off; and the blood flowing down [D 5] between his legs,' D 6. The response is scored twice, but only one Z is credited, that with the higher value. Thus, W F+ H; D FY+ Blood, 4.0.

'A little dog [Dd 22]; he's hiding behind a fur,' D 5.

'An animal [D 4] and he has paws on a stick', i.e., Dd connecting D 4 with the rest of the figure.

'As if someone put their arm in there [into D 1], a pipe; and they have four fingers sticking out,' Dd 26 and 28.

Distant Detail Z, 3.5

'Icicles hanging off a roof [D 4] and here you can see the water which has dropped down from the icicles melting,' i.e., the irregular Dd in the outer edges.

White Space Organized with Filled-in Elements, 5.0

'A map': the edge begins at D 2 and extends upward to about the level of the lower end of D 4; the outer white, along this edge, is the 'shore.' Not all *map* responses are Z, even though they usually involve solid with white, the latter as *water*. Many are unit reactions; the water is an incidental elaboration, very much as the body parts of an animal or human would be.

'Opening of a cavern, the light here [Dds 24]; the rest [D 1] is dark'; 'tunnels made by ice'—Dds 24, with D 1 as the 'ice' that hollowed out the 'tunnel.'

Not Z

'An impression of cloudiness, almost hopelessness.' Form does not enter into this reaction. Hence, no Z.

'Two snakes [D 4] coming down, ready to pounce on something.' There is a question as to whether this is Z because the 'snakes' are about to 'pounce on something.' However, no part of the figure is selected as the object of the attack; S is simply seeing the 'snakes' in a certain posture.

'Enormous trousers and the feet in them,' D 6. This detail is frequently seen as *boot* or some other form resembling a *human leg*. The 'trousers' and 'feet' are therefore in the class of precision elaborations.

'Somebody in his seven league books, stepping off.' No human is seen. The association has as its sole content 'a pair of boots.' The fact that a 'pair' is perceived does not constitute Z. The two D 6 when seen as *legs* are of similar form; they are not perceived singly but as a unit *pair*.

Z IN FIGURE V

W, 1.0

Bat and *butterfly* for this W are among the most frequent reactions in the test (cf. also chap. II, samples of instant W). Each would be scored 1.0. Other W, all with a Z value of 1.0, are: 'old-fashioned dining room picture of a fowl'; 'hide of game, stretched out to dry'; 'bird with wings spread out as in flight.'

Adjacent Detail Z, 2.5

'A woman dancing [D 7] with cape flowing out [D 4], the scarf shimmering, flung out of her hands': W, and also adjacent Z; the latter is credited. This response recurs with varying content but with the same structure: e.g., 'a masked dancer, with outstretched fabrics on his arms.' The middle (D 7) is the human in all these responses, and the lateral parts (D 4) are the appended decorations. Another example is 'animal with train of plumes.'

'A fur necklace or a cape made of a couple of fox skins.' What first looks like a simple W, with Z credit of 1.0, is instantly broken up by this S and reassembled—a relatively more difficult process in figure V. This is adjacent detail Z, credited 2.5. Similar instances are:

'Two rams bucking each other,' each D 4 being a 'ram.' W M+ A 2.5.

> 'A billow of smoke [D 4] reflected in the water,' i.e., at the midline, and including a small adjacent portion of the other D 4.

Distant Detail Z, 5.0

'Two people [each Dd 24] following each other around a mountain,' D 6.

White Space Organized with Filled-in Elements, 4.0

'A nautical chart [W], land surrounded by water, or water surrounded by land.' A similar example: 'The whole thing is an island of dreams, washed by the sea,' i.e., by the surrounding white space; 'canal or inland bay [Dds 29] from the ocean [outer white] into the land.'

> 'A shore line [white space at D 3 side] and this would be the hillside [W] with the trees . . . and bushes that naturally grow on the hillside,' i.e., Dd within D 4. Three kinds of Z are here achieved: W, white space, and adjacent. The highest of the three is credited, and the scoring is Ws FV+ Ls, 4.0.

Not Z

'Typical of depression, or of blueness, because it is black.' Form does not enter into this reaction; hence, no Z (cf. chap. x).

Z in Figure VI

W, 2.5

Chapter II offers samples of instant W in this figure. Each of those responses would receive a Z credit of 2.5. Other examples are:

$\lor$ 'Silhouette of a tree; here [D 8] might be the roots'; 'bass viol cello'; $>$ 'wild duck or goose, flying'; $\land$ 'leaf-imitating insect'; 'cross with something thrown over it'; 'statue.'

W with Adjacent Detail Z, 3.5

In this figure, the Z that is at once W and adjacent detail Z has been found to occur frequently enough to warrant estimating a separate statistical value for it. The response occurs less frequently than either W or adjacent detail Z alone. It therefore has a higher value, 3.5 (cf. similar treatment of double Z in fig. II). Examples are:

'Worm, squashed; this [D 5] is the body part, and this, the segment,' i.e., all portions lateral to D 5; 'a shield; the design on a coat of arms [D 8] and the second part has a heavy, shieldlike aspect of strength and durability,' D 1; 'an aeroplane picture of the ground [W], showing the road [D 5] through the ground'; $<$ 'land-scape reflected in the lake': the midline is the shore line at which the 'reflection' is effected.

Adjacent Detail Z, 2.5

'A shaft [D 5] rotating, and the rotation is causing waves,' i.e. the Dd in D 1; 'a channel [D 5] and this [D 11] is an obstruction—a rock or two rocks in the channel'; 'an airplane view of a river [D 12], here are steep sides [D 4], the canyon.'

$<$ 'A snake [D 2] crawling, and the reflection as it raises dust'; i.e., the 'snake' is continued in D 12, where, however, it is hidden in the 'dust'; one D 4 is 'reflection' of the other.

$\land$ 'A person's form'—lower third, approximately, of D 2—'with a light in back of the head,' i.e., the adjoining gray.

'Someone [D 2] stuck up on a crucifix,' D 6; 'lamp stand [D 5], clustered with jewels,' D 10 and Dd 21; 'grasshopper [D 2] standing on a stone,' D 1; $\lor$ 'two little heads [D 10] of people, huddled.'

'Two lady dancers': D 2 is seen as 'two dancers,' the detail being broken up and reorganized meaningfully.

$\lor$ 'Two apes back to back [each D 4] with a tuft of hair [Dd 21] on the head; and they have their arms extended [D 9]; the apes seem to have been hung on some sort of post,' D 5. In this response S twice organizes adjacent details meaningfully: 'the apes are back to back,' and they are suspended from a 'post.' Cumulative Z credit would be justified, but since the second Z is an elaboration of the one response, it is scored only once.

'A candle stand [D 1]; this could be the candle [D 2] that's in it; and this could be the reflection of the light'—portions of D 6. Three adjacent detail Z. The 'reflection' is elaboration of the response already credited with Z. However, there is ground for one additional Z credit. Thus, 'candle stand,' D F− Hh; 'candle,' D F+ Hh, 2.5; 'reflection,' Dd Y Fi, 2.5.

'A lighthouse,' D 8, with D 2 as the 'tower,' and D 6 as the 'rays.'

Distant Detail Z, 6.0

< 'Like out on a farm . . . you take a picture on top of a hill . . . and here are trees [D 6] and there is a little river [D 12], water.' The response was to D 1 generally, with the component Dd of D 6 brought in meaningfully as the 'trees.' Hence, distant Z. Adjacent detail Z is also used: the 'little river' in the landscape. The distant detail Z, being the more difficult, is credited.

White Space Organized with Solid Detail, 6.5

∨ 'A couple of eggs [D 10] nesting in a cavity [Dds 30] or in a tree in a crotch [Dds 30] between two limbs,' Dd 28.

Not Z

'A bird,' D 3, with D 2 as 'body' and D 6 as the 'wings.' S does not grasp any new meaning in the related material. Hence, no Z.

'A skeleton inside,' D 5. This is a descriptive 'inside.' The 'skeleton' is not seen in any relation to the rest of D 1.

'Whiskers [Dd 26] and wings,' D 6. Chain association without Z, reflecting the seriously hemmed-in mental state of the depressed individual who gave this response. He could not perceive the 'whiskers' and 'wings' in an organized whole. The feebleminded also show this inability to organize, though their psychologic weakness is of a different kind. As one example, 'water,' Dd in D 4, lateral to D 5, and 'water' for the similar Dd on the other side of D 5. Both responses were followed by 'pipe' for D 5; but the 'pipe' and the 'water' were not built into a meaningful unity.

Z IN FIGURE VII

Some W in this figure are, at the same time, organization of distant detail: *the two women gossiping*. The statistical credit for distant detail Z in this figure is higher than for simple W—3.0 as compared with 2.5. Hence this higher value, 3.0, is scored for the W that also employs distant detail organization. Some W utilize adjacent detail organization; the *women* are *on* something. The statistical value for this was found to be 3.5, and the response is so credited. The possible values where W is involved are therefore: simple W, 2.5; W with adjacent detail Z, 3.5; W with distant detail Z, 3.0.

W, 2.5

Chapter II affords samples of instant W, all of which would receive Z credit of 2.5.   Other examples are:

∧ *Cloud formations* seen from locations 'high enough to get a good view of the clouds'; 'formless piece of molding clay'; 'piece of coral'; 'isles of the sea'; 'torn paper'; 'map' (of islands); 'rock opening up.'

W with Adjacent Detail Z, 3.5

'Acrobatic performers [each D 2] standing on their heads; balanced on balls,' i.e., on D 10.

'Two ladies sitting down . . . as if there were a chair there . . . sitting on a rocker [D 10] and their knees touching,' at D 6.

∨ 'Two dancing dolls [each lateral half], their heads together,' at D 6.

∨ 'Two dogs [each D 2] balancing two objects [each D 10] on their noses.'

W with Distant Detail Z, 3.0

'A couple of ladies gossiping at a tea; they are large-bosomed, and dressed as of the nineties.'   Each lateral half is one of the 'ladies.'   No adjacent relation is organized.   This is the response pattern of essentially all the W that are also distant Z.

Adjacent Detail Z, 1.0

> 'Two animals caressing each other'—i.e., D 3 and D 10, 'because of the contact' at Dd 28.

'Two elderly women, faces squashed; they have had their teeth out . . . light is coming from the back.'   The only Z is in the 'light' i.e., Dd on D 1.

'A woman dressed in black [D 6] coming out from a distance, and clouds in the background,' D 4.

'Cliffs [D 6] and water rising through,' Dd 25; 'a tree [D 8] growing on top of a mountain,' i.e., adjoining portion of D 1; 'rocks . . . piled on top of each other,' i.e., the several D on each side; 'two Indians [each D 1] standing on rocks [each D 3]; these creatures [D 3] look as if they are just leaping off of a rock,' D 10.

'Indians [D 1] with feathers sticking out' [D 5].   While D 5 is frequently perceived as a unit with D 1, it is given its own meaning here, even if incidental to that seen in D 1.   The content is frequently 'coiffure,' 'high comb,' or similar elaboration of 'woman's head.'   A Z score of 1.0.

Distant Detail Z, 3.0

'Two women facing each other, as if in anger': each D 2 is one woman. This response, with variation in content but identical structure, is the most frequent one. The content need not be human forms: e.g., 'two little animals facing one another in a semiquarrelsome way, ready to fly at each other.' In some instances only D 1 or D 3 are selected: 'two old ladies waving good-bye'; 'two men looking away [both D 3] as though they had been angry; they had an argument.'

White Space Organized with Solid Detail, 4.0

'A big pot [Ds 7] steaming on the fire,' D 6 and D 10 being 'fire' and D 8 with Dd 24 being 'steam.'

'The outline of a lake [Ds 7] with the top of the mountains sticking up [sundry black Dd]; white clouds and black mountains.' S includes all of the blot figure. Ws FV+ Ls, 4.0.

'A globe of a kerosene lamp [Ds 7] and its base,' D 4.

'A motif . . . decoration on a building . . . sort of fountain . . . that [D 1] being the face, and that [D 5] a horn; and you could spill water in there,' Ds 7. Another W in organization with white space.

∨ 'An archway': Ds 7 is where 'a canoe can go through' and D 4 is 'the arch.'

'A path,' Ds 7, and 'someone coming down the path, a butler [D 6] and he's carrying a tray'—tiny Dd at left of the 'butler.' This 'tray,' even though elaboration, would be scored as adjacent detail Z had not credit already been given for the more difficult white space Z.

Not Z

< 'The British Isles [D 2]; it's the way England goes, bulged at both ends and narrow at the middle,' i.e., D 1 and D 3. Experience has shown this response to be a unit percept of D 1 and 3. Commonly it is 'North and South America,' occasionally 'Spain and France.' In all these there is no new organizing activity on the part of S. When, however, new meaning is added, e.g., the junction between D 1 and 3 as 'Panama Canal,' a new relation has been perceived, and Z is scored.

'Butterfly' for D 4 is not Z. This holds also for any other 'winged creature.' Even when D 6 is selected out as 'the body' and D 10 are 'the wings,' as in 'a caterpillar . . . his little body up here [D 6] and his wings [D 10] and as though he has some little feelers under his wings, where he steps on something,' the response is typically one in which the body parts are the apparent Z.

Z IN FIGURE VIII

W, 4.5

Examples of W in figure VIII are found in chapter II. Others are:

'Design for wallpaper, a heavy unit design, as for a downstairs gathering place.'

'Heavy foliage, bright colors . . . delicate leaves.' This may be contrasted with the 'disease' association among the not Z examples (below) dictated entirely by color.

'We have a man's chest, his lungs; the red on each side might be the rib laid open.'

'A statue with two carved mice on the sides': this is W and adjacent detail organization; credit, 4.5.

Adjacent Detail Z, 3.0

'A bear [D 1], climbing the tree,' D 4.

'A dress, the shoulders [D 5], the girdle and skirt,' D 2.

∧ 'A woman weeping; she has a green hat on': the tiny projection upward between both D 6 is the 'woman' and the tiny green Dd in which this projection ends is the 'hat.'

'Hands [Dd 22] reaching out, taking hold of the mice' [D 1].

'The unicorn and the lion holding up the crown': D 4 is broken up and reassembled with an original meaning.

'A tree [D 4], and two animals [D 1] are holding on to the branches with four feet and are standing on rock' [D 5 and D 2]; two entirely independent Z are achieved, and each is credited. Scored D F+ Bt, 3.0; D F+ A P; D F+ Ls (rocks), 3.0.

'A sea lion [D 6] peeking over rocks' [D 7].

Distant Detail Z, 3.0

< 'Animal [D 1] with feet resting on rocks [D 5, 2] looking down at something.' The 'something' is within the scene but not any detail in contact with the 'animal.' Either adjacent or distant detail organization can here be scored; credits are the same, 3.0.

'A fir tree in the distance [D 4]; at the bottom a forest fire [D 2] beginning to creep up'—i.e., toward the 'tree.'

White Space Organized with Filled-in Elements, 4.0

> 'An animal [D 1] stepping from a rock [D 2] over a brook [Dds 28] onto the bank on the other side [D 5], with a log coming out [Dd 22], this is the reflection at the bottom.' Much organization goes on here: adjacent details at least three times, possibly four (it is not certain that the 'log' is organized with anything; it is certainly a part of the scene); white space, once; and all the material is built into a whole. The scoring is for the highest of the possible values, W or S, either of which rates the same in figure VIII. Ws FV+ A, Ls P, 4.5.

∨ 'Two people, children, leaning against each other': in D 3, the white, the lower halves of the white spaces when the card is $\vee$. Each of these two Dds is one 'child.'

'An old-fashioned lamp post [tiny projection upward between D 6]; the globe would fit in here'—Dd 29, with the space within.

'A crystal rock [D 2], the background [i.e., white space] is sand.'

'Two wolves [D 1] catching their reflections in the lake': all the interior white spaces are the 'lake.'

Not Z

'The color scheme is offensive . . . it looks like a disease.' Color only dictated this response.

'A rainbow, because the orange [D 7] shades into the red [D 6], the red to blue [D 5], and the blue to gray [D 4]; that color goes through' D 7 and D 1. Again, color alone sets off the 'rainbow' association; form is not involved.

'Pair of drawers' for D 5—an apparent combination of two details that are, however, usually seen as paired, e.g., 'butterfly wings.'

'Butterfly' in D 2 and 'insect' in D 4 are not Z, even when the 'body' and 'wings' are patterned out. The responses are to the unit details. These details are regularly perceived as units, and as *butterfly* or similar form. The wings, etc., are elaboration, not construction of new relations. Similarly, D 3 may be seen as skeletal form, with or without attention to the included white spaces, and with or without Dd 21. When these Dd are included, they form one unit with the 'ribs' and do not introduce any new relation. Hence, no Z.

Z in Figure IX

W, 5.5

'Composite flower'; 'a futuristic painting'; $\vee$ 'old woman, all dressed up in the fancy clothes of 1890–1900; she has a green jacket, with shoulder puffs [D 1], and the purple [D 6] makes a collar'; 'A woman gazing into a mirror, and seeing her reflection.'

$\wedge$ 'A relief map, various heights shown by the color; and the center might be a peak; the white, lowlands [Ds 8]; it might be snow; the brown, arid land; and the green would be fertile.' Three kinds of Z—W, adjacent detail, white space. The highest, W, is scored—Ws CF+ Ge, 5.5. See also Chapter II describing the organized W in figure IX.

Adjacent Detail Z, 2.5

> 'A female figure [D 4], sitting on the carrier of a bicycle' [D 10].
> 'A fat man [D 1], riding a bicycle, climbing uphill,' [D 3].

$\wedge$ 'Two girls in old-fashioned costume,' i.e., D 1 are the full skirts, D 2 are the 'heads' of the girls; they are dancing a 'minuet.' This is credited as adjacent rather than distant detail Z, because the contact of the two D 1 led to the 'minuet' idea.

$\vee$ 'A parrot [D 3] sitting on a twig' [D 7].

$<$ 'A girl [D 7], falling off, and two people hanging over, trying to save her' [Dd 26 and Dd 27].

'Like a thistle, a motif from it; the brown [D 3] being the prickly part, and the green the dense part.' This S is organizing details not seen as units; the meaning he sees is his work.

$>$ 'A landscape': D 3 as the 'hill,' with D 1 as 'trees merged in the distance, reflected ... to account for the reproduction of the same outlines.' The question is whether the Z is of the distant detail kind, since the two D 1 do not actually touch. But all *reflections in landscapes* have been found to be adjacent detail Z and they are so scored as a general rule.

'Two people kissing each other': D 3 and D 1, on each side, is one 'person'; the 'nose' is at Dd 28; they are 'kissing' at the inner junction of the two D 1, i.e., at Dd 30.

'A rock [both D 3] and a tree inside' [D 1]; 'inside' in the sense of growing out from it.

$\vee$ 'A sort of lamp shade [D 9] with a pedestal, and the colors below are the shadows thrown by the lamp.'

Distant Detail Z, 4.5

'Things reaching toward each other,' D 7 and Dd 25 as a unit, on one side, 'reaching' toward the corresponding unit on the other side; 'or a sort of bridge structure, incomplete.'

'Two curious creatures, with claws and breasts of birds, conversing,' D 3; 'two creatures squirting something at each other,' D 3.

'A chicken that's being cooked ... put on a spit and opened up'—D 1 and D 3 as a unit form half of the 'opened-up chicken' and D 5 is the 'spit.'

'Landscape; if it ain't landscape it must be rocks'—both D 3. S is in some doubt, but he does organize his 'rocks' into a 'landscape.' In the inquiry he gives further evidence by calling D 3 'hills' and fitting D 5 in as 'river.'

'A little bridge [Dd 25]; where they connect is the arch that makes the bridge.' Actually they do not connect; S closes the gap.

'A candle [D 5] leaving shadows [D 1, 3]'; 'fire with smoke coming out [D 5], and on the side two trenches [D 1], and they built a fire in the middle.'

White Space Z, 5.0

'Mountains [D 3] and a valley [Ds 8]; it is a vista.'

∨ 'A map, with the surrounding water': D 7 and the white space around it.

> 'A landscape with water [Ds 8] and the hills in the distance' [D 5].

< 'A brook,' one of the white spaces forming Dds 23; 'a stump is over it,' the immediately adjoining Dd; and there is a 'reflection,' i.e., the Dds 23, that is the lower one when the card is <. Distant Z is also used, but the white space Z has the higher value.

'An arch,' the two D 7 as a unit, "with a very deep drop in between,' Ds 8.

> 'Looks like a lake [Ds 8] and hill [D 3] and the sun rising': the orange Dd, outward to Dd 22, and adjoining D 2 (at the 'neck' of what is usually an 'animal') 'is the sun, rising in the morning, and the moon too, in the evening, the quarter-moon.' Dds 23 is the 'moon.' In the inquiry S added, 'One is reflection of the other in the lake,' i.e., portions of the other D 1, D 3, and the other Dd 23 are reflection. The Z here includes (a) adjacent detail twice, in the 'reflection' and the 'rising sun,' and (b) white space twice, in 'the lake and the quarter-moon rising in the evening.' The best scoring would be Ds FV+ Ls, 5.0, for the 'lake scene,' and Dd CF− Ls, 2.5, for the 'sunrise.'

> 'When you're out in the wilds and the sun [D 3] is going down, and this blue fringe [D 5] is like a lake, and it is reflected in the water' [Ds 8]. Distant and adjacent white space Z in the one response. The highest, i.e., white space, is credited.

Not Z

'A fountain, and water shooting up' [D 9]. This detail is frequently seen as a unit—∧ as a 'fountain,' ∨ as 'tree'. The percept is not new Z.

'Mountains,' D 3, and, in the inquiry, 'because there is water in between.' The response, given by a feebleminded subject, reflects an approach to Z that does not become Z. The fact is grasped that there is a relation between the two associations—they are 'mountains' because of the 'water' between; but the several D are not organized into a larger unit. Then too the 'water' is first seen in the inquiry, indicating that the relation was only sensed in the inquiry, and hence could not be scored.

'Two dogs with a stick between them,' D 3 and D 7. The proof of a meaningful relationship suggested by 'between' was lacking. The language was descriptive. The burden of proof is always on the response, before it can be scored Z.

Z in Figure X

W, 5.5

'A menagerie ... beetles, crabs.' The many details composing this figure are frequently reacted to indiscriminately as 'bugs,' 'animals,' 'fish,' or 'plant life.' Such response is not Z, unless they are also seen in some unifying relation, such as the 'menagerie.'

Other examples are: 'view of the bottom of the sea ... crabs, sea urchins, and all kinds of different things'; 'aquarium'; 'carnival of animals'; 'botanical exhibit.' Of the same order, but more original, and packed with content revealing creative potentiality, are 'dance of the caterpillars'; 'dance of the lower orders floating in liquid air.'

Other Z of the W type in this figure are: 'coat of arms'; 'dance arrangement'; 'wallpaper design for nursery'; $\vee$ 'orchid'; 'figures in tapestry'; 'bursting of fireworks when in the air.'

Adjacent Detail Z, 4.0

'Insects fighting each other,' the two D 8; 'people [D 8] dancing around a Maypole,' D 14; $\vee$ A man flying [D 5], the arms seem to be human wings [D 4], as if attached.'

'Two clownish figures [D 9], joined by a blue hand [D 6], which is continuous with a penis'—the Dd projecting from D 9 and touching D 6.

$\vee$ 'Two people [D 6] jumping from something to a cliff ... a running jump, and they have their feet on that'—on D 9, which is the 'cliff.'

'A cloud going across the yellow sunrise,' D 15; the black Dd is the 'cloud.'

$<$ 'Peacocks or unicorns [D 4] rising on each side of a manlike figure,' D 5.

$\wedge$ 'Two birds flying toward each other,' D 6; 'creatures [D 1], waving something green,' D 12.

'Two animal bodies [each D 2] and baby faces in them,' Dd 33; 'two dogs [D 6] with a bone,' Dd 34.

$>$ 'An ocean [D 9] and people in the water': various Dd of D 9 are 'waves' and heads of the 'people.'

'Like clowns [D 2] and they are holding on to the curtain [D 9], a stage curtain, and swinging.'

Distant Detail Z, 4.5

$\vee$ 'A flower,' D 9, with D 10 as the 'pistil'; $\wedge$ 'beetles or scarab [D 12] worshiping the central figure [D 11], about to prostrate themselves'; 'two animals leaping at each other,' D 7.

'A soldier,' Dd protruding on the edge of D 9 nearest to D 1, 'leaning over a trench, ready to shoot; other soldiers lying dead,' i.e., other Dd protruding on the edge of D 9.

∨ 'A man [D 5] diving into a chasm, trying to get his hands above his head; he's a short, fat little fellow; directly below . . . it looks as if it might be a hole [Dd 34] but not big enough to get a man through.'

'Two policemen breaking into a door.' S effected several Z: the 'police' are D 9, with D 8 as 'caps'; the two D 6, the 'top of the door'; D 3, the 'door knocker' they are swinging. This latter is distant detail Z, which is credited.

White Space Organized with Filled-in Elements, 6.0

'A purple vest, open, with some gaudy skirt underneath.' Dds 30 is the 'skirt', and portions of D 9, with D 6 and D 3, are the 'purple' and the 'gaudy' vest.

'A huge canal system [Dds 30], like the Panama Canal, and a system of locks,' D 10, D 6, and D 3.

Not Z

'A curious fish,' D 10. This detail, while frequently broken up and resynthesized, is also seen often as a continuous unit, as here, or as 'a lyre.'

A similar problem is presented by D 11, which may be perceived as one unbroken form—'a chandelier'; 'the Eiffel Tower'; 'a tree.'

'All kinds of worms, different insects.' As contrasted with 'collections' and 'menagerie' (above) in this figure, no unity or common factor is grasped in the present response. Hence, no Z.

CHAPTER VII

APPROACH AND SEQUENCE: Ap and Seq

Two of Rorschach's important indices for his test, approach and sequence, are derived directly from the W, D, Dd scorings. The normative basis for these two indices rests, therefore, on the reliability with which the investigator scores W, D and Dd. In finding the approach (Ap) the rule is again a simple one of (a) counting the number of W, D, and Dd in the record, and then (b) estimating the proportions of each. In a normative adult population with a mean productivity (R) of 32.65, the Ap was found to be W: 6, D: 23, Dd: 3.[7] I always use this formula to find the expectancy for each of the three location categories, as proportion of R, and so I arrive at S's Ap. For example, in a record of R 32, with W 10, D 19, Dd 3, Ap is W! (D) Dd. With R 49 the expectancy would be W 9, D 35, Dd 4. Or with R 49, we may have W 6, D 41, Dd 2, and then Ap is (W), D!, (Dd). The exclamation point designates excess emphasis; a score in parentheses signifies insufficient attention to, but not extreme disregard of, the particular item.

The D!! finding represents a disagreement with Rorschach, who says, "I have never found a pure D type, Dd type" (ref. 27; p. 45). This is contrary to my own experience. I have numerous records in which W and Dd occur not at all or in too small measure to form part of Ap. In respect to the Dd type, my run of cases confirms Rorschach. Another departure from *Psychodiagnostik* is in respect to the W+ as against the W− types. The plus and minus scores in the test distinguish between kinds of F. To introduce them into the *Erfassungstypus* discussion is to mix the variables. True, a W individual who is also dominantly F+ differs critically from a W subject with mostly F− perception. The one is likely to be superior and healthy, the other in a condition of serious functional breakdown, such as is seen in brain pathology. But all this has to do with the personality as a unit, and the manner in which it manifests itself in the several Rorschach test variables. For purposes of exposition, the variables are best demonstrated separately.

Weakness in my formula exists with respect to the possible changes in the normal proportions with increased R, especially at highest productive levels. Instead of a straight line shift in quantities of W, D, Dd, which the formula assumes, we may have a curvilinear relationship. It will take *ad hoc* research to establish this.

The question is in order, too, whether the formula is equally applicable to all ages, a question especially important in using the test with children. However, it is a standard rule to use the formula, and the reasoning for this is stated elsewhere (ref. 8; p. 256). The frames of reference for the basic formulae were provided by 155 normal, Chicago school children[33] and 157 normal adults.[7]

The general rule for establishing a patient's Ap is that it is a function of (a) the actual findings of W, D, Dd, in his test record, and (b) expected findings in accordance with his total scored productivity. Concerning how great a departure from expectancy amounts to being a meaningful excess or inadequacy, for D the percentages are 87.5 and 112.5. That is, when D is 87.5 per cent or less of expectancy it is relatively ignored in the approach; at 112.5 it is overstressed. With the usually smaller totals of W and of Dd the obtained percentages range much more widely; this difficulty is especially marked in records in which total associational production (R) is small. For example, with R 20, expectancy is 4-14-2 (the actual slide-rule figures are 3.7-14.4-1.9). If S produces a record with W 3, D 15, Dd 2, his W is only 1, in absolute count, away from expectancy, but yet it is 75 per cent of expectancy. D and Dd remain close enough to the expected so that we cannot mark their totals as departing from normal. The Ap here is (W), D, Dd. For his loss of W, this S is not notably compensating by accenting either the D or Dd. The excess of one D is within a leeway range. In practice, it is noted that the compensating imbalance in this pattern is toward the D direction and the interpretation is so influenced.

Sequence is a statement of the order in which W, D, Dd are attended to in the ten test figures. Findings of sequence can, therefore, be reliable to the extent that W, D, Dd have been objectively (statistically) established. The examiner's judgment becomes a factor here, however, since no quantitative formula has been worked out by which to delineate the methodical sequence as differentiated from the Irregular, and the Irregular from the Confused. It is a learned process for each examiner, derived from his own growing experience, although he can also use the published sequence findings of others as points of reference.

Sequence is classified into three grades—methodical, irregular, confused. These are essentially Rorschach's *geordnet*, *gelockert*, and *zerfahren*. His *straff*, or "rigid," and *umgekehrt*, or "reversed" sequences do not occur with sufficient frequency to warrant separate categories. When an inverted sequence is found, it is more likely to be confused; i.e., S will first attend to Dd in several cards, but is pretty certain to start in some with D, and once or even twice with W. Theoretically, there is no reason why a methodical sequence cannot start in all or nearly all the figures with Dd, proceed to D, then to W. But it just does not happen. Most individuals who are capable of W start with W, then attend to D, then to Dd. That is, they (a) make a general survey of the problem, (b) look over the obvious elements, and (c) study the minutiae. This is the methodical sequence (*geordnet*). In some subjects this order breaks down severely. There is no discernible logic in S's attack. As one inspects his procedure in the ten

TABLE 2.—*Ap and Seq*

I	II	III	IV	V	VI	VII	VIII	IX	X	Totals	
W	W	D	W	W	W	W	D	D	D	W	7
Dd	Ds	D	D		Dd	D	D	D	D	D	17
	Dd	D	Dd			Dd		Dd	Dd	Dd	9
			D					W	D		
								Ds			
								D			
								Dd			
								Dd			

Ap. The expectancy is: 6-23-4. Findings are: W (D) Dd!

Seq. In 6 of the 7 figures in which S uses W, she starts with the W. Wherever she uses both D and Dd, she always first sees the D. The fluctuation of Seq in figure IV is minor. In figure IX we have the one real irregularity: a Dd even preceding the W. As a whole this is one of those fluid sequences—with even a slight trend to rigidity—most common in the healthy normal subject. Seq is *methodical*.

TABLE 3.—*Ap and Seq*

I	II	III	IV	V	VI	VII	VIII	IX	X	Totals	
W	W	W	W	W	W	W	D	D	W	W	11
D			D	D	W	D	W	D		D	9
D					D			W			

Ap. The expectancy is 4 W, about 13 D, slightly less than 3 Dd. Hence, the record shows heavy excess of W at the expense of everything else. Ap is W!! (D).

Seq. This record demonstrates the difficulties of establishing Seq when the responses are so few. W usually precedes D, where both are found; in figures VIII and IX. Seq is *questionably methodical*.

TABLE 4.—*Ap and Seq*

I	II	III	IV	V	VI	VII	VIII	IX	X	Totals	
W	W	D	W	W	D	D	D	Ds	D	W	5
D		D	D	W	D	D	D	D	D	D	21
D			Dd		Dd			D	D	Dd	3
									D		
									D		
									D		
									Dd		

Ap. The expectancy is 5 W, 21 D, 3 Dd. Ap is therefore just as expected.

Seq. W precedes D, and D precedes Dd always. If anything, this Seq approaches Rorschach's "rigid" category. But in any event it is *methodical*.

figures, there is no possibility of prediction at any point as to whether he will in the next card start with Dd, W, or D, or as to whether any one D or Dd or W will be followed by more of the same. This is the confused (*zerfahren*) sequence. The irregular sequence will come to be recognized qualitatively midway between the extremes.

TABLE 5.—*Ap and Seq*

I	II	III	IV	V	VI	VII	VIII	IX	X	Totals	
D	D	D	W	W	DW	D	D	Dd	D	W	2
Dd	D	D		DW	Dd		Dd	D	D	DW	2
Dd		Dd		D	D		D	D	D	D	21
D								D	D	Dd	12
Dd								Ds	Dd		
Dd								Dd	D		
									Dd		
									Dd		
									D		

Ap. The expectancy is 7 W, 27 D, and 4 Dd. The finding 2-23-12 thus shows a clear excess of Dd, with serious disregard of W. Ap here takes account of the 2 DW. Even 1 DW is really a deviation; a finding of more than that signifies a serious weakening of method of approach. Hence, Ap is DW (D) Dd!!

Seq. The major blot portions—W, D—usually precede the minor ones, Dd. But deviations are obvious: the 2 Dd following immediately on the D with which S starts in figure I; the Dd sandwiched in between 2 D in figure VI, and again in figure VIII; the Dd as first response in figure IX; fluctuation of D and Dd in figure X. Seq is very *irregular*.

TABLE 6.—*Ap and Seq*

I	II	III	IV	V	VI	VII	VIII	IX	X	Totals	
W	D	D	D	W	W	D	D	D	D	W	18
D	D	D	W	W	Dd	D	Dds	D	D	D	23
D	D	W	W	W	W	Ws	Dd	D	D	Dd	4
D	W	W	W		W	W	D	Dd	D		
W	D		W						W		
D	Ds										

Ap. The expectancy is 8-32-4. The finding, 18-23-4, shows heavy overemphasis on W at the expense of D, with Dd normal. Ap is W! (D) Dd. The question arises here of omitting D altogether in Ap. It would be W!! Dd. Actually the D found is 72 per cent of expectancy. As a rule o' thumb, we omit the symbol only if the finding is less than half of the expectancy; when it is between 50 and 85 per cent, we use the parentheses; when it is more than about 85 per cent, we treat it as a normal Ap.

Seq. In 5 of the figures D precedes W. But Dd is never selected before at least one D has been selected and is never the first response, although there is fluctuation of D and Dd. This Seq has, in its W, D order, some of the characteristics of Rorschach's "reversed" Seq. It is certainly seriously irregular, though, on analytic inspection, less so than appears. Seq is *irregular-confused*.

TABLE 7.—*Ap and Seq*

I	II	III	IV	V	VI	VII	VIII	IX	X	Totals	
Ws	D	D	W	W	DW	D	D	D	Dd	W	5
Dd	D	D	W		Dd	D	D	D	D	DW	1
	Ds	Dd	Dd		D	Dd		D	Dd	D	21
	Dd	Dd			W	Dd		D	Dd	Dd	13
	D	D							D		
	Dd								Dd		
									D		
									D		

Ap. The expectancy is 8-29-4, the finding 5-22-13. Since we count DW as D, S selects too few W, is excessively sensitive to Dd, and insufficiently interested in D. Ap is (W) (D) Dd!!

Seq. S starts with Dd in 1 of the figures, with DW in another, with W in 3 of them. In figure I, a Dd follows the W, and in figure IV, Dd follows 2 W, with no attention to D. A Dd follows the DW of figure VI, with the W at the end. D and Dd intermingle in figures II and X. Here there is too little central direction of attention. Seq is *confused.*

TABLE 8.—*Ap and Seq*

I	II	III	IV	V	VI	VII	VIII	IX	X	Totals	
D	W	Dd	D	W	W	D	D	D	W	W	5
W	Dd	D				Dds	D	Ds		D	10
								D		Dd	4
								Dd			
								D			

Ap. The expectancy is 4 W, 13 to 14 D, 2 Dd. The imbalance is thus in the accent on Dd and in the neglect of D. Ap is W (D) Dd!

Seq. This is an example of how a hebephrenic (a woman of 21) can confuse order even when producing only 19 responses. In the first four instances in which she gives more than one response per figure—figures I, II, III, VII—she never uses the same sequence twice. In figure IX her final response is to D 1, i.e., the D most commonly selected in this figure, following 3 other D and a Dd. Seq is *confused.*

TABLE 9.—*Ap and Seq*

I	II	III	IV	V	VI	VII	VIII	IX	X	Totals	
D	D	D	D	W	D	D	D	D	D	W	2
D	Dd		D	DW					D	DW	1
D	D		D	W					D	D	21
									D	Dd	1

The expectancy for R 25 is W 4.6, D 18, Dd 2.8. With the DW the total D count in this record is actually 22. Thus, a clear example of excess attention to D, with neglect of W and of Dd. Ap: (W) D!! Sequence is marked simply NEV—not enough variation.

Sequence is, then, determined by inspection. The situation in this respect is similar to what it is for some of the individual tests in the Stanford-Binet and in Wechsler's scales. We turn to the Terman-Merrill manual to decide whether we will score, say, a Memory for Designs with full credit, half credit, or no credit, as the case may be; or, similarly, with reference to the Paper Cutting, for definition of abstract words, and some others. Or in the case of the Wechsler, a patient's answers may serve as clinical leads in such tests as the Information, Vocabulary, Similarities, when the answers are compared with those which Wechsler has published.

Rorschach's published cases[27] are, of course, invaluable; so are the few that Oberholzer has published.[24, 25] In the one sample record which they included in their 1942 manual, Klopfer and Kelley[16] identify the Sequence. Among European writers, Bohm's German textbook[12] provides valuable examples; and among the French writers Loosli-Usteri does,[19, 20] as does also Schachter,[30] and my own texts.[6, 8, 10] Another, especially valuable source is the journal published by Huber,[35] including as it does from time to time full test protocols and their scorings, usually by Swiss writers, which makes available the current thinking in the test's country of origin. A practice which examiners will find helpful is to conduct reliability checks on themselves from time to time of their Seq judgments, using, of course, a number of their own cases. It is a help toward keeping one consistent in this procedure.

The white spaces in Ap and in Seq. As my statistics show (see p. 41), three of the space details in the ten test cards are true D: Fig. II (Ds 5), Fig. VII (Ds 7), and Fig. IX (Ds 8). In establishing the Ap or Seq in any one record, I therefore count the scoring of Ds among the D and the scorings of Dds among the Dd. Where error can creep in in this practice is in records in which a number of Dds are submerged in the scoring because they are part of a larger percept and have been scored Ds. An alert examiner will, of course, make his notes about these in his margin and they will contribute to his interpretative thinking.

Examples of Ap and of Seq, as derived from various response records, follow. Each table shows the order of W, D, Dd as actually selected.

The diagnostic usefulness of both Ap and Seq as originally described by Rorschach is very high. They pattern out a patient's intellectual fluidity or rigidity, his learned habits in this sphere, the psychologic defenses which these habits disclose, and what all this means in terms of changeability, which is to say, treatability. Both these test findings have been ignored by many American psychologists, to their great loss of clinical information provided by the test.

Chapter VIII

EXPERIENCE OF MOVEMENT: M

In the movement response, Rorschach makes his most original contribution to method in personality study. The response, as Rorschach understands it, really reproduces movements or activities that S is carrying on within his mental life. Since these mental activities are those in which we should like to engage in the outer world but cannot, or dare not, they are our wish-fulfilling activities. Thus, they are our fantasy life—which means that the associations encased in them actually project S's intimately personal living. The more original and deviating movement associations are representatives of very deep wishes, innermost psychologic activity. The content of the response is thus identical with the material of Freud's unconscious and of the psychoanalysts' dreamwork. Wells (F. L.) has called it an experimentally induced dream.

The psychologic activities that M projects to the surface are therefore of a kind that can only materialize in the image of a human being. The fantasies in which people realize themselves have their own likenesses, i.e., human forms, as heroes. Were we built in other shapes, it is likely that M would take these shapes. We are reminded here of the poem by Yeats in which the moorfowl, the lotus, the roebuck, and the peacock each speaks his mind concerning the Creator. Says the peacock (he is representative of the others):

> I passed a little further on and heard a peacock say:
> Who made the grass and made the worms and made my feathers gay,
> He is a monstrous peacock, and He waveth all the night
> His languid tail above us, lit with myriad spots of light.

The nuclear M or movement association is thus the one in which a whole human being is engaged. He may be actively engaged in it, or passively, i.e., acted on rather than acting. This scoring applies also to a posture, whether of the person in some tension, static, or lying down and still. The two essentials are that (a) it is an activity within the normal anatomic repertoire of human beings, and that (b) a whole human form, any that can be scored H, is seen. The most common M is the one elicited by the two manikins of figure III. Rorschach extends his M category to include associations concerning humans in whom activity is usually connoted, e.g., the "two clowns" of figure II. His language (ref. 28; p. 196) is: "It is also a movement response, M. Comparing it with a large amount of material it will always be shown that a kinesthetic component is essential in this association (the clowns), whether or not S has expressed anything concerning the movement in the clowns." I like to have S say that the "clowns," or whatever the humans perceived, are doing something, and any doubt can usually be resolved in the inquiry. Thus, in figure III the "two men" sometimes remain just "two men," forms without activity or other signs of life. This is scored F+. There is, however, justification for the M for the "clowns" and it takes not much effort in the inquiry to elicit from S that they are "clowns because that's the way clowns are," and a further question or two brings out the mimicking attitude or some related pose. "A person sleeping" is M. So also is "somebody dead." But "a dead body" would require closer scrutiny as to whether the percept is of a human being who has died or who has been killed; either of these can be M, but a simple percept of a human body without language to indicate that S sees it as having been the object of action or having recently died is not M.

M in part humans. M, Hd. The more usual body parts so scored are: the arms, or any parts of them, i.e., fingers, hands, fists. Eyes. The face is fairly frequent as expressing some emotion or other state of mind. Somewhat less frequent are lips as "kissing," or "blowing," and teeth as "biting"; also the legs or feet, and occasionally the toes. Activity characteristic of these human body parts needs to be part of the association if M is to be scored. Also scored M is the male genital in erection or in process of penetrating a vagina—rare but it occurs. The female genital is frequently seen, by itself, and usually is not M. Now and then the percept is as of a woman's thighs exposed for intercourse or for childbirth. These two are M. My rule is to score M, Hd whenever the percept includes any part of a human and the part's normal activity.

The selected area and M. Whether the movement is seen in W, D, or Dd does not affect its scoring as M if the above descriptive definitions of M are met.

Movement in animal associations. M, A. Here is included all movement in which either of the following two conditions are met. The activity is (a) one specifically characteristic of the human species, as 'two birds talking' for figure VI (D 10), or (b) it is an activity in the human anatomic repertoire, of which the 'boxing bears' of figure II is the most common; while another is for figure X, the upper grey details (D 8): 'two bugs having an argument.' To score M in part animals, Ad, the same rules hold as do those for M in whole animals. The activity must be a specifically human one or such as humans can anatomically perform. (See p. 91 f. for animal activity that is not M, and compare also p. 87 f. for some that are M.) Examples: in figure II the jowl detail, upper outer corner of the black mass (Dd 31): "an ape's mouth, grinning,' is Dd M+ Ad; in figure X one of the tentacles of the upper blue (D 1) is 'a lobster's claw, tickling the back of this man's neck,' scored Dd M+ Ad, Hd.

A serious source of error with regard to M in A is contained in Klopfer's FM category. This scoring sign is being routinely applied to any animal activity, e.g., "a bullfrog croaking" (ref. 17; vol. I), but this scoring may impute to the patient a dynamic psychologic process in M, such as a strong wish or fear, where there is none. (See p. 76 concerning Rorschach on animal movement that is not M.) Klopfer says of FM that it provides indication that "a subject is emotionally infantile, living on a level of instinctive prompting below his chronologic and mental age" (ref. 16, p. 279). This is a correct statement for animal content that is a true M. A fantasy invested in an animal actor is in fact a dream reality, and therein lies its dynamic quality. It has so much valence to the subject that he must disguise it in subhuman content. All M has, *ex hypothesi*, a latent meaning differing from that in the manifest content. That is, it screens something from the S's system of conscious thinking, even as the M's in human form do. In the M with animal form S must keep the meaning much further away from his system conscious. He is more effectively concealing the wish or the fear. It is essential, therefore, to take account of the deeper significance of the M in animal forms as possible leads to ideas against which the patient is doubly defending. However, to score FM, i.e., M, for animal activities as a general rule is to take in also much M that is non-M (e.g., 'bullfrog croaking'), with resulting diagnostic errors. It is to say of a person that he is living a wish fulfillment, or mulling over an anxiety, when he is in fact living no such experience. Another drawback of this scoring is that it is a detriment to the psychologist's learning experiences. Depending on rote signs, he does not have to search for psychologic processes, to think through the dynamics in an association. It is an easy way out. But it stunts growth.

Expression of emotion as M. The S's percept may be only of an emotion; however, this always means a human emotion and they are scored M. They may be seen as if in human or in animal forms, whole or part humans or animals. Thus, in figure IX, the end pink detail (D 4): 'an elderly man, with a kind benign smile,' D M+ Hd P. In figure X, the lower green detail (D 4): 'a caterpillar with a sense of humor, smiling, whimsical.' For figure IV, the upper lateral projection (D 4), card on its side: 'an arrogant cobra.' In figure IX, the small Dd in the large green detail (D 1): 'two eyes looking toward me, vacant, looking past me.'

Abstract emotions. The emotion may be directly abstracted from the color or the shading. Thus, figure III the upper lateral red detail (D 2): 'the red is anger,' and the patient later related it to anger in the human figure earlier seen. A scoring here is D M.C− Ab. For the entire of figure IV: 'this blackness, it is depression.' Scored W M.Y Ab. For the entire of figure V: 'looking down from a fearfully great height, upon a lake, cavernously deep.' Scored D M.V— Ls.

M in the inanimate and in natural forces. Klopfer's and Piotrowski's *m*. In some associations, S reports in inanimate objects an activity that could be one in which a human engages; or he describes it with a vividness intense enough to indicate that he is identifying with it. The subjective element can be large in scoring these. Some examples: in figure VI, the center little gray details (D 10) with the card on the side: 'a bullet moving with great speed and here is its path.' The scoring is D M.Y+ Oj, Ls. The activity may be ascribed to a plant form. Thus, in figure X, the upper two gray details (D 8): 'two walking black tulips . . . miserable creatures', D M.Y— Bt. In figure III, the small details extending inward in the bottom detail (i.e., in D 7): 'reminds me of the wind blowing', Dd M Na. To the entire of figure X, the following two abstractions: 'music of the spheres,' and 'tension of geometrical forces'; W M+ Ab., both. These two responses were produced by different persons, and, as may be guessed, both were of very high endowment, working in professional fields. Earthquakes and other cosmic calamities are sometimes M, sometimes not. In establishing the determinants for these, we are entirely at the mercy of S's language, and the subjectivity element waxes large. Rorschach's language in defining M is, "We are really dealing with one's *feeling himself into the movement.*" The German is *Erfühlen der Bewegung.* The italics are Rorschach's. I myself score M when S's language in the free association or in the inquiry indicates intensity of feeling and permits the judgment that the subject is living the scene he is describing. For example, in figure VII, the two lowest sections (D 4): 'this looks very solid or massive . . . a fist driving forward? Moving irresistibly? A pushing or solid force.' The scoring D M— Ab.

Human purpose. An animal activity that is usually scored F may be elaborated by the S to express some strictly human purpose. Thus, in figure VIII, the lateral animal detail (D 1), frequently seen as 'climbing the sides of some rocks,' is scored F. But 'they are climbing to see who will get to the top first' is scored M. Similarly, 'hanging on to the sides for dear life,' is M. Another example, in figure X, the upper blue (D 1): 'these two spiders are plotting something.' Doubt arises with respect to some 'fighting' associations. Animals are frequently seen as carrying on this human, all too human, activity. When they are doing so in accordance with their own style of combat, one which is not anatomically available to humans, the scoring is F. Thus, for figure V., as a whole, "two deer bucks locking horns in combat," W F+ A. Yet the similar response to figure V., whole: "two bulls crashing head on, in mortal struggle," is

W M+ A. In this latter, the emotion implicit in 'mortal struggle' casts
the vote for the M, and the vigor in the expression 'mortal combat' rein-
forces the judgment. The decision must be made from the patient's
language, and in instances the subjective element is present. I use the M
scoring when the language is expressive of a strongly sensed feeling (as
described by Rorschach; and see also Schachtel's[29] emphasis on identification in his theoretical discussion of M). The data of observation consist of
verbal behavior, whether in M or in any of the other scoring categories.

Not M. Rorschach's basic rule is explicit and its psychological rationale
is so consistent with dynamic theory of personality as to leave no problem
in identifying the obvious non-M. To reiterate the rationale, the movement determinant, M, discloses a wish or a fear, i.e., it is something that
the S is living and that has an engrossing emotional significance for him.
S cannot, however, face this fear or the wish consciously. His self-respect,
the ego, will not let him. So he transforms thought, as in dream work,
into an association which he does not recognize for what he intends. This
is the fantasy which we score M. Concerning non-M, Rorschach writes:

> One must not be misled into deciding that every verbalized or acted out move-
> ment is kinesthetically determined. S's will name objects that are quite animated,
> yet what we are dealing with here is not kinesthetic responses. Associations such
> as, 'a duck going into the water,' 'a dog snapping at a butterfly,' 'a flying bird,' 'an
> airplane in flight,' 'a mountain emitting fire,' and the like, are, to say the least, in
> by far the greatest number of instances, not at all M responses. These are form
> responses, characteristic of the form of the figure alone. The observation in terms
> of movement is usually only a rhetorical elaboration of the response, a *secondary*
> association. This is the case in fact even in those instances when the movement is
> demonstrated in any way whatever. What we are dealing with in these instances
> is an associative recall of what has been *named*, not a feeling one's self into the move-
> ment.*

Common examples of not-M will be found on pp. 91 f.

The burden of proof regarding M or not-M is always on the individual
response. The examiner must elicit language from S, verbal behavior,
that establishes M. It must also establish beyond peradventure that the
perceived activity is not the memory reproduction of activity in a subhuman creature (Rorschach's rule). This burden of proof applies even
to the human movement responses when the association raises any doubt
on this point. We say too much about a person psychologically when we
score M to risk such scoring without adequate evidence.

In associations in which the doubt between F or M cannot be resolved,
the practice in Zürich, including Oberholzer's, has been (a) to postpone
the decision until the entire protocol has been scored, then (b) if S pro-

---

* The italics are Rorschach's (ref. 27; pp. 25–26).

duces a substantial number of M associations, i.e., if he is an "M person," to score the doubtful associations M. If (c) he produces few or no M associations, score F. This is to say that a scoring judgment is made on data extraneous to the particular response. Strict empiric thinking resists such a procedure, but there is more truth than poetry in the Zürich approach. That is, in a freely imaginative person, an association that is on the fence on the question of fantasy structure has more psychologic probability of being M than not; contrariwise, in a nonimaginative person, it is more probably F. Further, an error in scoring M in a record already studded with them will not be serious, but it can be a large error to add even one unwarranted M in a record with only two, one, or none.

The stance in the M. Rorschach identifies two stances taken by the actor in the perceived movement: extensor (more literally, "stretch"; the German is *streck*) and flexor ("bend or bow"; German *beuge*). No scoring sign attaches to these. They are of great importance in interpretation, disclosing S's attitude in his unconscious in relating to others as self-assertive or submissive. It opens up, in Rorschach's interpretation, a view to an even deeper personality nucleus: S's sexuality as dominantly masculine or feminine (see Rorschach[28]; compare also Schachtel[29]). Stance is identified from S's language according to whether the direction of the movement is toward the center of the blot's axis, centripetal on flexor; or away from the blot's axis, centrifugal or extensor.

Samples of extensor M are: figure I, W, "an angel spreading out a lot of wings"; the upper half of either lateral section (D 7), "a soldier, a sentry, looking out"; figure VI, inverted, the larger lateral extension (D 9), "a figure someone stretched out, the arms outstretched"; in figure III, W, "a sense of motion, as though the wind were blowing out." Examples of flexor M: figure X, the large pink mass (D 9), "a lovely lady, in an evening gown, she is sort of bending over," and it is no accident that the same patient, a neurotic young woman, saw a smaller portion of D 9 as "two more girls, they look like slaves, girls in position of obeisance'; figure IX, inverted, entire excepting the outer pink profiles (excepting D 4), "two women at a tea table, conversing with their heads almost together'; in figure VI the two gray details in the center (D 11), "two little figures huddled together.'

Some flexor M are very frequent and obvious, such as the "clowns clapping hands," or the like in figure II; also the "bears kissing" in this figure. In figure III, it is the two humans greeting each other or in a formalized posture such as a dance or a comic or caricatured attitude, associations which are readily elicited here. The configurations of the blots, particularly figure II but also, in varying degrees, figures VII, IX, X, and I, facilitate the observation of flexor movement to such a degree as to require minimizing the significance of these associations. They are a function of the stimulus and not of the S.

In some M the stances are mixed. Not infrequently, what starts out as a flexor M, so channelized by the configuration of the blot, develops also a clear-cut extensor activity. For example, in figure II, W, "like two witches fighting with each other, the hands raised in battle"; and in figure III, the two human forms, while "facing each other," are seen as in "a tug of war, each pulling at something," or they may be "tearing something apart.'

In figure VII, the inward-facing feminine figures are seen as "pointing in opposite directions.' Or they may be "dancing, looking toward each other, but their bodies turned away from each other," i.e., the direction of the movement is both centripetal and centrifugal in the same association. This is one of those exceptions to the rule, as trying in the test as exceptions are in life generally. The association uncovers the ambivalent stance of some neurotics. A nice example of such, in figure I, the central detail [D 3] is: "a nude female, looking back, facing the other way," i.e., facing away but looking back toward the S.

Another kind of discrepancy is that between stance and content. Thus, in figure I the association of someone "with hands up, in prayer" is extensor movement, but the "prayer" motif is found in passive, dependent individuals. As always, the meaning of any one association is derived from its context in the whole personality. Sitting persons and all that are perceived as lying down are flexor M.

To interpret extensor and flexor M as Rorschach does there must be no room for doubt about the direction of the movement intended in S's language. When there is doubt, we cannot use this interpretation. The conclusions drawn from it concerning the personality are too far-reaching. The fact is that many M cannot be clearly judged as extensor or flexor.

One other M stance is found which Rorschach does not discuss. It is the dead-center, static one. The actor in the percept is in upright posture, motionless, perhaps rigidly fixed. Examples: figure I, the center detail [D 4], "a little boy standing"; figure I, inverted, middle detail with accent on the inner darker portions [D 3], "a child in swaddling clothes, actually a figure holding the child"; in figure VI, the upper part of the central black [D 2], "a little man closed up in a plastic bag, arms straight, eyes closed, tied up to the wall." The crucifixion association elicited occasionally by the entire upper section of figure VI [D 3] is usually M, and static. These static M have their source in an ambivalence in S, an ambivalence which cripples him when it comes to decision-making, throws him into dead-center between two alternatives.

The energy in the M activity. This concept grows out of experimentation by D. M. Levy with ink blot stimuli which he constructed, using Rorschach's M for his point of departure. Using this Levy concept, I have been evaluating all Rorschach M responses in accordance with an eight point (0–7) scale which his co-workers have developed. The procedure and this scale have pitfalls, described in a former publication,[8] but I have been finding them useful in providing leads to the intensity of feeling invested in the wish or fear concealed in the M.

In using the scale I have started with the assumption that the amount and vigor of verbalized activity is indicative of the degree of feeling invested. Thus, an energy rating of 7 would point to intense feeling, one of 0 to none, or 1, to a small degree. Examples of each rating are listed below.

However, this rule frequently does not work. In some M that are of low energy rating, the thinking is nevertheless obviously centered around a topic of high emotional tension. For example, 'a fallen cow' (figure V, D 4). The rating here is 2, but the latent significance of this response is the attitude of an adolescent boy toward his mother (case reported in full in ref. 8, pp. 69ff). 'Someone lying on his stomach; and might be the rectum' (figure I, Dd 22). Rating is 1. (For full report, see ref. 8, pp. 148ff). 'A beheaded female' (figure I, D 4). Rating is 0. The boy who gave the 'fallen cow' response also produced this one.

My solution has been to judge feeling investment both from content and by the energy scale, The possible combinations are:* (a) energy measure is high (4 or more), theme meaning is significant; (b) energy measure high, theme not significant; (c) energy measure low (3 or less), theme significant; (d) energy measure low, theme not significant. The interpretive lead is clear in (a) and (d) where the two kinds of observations converge. In (c) I take my clue from the content and interpret as vigorously felt fantasy any which has a strong hold on the patient. It is in respect to (b) that there is most room for uncertainty. When the fantasy is of the stereotyped kind, I disregard it for purposes of gauging the energy loading. In all other instances, I make the assumption that high energy rating discloses relatively high feeling investment in the wish or the fear.

Examples of the several ratings by the Levy scale.

Rating 7: "Two dancing girls" (figure I) "swinging about some piece of gymnastic apparatus, with their draperies flying out as they whirl around the center."

Rating 7-6: "Two darkies (figure III, D 9, card is V), minstrels, dancing, kicking up their legs, in the stance of a dance in the high kicks.'

* This is a restatement of the exposition in my earlier publication.[8] It is a dependable procedure, as judged by clinical information about the patient. A systematic study of the method is something that still remains to be done.

Rating 7-6: "Two witches fighting with each other (figure II), hands raised in battle, clash of hands, as if each is trying to push the other."

Rating 6: 'Could be a woman dancing" (figure VII, D 2, card is V) "with this the skirt . . . the head . . . the arms . . . legs.'

Rating 5: 'Like a gorilla (figure IV) . . . looks like it wants to kill something or someone . . . way in which arms and shoulders are raised . . . and mad look in his eyes."

Rating 4: 'Two graceful animals (figure VIII, D) pushing toward each other, with some object in between.'

Rating 3: 'A little old woman (figure IX, D 1) hurrying to get somewhere.'

Rating 3-2: 'Like human figures with white caps (figure X, D 9), heads down . . . carrying something . . . in balance.'

Rating 2: 'Two King Neptunes, in the sea, laughing at each other' (figure IX, D 3).

Rating 1: 'Two apes back to back (figure VI, D 9, $\vee$), and they have their arms extended."

Rating 0: "Two men, lying back to back (figure V, D 4), sleeping."

Affective quality in M. This tells of the feeling quality bound in with the perceived activity and hence with the experienced fantasy. The two poles are, of course, pleasure–pain. At the one extreme would be the florid fantasy of a young schizophrenic male who saw figure X as "heavenly hosts presiding over his marriage" with his beloved; the large pink masses (D 9) were himself and his bride, and the other details of this populous test figure were the angels and other inhabitants of heaven. At the other extreme we have the panicky dream associations, the most obvious being is that in which figure IV, W, is seen by the S as an advancing monster, with variations in the degrees of threatening aspect that are verbalized. In between these extreme affects, S's ventilate all degrees of pleasure and pain known to human experience. The judgment concerning the affective quality is usually clear.

Summary of M observations. The observations that may be made with respect to M in any one test record are: total number of M; total M in proportion to the total scored productivity; Experience Balance and Experience Actual (see below, p. 100); structural quality, i.e. M+ or M−; M perceived in minor details (Dd M); M perceived in part humans (M in Hd); M in animal content (or in part animals, Ad); M as extensor or flexor activity; the amount of activity, or energy, that makes up the M; the affective quality in the content of the M; the theme in the M.

These are the many dimensions of this one test behavior which informs us concerning the psychological events within a person. We can see, therefore, why Rorschach devoted so many pages out of his small book to M and its derivative, Experience Balance (EB). What I now call the Experience Actual (EA) is a derivative from the EB.[10]

Examples follow of all M responses:

MOVEMENT CERTAIN

Figure I

'Two people standing together, two girls [D 2]; something in the middle, I don't know what it is. Like both of them are going round in rings. They have their both feet together, and their both heels, and they are way spread out.' W M+ H.

'An angel spreading a lot of wings.' W M+ H, R1.

'A woman [D 3]; she's standing erect.' An example of M without noticeable action. Attitude, in humans, is M in Rorschach's sense. D M+ H.

'A man, with his hands, ready to spring on you' [D 4]. D M+ H.

'Looks like two witches [both D 2] flying on a broom.' This impossible feat is always on inquiry found to be M. It is one of those childhood realities that become fantasies common to our culture. D M+ H.

∨ 'In the center, a Buddha, sitting down.' [D 4, from about the level of Dd 27, which is the 'Buddha's opening' (eye), to D 1.] D M+ H, R1.

∧ 'From the hips down, there's a military figure [D 3] because of the stance of the legs, and the form of the trousers.' D M+ H P.

Figure II

The percept of *two humans* in some action constitutes a very common M response here. It is scored W M+ H P, occasionally D M+. Examples showing variations in details only, are:

'Peas porridge hot.'

'Like two comic strip characters talking to each other, or two people playing, looking down at a flower.'

'Like two women sitting down on something, with their hands against each other, and their knees together.'

In some instances, only D 1 are the *people*, e.g., 'like two people kneeling or fighting.' Scored D M+ H.

Other examples of M in this figure are:

∨ '. . . feet . . . of a boy running', D 2. Scored D M+ Hd.

'Two figures of Oriental type, back to back' [D 4]. The question to be determined in the inquiry is whether 'back to back' is simple description; or perception of a position taken by the 'figures', as was the case here. D M− H.

'In the center white space I see a dancer; she seems to be twisting and both legs seem drawn into one as she twisted.' Ds M− H.

'A man sitting in an armchair' [tiny Dd on inner edge of Dd 28]. Dd M H.

'This light-colored portion' [the lighter red Dd joining D 2 to D 1] "the midriffs of a dancing girl, the skirt here and the upper formation here.' In the inquiry S included all of D 2. Dd M− Hd.

Figure III

This figure evokes the most common M response in the test—the paradigm M. The content varies widely in minor aspects, but fundamentally the response represents D 1 seen as *two persons* in some activity. The scoring in the examples following is uniformly D M+ H P (see, however, p. 16).

'Like two figures, somewhat distorted people, bending toward the front and holding something between them.'

'This looks like the game where you hold hands and go around in a circle.'

'A comic picture of two men, each carrying a basket, meeting each other and bowing in a silly manner.'

'A man and woman "going to town." Then again, like two women; a woman's hand . . . more like a man and woman . . . in coitus.'

'Two dolls facing each other, performing some sort of dance.' The reason for citing this response is the content, *dolls*, which, being inanimate, may raise doubts as to whether this response is M. But the human forms involved, and the activity in which they are engaged, are evidence that this is one of the usual M responses with an original twist to the content. D M+ H, Rc P.

Another common M in figure III occurs as follows, the card always ∨: 'two figures kicking their legs over their heads; they look like very primitive Negroes.' D 4 are the 'heads,' and the rest of D 9 completes the figures. The variations are in minor elements. All are scored D M+ H. D 5 is usually the *kicking leg*, but not necessarily; as in 'two rather haughty Negro people walking away from each other, almost as if marching,' with D 5 *as hands*.

Other examples of M in figure III are:

'A girl doing a back dive' [D 2] D M+ H.

∨'Dolls, . . . their heads drooping . . . they're figures of people, arms' [D 2]. D M+ H.

∨ 'Hands outstretched' [D 5.] D M+ Hd.

∨ 'Looks almost like some person, as if someone in a heavy sweater, rolled up, standing at a bar or table.' D 5 are 'person's hands,' D 4 his 'eyes,' D 3 his 'tie.' D M+ H.

∨ 'There's a soldier in the middle, the white space is his hat, he's moving down; here's his shoulder'—Dds 24 for the 'soldier,' smaller portions of this space as 'hat,' 'shoulder.' Dds M— H.

Figure IV

'A big shaggy bear doing a dance.' This bear certainly walks like a man and opposes no real difficulty to scoring the percept as M. Hence, W M+ AP.

'Like a monster coming at you; his face, and his legs; the feet protruding on either side.' Scored W M+ A. Like the 'shaggy bear' preceding, this monster is decidedly anthropomorphic in posture, and the content symbol could as easily be H as A. The two responses exemplify many similar ones evoked by this figure—all M. They differ only superficially from the typical M of the following:

'A man in a large bearskin coat walking away, in a Charley Chaplin walk; his head is buried in the collar of his coat. I don't know where his arms are, but it gives you the idea he's flapping his arms in a comical manner.' W M+.

Other M responses in this figure are:

∨ 'Again, a feeling of supplication' [Dd 26]. 'Here's a dancer; here's the leg, just her legs' [Dd 26]. 'A good caricature of Mussolini making a speech [tiny Dd in lateral portion.] All three responses are scored Dd M H.

> 'Reminds me of an old person [D 2] as though praying.' D M+ H.

∧ 'Somebody in his seven-league boots' [D 6]. In the inquiry S said she saw no human—only the 'boots in motion, stepping off.' Fairy tale themes, being a priori a medium for projecting inner experience, are scored M when they fulfill Rorschach's requirements of (a) human content and (b) activity physically possible for humans. D M+ Hd.

Figure V

'A woman dancing, with cape flowing out, the scarf shimmering, flung out of her hands.' A frequent theme, with variations. In all of them, D 7 is the human figure and D 4 the extravaganza costume, with the other details entering in more or less. All are W M+.

∨ 'I have to suppress the idea of a man bowing, but why, I don't know' [D 1]. D M— H.

∨ 'That could be the phallus, hanging down, not the erect position' [Dd 26]. Dd M Hd.

∧ 'A pigeon-toed small boy; a toe dancer' [D 7]. Similar reactions to this detail are the following, each scored D M+: 'a man in the middle with a soldier's hat on; he has skinny feet and he is walking away'; 'a girl standing on her toes.'

> 'A picture of Santa Claus reading the mail [Dd 23]. He does not have his hat on; his hand seems to be resting on something.' Dd M− H.

∨ 'Legs [D 2] like a young kid's legs; they are tiny and tender, slim, and they are apart; it is someone supporting a baby.' D M+ Hd.

∧ 'And here are legs . . . of a chorus girl [D 1 and Dd 22] and they are in that position,' seen immediately after the 'dancer' in 'the finish of some number on the stage.' Although overtly static, there is no doubt that the 'legs' of this 'chorus girl' are part of the act. D M+ Hd.

After seeing the usual *bat*, S elaborated: 'And he has his wings folded around two women'—on each side, D 5 and D 11, and D1, form 'one woman,' as 'head,' 'bust,' and 'leg.' The M pertains to 'women,' an instance of someone being acted on. D M+ H.

'A boy formation, with the folded arms' [D 5 with D 11]. This blot area frequently elicits an inactive M, e.g., *reclining person*. D M+ H.

Figure VI

'A projectile that has gone through the center and has left a path in its wake . . . a sense of motion.' One of the rare M responses in nonliving associational content. Rorschach observed them (ref. 27, p. 26). They are found almost exclusively in persons of the highest intelligence range. The scoring here is D M+ Ab, motion.

V 'A great diving thing, with arms way outstretched, and its feet together; a big villain.' W M− H.

∨ 'Like a toe dancer very carefully balanced' [D 12]. Scored D M− H.

∧ 'A human figure [D 2] in a coffin [gray Dd exterior to D 2] or else behind a curtain.' D M+ H.

∨ 'A skirt and the bottom of somebody's legs [D 8], as of someone walking away and you see only the back.' The 'legs' are D 8 and the edges of Dd 31 form the outline of the 'skirt.' D M− Hd.

> 'An old woman who has her face in her hands' [D 9]. D M− H.

∨ 'A man and woman kissing, affectionate—kissing on the cheek, a lovers' farewell' [D 10]. D M− H.

Figure VII

'Two old-maid gossips,' each lateral half being one of the 'old maids.' S adds that she can 'see them gossip.' W M+ H P.

'Two women facing each other [D 2], with plumes in their hair, as if in anger or excitement, judged from their position.' D M+ H P.

Hoydenish, sometimes *Victorian ladies* represent the most common response to this figure. Whether the percept is F or M is not always clear from the original association, in which S may say no more than that they are *looking at* or *facing* each other. The critical point between F and M is in the sensing of an attitude in the figures. The inquiry is therefore most important. The response following, as first given, left some doubt as to whether it was M.

'A face here and a face there; they're looking at each other; it's the face of a woman ... I don't know why I get a woman's sex out of the face ... looks like it ... like a woman.' Only D 1 is involved and the accent is very much on form, and static. In the inquiry S elaborated, 'They are antagonistic, saucy.' D M+ H P.

Other M responses in this figure are:

> 'Kicking legs ...like various people's and animals'.' D1 and Dd 21 are the 'legs.' Scored D M− Hd. The M inheres in the *human* legs; the *animal* legs may here be considered incidental to the first association, and disregarded. If scored separately, for the purpose of indicating the Dd, they would be denoted Dd F− Ad.

∨ 'Two dancing dolls,' each lateral half; 'they would be female dolls, dressed in the old style, with bustles; look untidy, because they have no feet.' Scored W M+ H Rc (see note on *dancing dolls* in figure III). S followed this response with the following alternative: 'Again it reminds me of two Siamese twins I saw in the museum, joined together with their heads—with a common head.'

∨ 'Two old men [D 3] with long beards ... they're smoking.' D M+ Hd.

∧ 'Someone, a woman [D 6] wedged in between two rocks.' D M+ H.

'A man [Dd 26] ... a house [Ds 7] ... he's coming out of the house ... walking toward me.' Dd MV− H.

< 'A lady, kind of cross, standing there very rigid,' [Dd 21]. Stance only, but a true M. Dd M− H.

Figure VIII

'People climbing for the mountain top'—on the outer edge of D 4, the elongated Dd just below Dd 24. Dd M H.

'The two animals [D 1] are pushing these two sides together to keep them from splitting.' The M is not in the 'animals pushing' but in the 'sides' that are being kept from splitting. D M+ Ab. No human activity is involved (but see in figure VI 'projectile that has gone through' the center, and note concerning M in nonliving content).

'As though Gertrude Lawrence in wide-skirted frock, looking at herself in a mirror [D 4], making herself very long and slender'; i.e., 'it would be as when looking into a distorted mirror.' D M— H.

'Looks like a dancer; she is tall and thin and standing on her toes' [D 21]. Dd M— H.

'Like these two hands [Dd 22] are reaching out to take hold of the mice, on either side.' Dd M+ Hd.

Figure IX

> 'The green reminds me of the silhouette of a very fat man riding a tricycle—rather, a motorcycle.' D M+ H.

> 'This' [D 4 together with D 10, or half of D 6,] 'might be construed as a female figure sitting on the carrier of a bicycle; her face strikes me as particularly foolish.' D M+ H.

> 'Someone taking water out of a pail' [Dd 26 and 27]. Dd M H.

∨ 'Adagio dancers' [Dd 30]. Dd M— H.

∧ 'Here's a person creeping along [D 1], a kind of awkward stealthiness.' D M+ H.

'Like pictures of goblins or witches [D 3] concocting some kind of brew over this center portion [Ds 8]; incantations of some sort . . . the Macbeth scene, the cauldron.' D M+ H P.

'Almost like two hands [Dd 21], I don't know what they would be doing; they are leaning on something, as if the knuckles are bent.' Dd M+ Hd.

'A Degas suggestion, four ballerinas dancing, the four sections [of D 6]; fluttering through here.   They are airy; the two in the center as in impressionistic art.' D M+ H.

Figure X

'A suggestion of two fat men [D 6] hanging on to rocks with one hand and reaching a towel with the other.' D M+ H.

∨ 'A man doing calisthenics with his arms over his head' [D 5]. Scored D M+ H.

∧ 'These red things [D 9] are leaning backward, they seem to be opposing each other; people . . . they're facing.' D M+ H.

'Like pictures of Egyptian gods dancing' [D 8]. D M+ H, R1.

'Like a clown sitting on a trapeze, tattered' [Dd 28]. Dd M+ H.

∨ 'As though a man, flying [D 10]; the arms seem to be human wings [D 4]; they are not attached but mechanical.' D M+ H.

∧ 'A nude woman [D 14] standing with her hands up.' D M+ H.

∨ 'Kind of a chef [Dd 26] barbecuing a chicken' [D 6]. Dd M+ H.

∨ 'A parachute [D 3], two parachutists landing.' D M+ H.

∧ 'Two chattering women [D 4] that have just been interrupted, and are surprised; dressed in a Victorian styles, with sheath gowns; it is a very tight gown that swirls up.' D M— H.

V 'A person with arms up . . . blessing or asking for blessing'—Dd projecting from the bottom (∧) of D 8. Dd M— Hd.

V 'A man hanging on to two things [D 5]; suspended in the air; looks rather like an Eskimo.' Scored D M+ H. An example of a passive status that is a good M.

∧ 'They look like lovers [D 9] that are leaning toward each other, and are also held apart by the blue [D 6] and they are pushing against it.' Really two M—the lovers, and the force that keeps them apart. The latter could logically be scored anew, as D M— Ab, force. But it is well to avoid overscoring, and the single score D M+ H, with marginal notation of the additional M activity, is sufficient.

THRESHOLD MOVEMENT

Figure I

'A couple of wolves, dancing' [D 2]. A human activity in an animal, perceived in a detail frequently seen as a human. The inquiry also brought out 'faces of wolves, wings of wolves,' i.e., 'they are dressed up.' This is a mixture of human and animal characteristics (in a child of 8) and possessing the human forms necessary in the *dance*. D M+ A.

Figure II

'Those are two bulldogs' [D 1]. *This as it stands would be a simple* D F+. But S, a schizophrenic woman, continued with 'looks as if they are standing at a bonfire' and added in the inquiry 'they are carrying on secret societies in connection with Harvard.' The 'dogs,' by mediation of the archaic thought process of schizophrenia, are participating in a purely human activity. The upright position of these details aids in this contamination. D M+ A.

Figure III

'Two grotesque figures . . . like head of an ostrich and the body of a man' [D 1]. Had S left the association with these words, it would have been scored: D F+ H. The content is *animal* and *human body parts* without activity. But she returned to the figures and elaborated: 'The men are bent over and each one is holding something.' Thus it becomes the common D M+ H P. The 'ostrich' head need not be scored, being a by-association—contaminatory—that S quickly absorbs in the healthy response.

A similar, more common kind of association is 'these two black [D 1] are like cartoons; a duck, dressed like a human being; as though they're carrying satchels.' The animals in human clothing are likely to be M, but the burden of proof is greater. In this response, 'carrying satchels' came out only in the inquiry. D M+ A H.

'Like two Teddy bears [D 9]; they're killing chickens.' The 'bears' are in a human pose and engaged in a human activity. The mixing of categories, or contamination, is simply an index to the uncritical mentality of this feebleminded girl. D M— A.

Figure IV

'Legs [D 4], a woman's legs.' She is 'on her knees' (added in the inquiry). In the doubtful range because not a whole human. While much Hd is M, the burden of proof is greater. The inquiry brought out the necessary evidence. D M— Hd.

V 'Two women in rather conventionalized sunbonnets [D 7], looking at each other.' The term 'conventionalized' is accent on form. These two feminine figures are more commonly seen as M, and the expression 'looking at each other' is evidence—just barely enough—of an attitude. D M+ H.

Figure V

'Here's a pointing hand, and here's the finger [Dd 22] coming out here.' This is threshold M, being so largely descriptive and resembling other responses of S in which the participle was entirely descriptive. Also against an M scoring is the fact that S had few such responses. Further information was not obtained in the inquiry. The scoring, very much on the threshold, must depend on the activity that inheres commonly in a *painting hand*. Hence, Dd M— Hd.

'Someone's leg [D 1] or else the leg of an animal being enveloped behind the wing; snatched in the air behind a sinister wing.' There is heavy accent on animal parts. But the first percept is a human detail and in changing it to an animal portion, S is merely revealing the impoverishing influence of an anxiety. Scored here D M+ Hd, Ad.

Figure VI

V 'Like some kind of animal [D 4], a shaggy dog or bear or lion or gorilla standing on its hind legs; the nose is here, the snout and topknot; it's got a paw stretched out and I think of Siamese twins' [both D 4]. The slow development of the M is no indication against it; it is valuable in giving additional information about S and the crippling anxiety for which he was being treated. Thus, he at first flees from his M, i.e., from his wish-fulfilling fantasy, by the medium of the several animal associations, which finally develop into humans. D M+ A, H.

$\vee$ 'At the very, very top of the tree, in the center, I see two little heads [D 10] and two little hands' [Dd 28].   In the inquiry S added 'of two people huddled.'   D M— Hd.

Figure VII

'Looks like two women making faces at each other . . . or the statues of two women making faces at each other . . . or the busts of two women making faces at each other . . . mounted peculiarly on a rock.'   The doubt is created by the changing of the 'women' into 'statues,' then 'busts mounted,' i.e., lifeless objects.   But S opens with a movement response; and even the new content, 'statues,' in being an artistic creation, is material represented in the test by M.

'If the design is viewed from a teleological point of view, it has a weakness right here; it seems about to break' [at Dd 28].   S reveals between D 1 and D 3 a feeling of motion in the sense described by Rorschach as the essence of M.   The associations 'teleological,' 'weakness,' 'about to break,' tell part of this young man's story and thus exemplify M in its function of inner experience.   The absence of any overtly expressed human movement and the thin actual movement in 'seems about to break' are the reasons for classifying this response as threshold rather than unequivocal M.   Dd M Ab, weakness.

'Like the heads of snarling animals in a death struggle [D1], caricatures of animals, enjoying some joke hugely, as if they had been drinking and are letting themselves go over the situation or over some joke.'   The characters in this action, animal heads, would be scored F.   But activity as human as that here described can only be M.   D M+ A.

$<$ 'This [D 5] looks in a sense as if it is towing this [D 2], because [Dd 29] is as two strands of rope.'   There is no doubt but that *towing* is a motion.   Also it is a human activity; and the manipulation of tools is here explicit.   I am here discarding a former scoring, and using one more in accordance with similar responses clinically known to be M.

Figure IX

$\vee$ 'I can almost imagine a figure with head and body and feet . . . caressing each other.'   Each lateral half is the figure.   S could not say what the figure was but it was not human; and D 6 is an 'elephant's ear.'   Yet the position of the figure is anthropomorphic, and the caressing, in the upright pose, is a human activity.   D M— A.

'A couple of sea horses spraying water on each other' [D 3].   This behavior is characteristic of humans.   The M potential is strengthened by addition of *expression* in them (in the inquiry).   The animal content places on this association a burden of proof greater than is found in S's language. Hence this association was formerly set down among the 'threshold, not movement.' But in the light of experience in the intervening years, clinically validated, these human activities are clearly M. Hence, D M— A.

∧ 'The impression of things reaching toward each other . . . tentacles, or a sort of bridge structure, incomplete.' D 7 with Dd 25 are 'reaching'; this, judged in the light of certain other associations of S, is an active effort. 'Tentacles' in this instance is the secondary association. While the M value is decidedly on the borderline, the chance of error is much greater in not so scoring. Hence, D M+ Object.

∨ 'Here's two little things that might be like men that might stand opposite each other'—the green Dd immediately adjacent to Dd 30, including the peaked Dd that touch D 10. 'They're dressed up like devils, sort of creatures of the world of fairyland. They have the body here and the peaks here.' A very doubtful case, owing to the emphasis on form elements—'body,' 'peak'; but 'stand opposite each other,' with its dynamic quality of opposition, is M in the true Rorschach sense, and the content is human. The scoring is Dd M— H.

'Like teeth [Dd 21] and they're biting something green' [D 1]. The doubt lies in whether the 'teeth' are human or animal. E did not push the questioning far enough. But certain other of S's associations, related to this one, indicate human teeth. Hence, Dd M— Hd.

Figure X

'Sort of insects fighting each other' [D 8]. The animal content dictates caution, but the anthropomorphic stance of these little figures warrants M when the activity is so strong and so human. Scored D M+ A. S's next response but one was 'there are more opposing insects' [D 4]. In the inquiry he added, 'It might be love or hate'—critical evidence of the inner living process that is projected. D M— A.

'These green figures [D 12] look like beetles, or scarabs, worshiping the central figure [D 11]; they seem about to fall down or to prostrate themselves.' Here (a) the animal content and (b) the art forms raise the question whether S is not reproducing, in static form, memories of art objects he has seen. It happens too that S, though not an artist, gives several art associations. The association itself is, however, too much a human activity, too vigorous as regards the activity perceived, and too original as compared with what is usually seen here. Hence, it is judged as expression of experience in which S is engaging—a true Rorschach M. Scored D M— A, Art.

'The blue [D 1] is like an insect, shown at a dance, waving a large leaf'

[D 12]. This D is frequently seen as a nonhuman in a dance or other human activity. The M here has been validated sufficiently. D M— A.

THRESHOLD, NOT MOVEMENT

Figure I

'A fat woman [D 4] and a thin woman' [D 3]. Persistent efforts on the part of E could not evoke M in this response; it must be scored F—this in spite of the fact that S produced the extraordinary total of 19 M, and even though when, after the examination and inquiry were fully completed, E again called the response to attention with the question "Are these women doing anything?" S answered with 'they are standing.' Since E's question carried the suggestion of movement, this reply cannot affect the scoring. This kind of question cannot even be asked until all problems of scoring have been disposed of by the usual, nonleading method.

'A woman [D 3]; she has no clothes on.' The circumstance *no clothes* frequently overlies an M that quickly emerges in the inquiry. None was here elicited. D F+ H P.

'Hands [D 1] with mittens on.' Frequently an M response, but not here. D F+ Hd.

'A series of hidden faces, grinning faces, as though angels in the clouds of the Italian painters'—various Dd, in the lateral portion, adjacent to D 9. Laughing, smiling, and similar facial activity are in some instances M. In the present response, they simply recall art forms that constitute part of this very superior S's mental furniture. Confirmation of this conclusion is given in the inquiry, when he changes the human to nonhuman forms: 'they are really cats.' Dd FY Hd, Art.

Figure II

'Two animals with their feet up against each other ... the ears ... as if standing on their feet ... or tail' [D 1]. The pose is upright, but the description is only too clearly an example of Rorschach's "memory recall of the animals." D F+ A.

Figure III

'A couple of roosters fighting' [D 11]. This would usually not be considered as raising the M problem, but D 11 consists of nearly all of the usual *human* figure and the posture is anthropomorphic. Yet there is no evidence that the apparent activity is more than description of an animal posture. Rorschach's rule is being followed in scoring it D F+ A.

'Goats leaping through the air, way up high' [D 2]. The very vigorous activity throws this response into the threshold group. But, still sticking to the rule, in the absence of more substantial reason for honoring it in the breach, the scoring is D F— A.

Figure IV

'Here's a gnome, an elf' [Dd 21]. The little people of fairyland are usually seen in action, so much so that M is likely to be taken for granted. None was elicited here. Hence, Dd F+ H, My.

Figure V

'Like the leg of a dancer' [D 1]. S modifies the usual *leg* seen in this detail by making it that of a 'dancer.' There is no evidence of his perceiving any activity. The originality lies in the content, not in the inner creativity. D F+ Hd P.

Figure VII

'The inclosed space can be made to look like a pot steaming on the fire' [Ds 7]. In the inquiry S elaborated, making D 8 and Dd 24 steam, and getting a sense of motion with D 10 as 'fire' and 'heat coming from it.' This is the S who produced the moving projectile cited above as an example of certain M in figure VI. Here the *sense of motion* is entirely new inquiry material and therefore not scored. Were it free association I should still not call it M, since it is too much a by-product of 'fire.'

∧ 'One of the best dogs' [each lateral half]. 'Here's his tail, and the dog's tail is lifted [D 5] as if he's defecating.' Activity, but in an animal, and not in the position taken by humans. The temptation to score M inheres in (a) the importance of excretory activity to personality formation, and its influence on unconscious mental life, and (b) the function of M in the Rorschach test as representative of the unconscious. But in view of this importance of M, so much the more caution is necessary in identifying it. See note on 'rodents' (p. 97) in regard to hazards of a priori interpretation and scoring. D F+ A.

'A little doll, like, the figure in the middle' [D 6]; in the inquiry, S added 'it is standing up.' This raised the question of M, with the doll as substitute for a human form. *Doll* is a lifeless object, however, and S did not give her life in seeing her 'standing.' The score D F+ seems better advised. This may be contrasted with 'two dolls in a dance' in figure III.

Figure IX

'At this angle, the feeling of a moose [D 3]; I don't really see it; the idea of antlers, and the color too. It seems to be a running moose, because the lines are going in that direction.' In the inquiry S added 'there is a feeling of running in it'—Dd 28 being the 'hind part' of the animal—and 'it is quick.' Not M, for all the overt language. For one thing, it is an animal, and in a nonhuman position; for another, the motion is too much a function of the *lines*, i.e., of form. It is (Rorschach): "an associative recall of the *named* movement, not an experienced movement" (ref. 27, p. 26). D FC+ A.

Another S saw D 2 as 'a moose, swimming; only the head is visible.' The activity could be that of a human, but the association is entirely animal and the behavior characteristic of an animal. D F+ A.

Figure X

'There are pointing oxen . . . the head, and they're pointing forward' [D 12]. Description, with some activity, but entirely such as characterizes only the animal seen. D F+ A.

'This figure here [D 14] looks like a man in a tall hat, like a conventional figure in a funeral.' No further evidence of activity or living attitude was elicited. Probably the inquiry could have gone farther in this response. As it stands, only the form elements can be recognized, especially in view of the emphasis 'conventional.' D F+ H.

'Symbol for Halloween . . . a witch on a broomstick' [D 2]. Witches are more frequently M than not, but the evidence for M was lacking here, and S, in her spontaneous association, goes on saying that it is an art representation, '*symbol* for Halloween.' D F— H, Art.

Not Movement

Figure I

'Two bats fighting.' No human activity is involved. W F— A.

Figure II

'Here is someone's thumb sticking up here' [D 2]. *Sticking up* is descriptive. S does not in his association engage in any act. D F— Hd.

'A pair of dogs facing each other' [D 1]. Purely static description. D F+ A P.

'A couple of calves [D 1] sucking a bottle [D 4] or bears . . . some kind of animal.' In the inquiry, 'the bottle is on the nose, more on the mouth,' i.e., entirely the animal posture in the activity involved, and no evidence of any human form of behavior. Scored D F— A. The 'bottle' does provide strong temptation for scoring M. But see note on 'rodents' (p. 97) in regard to hazards of a priori interpretation and scoring.

Figure III

There are instances of D 1 as humans but not M.

'Two people; two men, with big noses; they're wearing high-heeled shoes. That's all.' In the inquiry S added 'they have suits on.' At no point is any movement sensed. D F+ H P.

V 'These two resemble long arms with gloves on' [D 5]. *Arms* or *hands* here, with card ∧, is frequently M. In this instance the percept was static. D F+ Hd.

∧ 'A couple of monkeys hanging from a tree by their feet' [D 2]. A quite nonhuman activity, and behavior of a pattern completely characteristic for the animal seen here. D F+ A.

V 'Like a trick seal [D 11] balancing something [D 4] on their tails [Dd 23] and standing on their front thing on a chair.' Representing an activity impossible for a human, the response demonstrates the soundness of Rorschach's observation: M is a living of a certain experience and therefore only actions of which humans are capable are M. S did not imagine herself 'a trick seal balancing something'; she remembered seeing an animal performing. D F− A.

Figure IV

'These are suggestive of arms hanging down from either side' [D 4]. The particle *hanging* is entirely descriptive, as though it were an adjective. D F+ Hd.

'Two ducks swimming'—in D 1, tiny gray Dd adjoining Dds 24. Animals in conventionally perceived form. Dd F A.

> 'This, a bent tree [D 4] leaning over a chasm.' It would not be necessary to cite this response, were it not that I have seen such percepts reported as M. It is not M in the Rorschach sense. D F+ Bt.

∧ *Ape* (or other huge animal) is not always M. Thus, 'something like an ape.' The inquiry could bring S only to indicate the ape's 'head, feet, arms, tail.' W F+ A P.

V 'These two dark remind me of nuns' [D 7]. Female forms in this detail are usually M. Only the form was the basis of this response. D F+ H.

Figure V

V 'Here I see a Greek or Roman god of the wind—the outline of his cheek, though the shading is very heavy' [end Dd of D 4, excluding D 1 and Dd 22]. Art forms with human content always raise the M question. There is no evidence here of anything but form determination. Dd F− Art, Hd.

∨ 'The heads of two rattlesnakes [D 3] looking down on a forest [D 4] from a high altitude.' D 3 are commonly seen as *snakes*, usually with heads upreared, as here. The percept denotes normal animal poses and in no sense involves a Rorschach movement experience. D F+ Ad.

Figure VI

∨ 'This is a sort of a suggestion of a dog . . . or a baboon [D 4], the forehead coming out here, the nose there.' This figure as *ape* is frequently M, but not here. 'Forehead coming out' is description, and everything else in the association is static. Note that the 'baboon' was first perceived as a 'dog,' confirming the indication against M. D F+ A.

∨ 'A shoot of water going this way in the middle' [D 5]. Another response that would not be cited, were it not that some workers do score this kind of percept as M. It should be scored D F+ or FV+.

∨ 'A bull, head down, bucking' [D 4]. An activity not physically human. D F− A.

∧ 'The general conception of the flying goose; you can see it drawn wing down and head protruding,' i.e., Dd out of D 6, on only one side of D 2. If proof is needed that this kind of response is merely the recalled image of an art form previously perceived, S provides it in her further free association: 'It is the sign on the auto that uses the goose; you see it drawn, wing down and head protruding, as though in flight.' Dd F+ A, Art.

Figure VII

'Two sheep . . . jumping around, without heads' [D 2]. Animals in a position frequently represented. Scored D F− A.

∧ 'Two penguins that have been squeezed together,' each of the two black Dd that make up D 6. Animal content, without any basis for M in Rorschach's sense. D F− A.

The two *women* are not always M: e.g., 'old ladies at the time of George Washington . . . bustles, hair all fixed on top'—S makes a movement with her own hand. Concerning acting out, see below, note on the response 'like two witches with long fingers' in figure IX. There is no evidence of M in the present association itself. Scored D F+ H P. Another form of this F is 'a couple of faces of clowns, two women's faces with hair up,' D 3 and D 1 separately seen as 'clowns.'

Figure VIII

'Like a couple of bear cubs [D 1] . . . climbing up the tree [D 8]; one paw is up.' This activity is a "rhetorical embellishment of the answer, a *secondary* association." (ref. 27, p. 25) D F+ A P.

Varying only in detail, but fundamentally the same, are the following examples (all seen in D 1, and all scored D F+ A):

< 'A woodchuck, and he's walking over uneven ground; he has two front paws over the surface, and seems to be trying to decide where to put his foot before losing his foothold.'

∧ 'Like two animals, or some sort of animal, reaching up, on either side.' S later changed this response to 'a wild boar, ready to spring.' This looks as though it has much dynamic tension. But it is simply descriptive of a characteristic animal posture, as is confirmed by S's own free elaboration 'one of the legs seems different from the others,' which is description and entirely static, and scored D F− A.

< 'Like a tadpole on the way to turning into a frog; like the quality of metamorphosis.' The leg Dd of D 1, which touches D 7. Thought of M can arise here because of the birth process involved and because of the metamorphosis. It has nothing of M in the Rorschach sense. Dd F Sc.

'These two portions [Dd 26] look like a hound dog peering around the corner.' Animal content, hence Dd F+ A.

Figure IX

'Here's a flying duck, this the body and head, and wings . . lifted up,' D 2 with adjacent Dd toward Dd 28. *Flying* and *lifted up* are simple instances of "secondary association" with an animal as conventionally represented. D F− A.

'Fountain going up; in the middle is a spray' [D 5]. Compare 'shoot of water' in figure VI, above, and note. D CF+ Ls.

'Yes, the whole thing does resemble a clown [D 3 only]; the one on the right is clearer than the one on the left.' No evidence of M in this *human* association, which commonly is M. The accent on form was maintained in the inquiry, in which S stressed the 'peaked' cap. D FC+ H.

∨ 'These two orange parts [D 3] look like fish; that is, if you stretch your imagination.' S added in the inquiry 'like fish' swimming under seaweed. A *duck flies* and a *fish swims;* the percept is that of another simple animal form in a characteristic situation. D F− A.

'Like two witches, with long fingers' [D 3]. S acts out. Some acted-out responses can be M. On this point my own experience is at some variance from Rorschach's since I have found many more of the acted-out associations to be M than would be warranted by his discussion. But without doubt many of them simply reproduce a remembered motion and do not have the inner personal significance of M. In the response here cited we have static description reproducing the conventional witch figure and no evidence of true M either in the spontaneous association or in the inquiry. D F+ H P.

Figure X

'The gray ones here are birds flying toward each other' [D 7].   Animals in movements or positions common to them only.   D F— A.

Similar percepts scored F are 'bears lying down' [D 13]; 'bulls or cows lying down' [D 12]; 'a dog stretching' [D 2].

'The little blue figures here [D 6] look like doves.'   In the inquiry S added 'they seem to be flying toward each other.'   Again perception of activity in which the animal in question is conventionally represented.   Scored D F+ A.   Another such percept is 'deer jumping' [D 7].

'These rodents or mice [D 8] are trying to squeeze through an opening and trying to get hold of something through this small object [D 14] with their teeth.'   The temptation here is to interpret the animals' effort to 'squeeze through' the 'opening' as very deep fantasy activity revealing the very core of S's personality.   As such it would be M.   To score M on this ground would be to commit the fallacy of interpreting first in terms of personality and then assigning the score that fits the interpretation.   It is possible of course that the *birth fantasy* is behind this response, but we are in no position to draw this conclusion, either from the response itself or from the general body of Rorschach evidence as it stands today.   Such interpretations are, to be sure, being made from Rorschach content, but those that have come to my attention indicate that their authors are borrowing from psychoanalysis and reasoning by analogy.   In the present response, the animal content dictates scoring D F+ A.   The more highly individualized content will interest the therapist and he will explore further in his patient with a view to establishing its significance.   But that is another step.   The Rorschach test has served well in offering S an implement whereby to evoke this mental activity, whatever it may mean to the patient.

Significance of any theme to a patient is really only known to the patient, latent though it may be.   Only he will make it known, aided, to be sure, by an appropriate therapy.

Chapter IX

COLOR NUANCES: C

The importance of the color response in Rorschach's test lies in the sector of the personality that is reflected in it: the individual's outwardly expressed feelings. The relation of color to affectivity was, of course, no new discovery of Rorschach's. There are signs that it was sensed in remote times, even in the earliest stages of culture. Rorschach simply made use of this connection deeply ingrained in the human mentality. By experimenting with colors in his test figures, and observing regularities of response in different personality groups, he obtained an index to that piece of equipment in our personalities wherewith we do so much and which so frequently does much with us. Rorschach's interpretation of the color responses has remained essentially unchanged. We still deal with these reactions as he has done in *Psychodiagnostik*.

What is a color association? The verbal behavior scored as indicating a color determinant is that in which the patient reports some hue in his percept. It must be *hue*, not black, white, or any of the intermediate grays (see chapter x). The color may be named in the free association, or for the first time in the inquiry.

Three nuances of color influence have been identified. For example, in figure VIII, the lower orange and pink mass [D 2], 'this round part, a flower, a pink and orange orchid'; figure II, lower red [D 3], 'blood, it's dripping'; figure IX, the large green mass [D 1], 'a green lake.' These three responses also demonstrate the information it is necessary to obtain in the inquiry in order to establish the relative weighting of color and form. S explained that both the color and form recalled the flower, but the form was what made him think of the orchid rather than another flower. The red was the most compelling fact in the 'blood' percept, but the form dictated the 'dripping.' The green was the only reason for the 'lake.' The three responses are scored respectively, FC, CF, C.

The difference between C and CF, between CF and FC, or whether we have any C determinant at all cannot in some instances be established satisfactorily. The levels of confidence are: the first, patient's spontaneous language in the free association. Second is the information we can obtain in the inquiry. Failing these first two, then, third, when there is a background of statistical experience warranting the C determinant, this directs the scoring; e.g., 'blood' is C when evidence to the contrary cannot be elicited; 'flowers' are most often CF; 'bow-ties' or 'butterflies,' FC. But

98

birds and grasshoppers may be FC, CF, or just F.   In these, and in others like them, it is safer to refrain from scoring any nuance of C in the absence of clear-cut evidence in S's language.   Should the doubt be unresolved between FC and F, the better scoring is F with a question of FC noted in the margin.   Similarly, we may know that C contributes but must leave the question open as to whether it is FC or CF.   As between CF and C, uncertainty is less frequent, since an undiluted C association is usually clearly such.

Language can be misleading.   S says, 'the red part is a necktie,' or 'the green is a caterpillar.'   The inquiry will show in many instances that the color does not contribute to the percept; it is used only in identifying the detail to which S is attending and is an F response.   But to some S's, it is a 'red necktie,' or 'a green caterpillar,' and the scoring may be FC or even CF.

An intriguing and promising approach to the problem of discriminating color from form as determinants is that by Baughman.[3,4]   It has the additional, stimulating value of demonstrating that laboratory technics can be devised to control the Rorschach experiment.   Here again, Rorschach had anticipated the control thinking; see his report of brief experiments in which he manipulated colors for some common animal forms, and the clinically logical results which followed (ref. 27, pp. 53–54).

Color naming.   To name the colors is not to perceive something color-determined.   It may, in fact, be the contrary: an avoidance of such association.   Color naming is therefore not scored.   Neither are spontaneous expressions made by S on being presented with one of the color cards of the test.   These vary from an exclamation such as, "Ah, colors," to a more explicit affect.   The latter may be pleasurable, "I love these colors," or "It's such a relief to have colors"; or decidedly unpleasurable, e.g., in figure IX, "What a horrible mess—these colors," or, figure X, "All these colors disturb me—they clash so."   Feeling in these reactions is strong and the language diagnostically differentiating.   However, none of these is scorable since they name no content.   They are reactions that are not percepts.

Some formulas.   In appraising the total influence of the color-determined associations in any one response record, each response is weighted, in accordance with Rorschach's formula, as follows: C, 1.5; CF, 1.0; FC, 0.5.   The sum of the weightings constitute the color sum; e.g., a test record includes 3 C, 2 CF, 4 FC, in which event the C sum is 8.5.

Information of importance concerning S's sensitivity to color stimuli is obtained from the freedom with which he responds to figures VIII, IX, and X as compared with figures I through VII.   This is his affective ratio.   It is obtained as a proportion of his total productivity in VIII to X over that in I to VII; e.g., R total is 40, with 15 associations in figures VIII to

X.   Hence, figures I to VII elicited 25 associations.   The affective ratio
is 15:25 or 0.60.

Experience Balance (EB).   This is set down as the relation between
the total number of scored M responses and C sum.   For example, in 40
responses, 7 are scored M, and C sum is 8.0; EB is 7:8.   C sum may be
3.0, or 1.0, or 0, with M 7, and EB would be respectively 3:7, 1:7, 0:7.
Or with any of these sums M may be 0, 5, or 15; and EB could be: 0:3,
or 5:1.0, or 0:0.   Any EB relation is possible.

Experience Actual (EA).   This is obtained by simple addition of the
two values making up the EB.[10]   Thus, with EB 7:8.0, the EA is 15;
with EB 3:7.0, EA is 10.0; with EB 0:0, EA is 0.

In summary, the following are the color variables to be observed in
interpreting any test record: the color nuances (C, CF, FC); weighted
total of the color nuances; number of color-determined associations, especially in relation to total productivity; color shock, and in what test
figures it is activated (see chapter XVII); affective ratio; themes in the
color-dictated associations; weighted color total in relation to number of
M responses, i.e., Experience Balance and Experience Actual, EB and EA.

The illustrative material that follows presents scoring samples of C, CF
and FC in the five test figures with color in them, and also samples of responses not C.   Most of these scorings were based on satisfactory information in the free association or the inquiry.   For the rest, judgment had
to be made from what was known from similar responses, the scorings for
which could be dependably established.   These, then, are scored by inference rather than from evidence in S's language.   No normative rules
can be formulated whereby all C, CF, and FC can be scored with unequivocal objectivity.   Some of the very associations which I am listing may
in another S be determined by one of the other color nuances.   Each
examiner must explore his S's percept and its determinants by appropriate
and clinically judicious inquiry.   The responses that follow are reported
only as a representative sampling of the experience of this examiner.

Figures II and III

'Blood,' 'fire.'   These are essentially always the themes when either of
these test figures elicits a pure C response.   There are variations on the
themes, e.g., menstruation, volcanic eruption, but they are variations
around these two most frequent percepts.   Scorings are always D C Bl
or Fi.

Figure VIII

'Reminds me of a rainbow, orange shading to red, red to blue, blue to
gray.   That color [D 1] goes through here,' i.e., Dd 25.   W C Na.

'Jello, the orange part' [D 7].   D C Fd.

⋀ 'For some reason the particular color of the blues [D 5] gives the impression of ice; seems to have the color of large cakes of ice.'   D C Na.

'The blue suggests grass [D 5] even if blue, as though there is spring in the land.'   D C Ab, spring.

Figure IX

'Just irregular smears of paint.'   Content such as *paint* is in some instances pure description, and not scored; in some instances, as here, something is perceived by S.   It is content, scored W CF + Art.   Even the association *ink* is in some cases not descriptive but a new percept and scored.

'The way you look at a futuristic painting, and you think it has meaning.'   W C Art.

'My first impression is green water' [D 1].   D C Ls.

'Pieces of pottery from this color' [D 1].   In the inquiry S emphasized: 'Color only: no particular shape to them.'   D C Hh Art.

'The green part is like a well cared-for lawn; it's an even green.'   D C Ls.

Sunset, as when you sometimes see it on a beautiful summer's evening' [D 6].   D C Ls or Na.

Figure X

'Meat, rather tainted meat' [D 9].   The darker parts of the detail indicate 'tainted.'   D C Fd.

'This picture reminds me of happiness because of the gay colors and delicate shades . . . rose color that you see in the ten-cent store . . . a sort of artificial flower.'   Gray details were excluded.   D C Ab, mood.

'A couple of blood spots on a handkerchief from bleeding' [D 9].   Color alone dictated the association.   Hence, D C Blood.

Color-Form Response: CF

Figure II

'A little flame' [D 3].

⋁ 'Dogs [D 1] breathing fire' [D 3].   Scored D CF+ Fi for the 'fire.'

'Blood splashed, blotches of blood.'   When in D 2 and D 3 of this figure, and in D 2 and D 3 of figure III, *blood* is seen as in any way spread, responses are credited with F even though further evidence of F is lacking in the particular instance.   The scoring is D CF+ Blood.

'A forest fire, beginning to creep up'—on D4, which S had previously seen as 'tree.'   'The lower colors [D 2] suggest the creeping up of the forest fire.'   Originally scored C because of S's emphasis on the colors, this response is now better understood as CF. The F is implicit in the expression 'creeping' as the perception of a movement by the 'fire.'

∨ 'A picture of a marine floor with the seaweed.' D 3 with adjacent Dd; the color of D 3 suggests 'dulce,' a form of seaweed. D CF− Bt.

∧ 'The whole thing gives me the vivid coloring of a modernistic painting.' W CF+ Art.

∧ 'Two devils on top' [D 2]. S first indicated color as the only determinant, then included form. Experience with D 2 as *humans* is broad, and would in itself have justified the F. Scored D CF+ H.

Figure III

'A red cat falling through the air' [D 2]. D CF+ A.

After seeing the two men 'getting ready for a boxing bout,' S continued with 'evidently fighting, because of the splashes of blood [D 2] back of them.' D CF+ Blood.

'Like a parrot [D 2] as if he's lost his neck, as if there's some blood squirting up and they're standing upside down and someone threw the body away.' D CF+ A.

Figure VIII

'Like a crystal formation' [D 7] because of its 'color' (in the inquiry) and the color variation. S names only color but spontaneously has noted formation. D CF+ Mn.

'The coloring reminds me of slides we used to put under the microscope, colored slides' [D 2]. S referred spontaneously only to 'coloring' but the inquiry left no doubt concerning the form element. Experience with this association for this detail also favors the CF scoring.

'A decorative vase.' W CF+ Hh.

∨ 'I get the shape of a flower' [D 2]. A case in point, showing how evidence in the inquiry may controvert an indication in the free association. There was no question but that color predominated, and that CF is the correct scoring.

∧ 'The color scheme of a dress.' D 5 are 'the shoulders,' D 2 'the girdle and skirt.' D CF+ Cg.

'He ['animal,' D 1, seen in preceding response] might be on the edge of a lake [D 5] because of this blue here.' The form element is in 'edge'; color is also spontaneously offered. D CF+ Ls.

'A design; would be a very nice wallpaper . . . heavy . . . as for a downstairs gathering place; a unit design.' W CF+ Art.

Some delicate marine creature of the jellyfish order'—entirety except for D 1. D CF+ A Sc.

Figure IX

'I am reminded of a fountain here' [D 5]. In the inquiry S added 'it has the color of water.' This detail frequently elicits *fountain*, usually form-determined. D CF+ Ls or Ar.

'These pastel colors running together remind me of paintings by a man named Stevenson; droll, quiet evening scenes with very few definite figures.' The F is a thin one but it is present, in the free association 'figures.' W CF+ Art.

∨ 'The color at the top [D 6] affects me; I see it on the water at sunset.' The importance of the inquiry is here shown. S speaks only of color; in the inquiry it was found that form helped in the percept. Scored D CF+ Ls. Support of this finding was given directly by S in his free association when he changed the sunset to 'meat, four slices of ham,' scored D CF− Fd.

∨ 'An old woman all dressed up in fancy clothes of 1890 to 1900 [W]. She has on a green jacket [D 1] with bustles or rather with shoulder puffs. The purple does not make a head; perhaps a collar [D 6]. Below the green shawl is a very pretty shade of brown, which might be a coat extended from under the top jacket [D 3]. The combination of colors is very beautiful, the brown and green particularly.' All the emphasis on color is taken as evidence that this factor has priority. Scored W CF+ H. Where a human form is in the associational content, the F element can be assumed. Inquiry is necessary only to establish priority of F or C.

'At the top it suggests northern lights, the way the lines go out,' Dd 25, because (in the inquiry) of the 'color.' Scored Dd CF+ Na.

Figure X

'Land in the sea, brown islands' [D 13]. D CF+ Ge.

'Lights hanging down from the chandelier [D 3]; it has the color of brass.' S accents color. Again experience, which is extensive as regards this response in this figure, dictates an F scoring. Many *chandelier* responses to D 3 are only F. The score here is D CF+ Hh.

'Chickens,' D 2. 'A marine scene,' D 10. Both these were found CF.

'A bursting of fireworks in the air; a rocket, shooting up, just as its bursts, and there's not the feeling of them dropping.' W CF+ Fi.

'Curious plumage [D 15], comic, from the tail feathers'—of D 7, just seen as a 'bird.' D CF− Ad.

'A butterfly with the different spots on the wings.' W CF−A.

'Taken as a whole it looks like a coat of arms; perhaps that's because so many colors are combined and because it's so symmetrical.' The term 'symmetrical' is a form concept, and this is the basis for the F in the scoring.

In the free association, S first noted the colors.   Hence, W CF+ Aq or Art.

'Like a purple vest, open, with some gaudy shirt underneath.'   Upper portions of D 9 with Dds 29 with D 3 and D 6.   'Gaudy' because of the colors.   Scored Ds CF+ Cg.

FORM-COLOR RESPONSE: FC

Figure II

'An impressionistic drawing.'   In the inquiry form was found to be the primary, color the secondary determinant.   W FC+ Art.

'A cap, the liberty of the French Revolution [D 2], fashionable several years ago for young ladies.'   D FC+ Cg.

'Strikingly like a red butterfly [D 3]; the symmetry gives two similar wings with varieties of antennae that butterflies have, streaming out behind.'   This *butterfly* is in most instances a pure form response; occasionally, as here, color contributes—'a red butterfly.'   D FC+ A P.

Figure III

'A red tie' [D 3].   Scored D FC+ Cg P.   Also 'a red bow.'

The 'tie' or 'bow' is in most instances only form determined (cf. the 'red butterfly' immediately preceding).

'Turkeys hanging in store windows around Christmas or Thanksgiving' [D 2].   D FC− A, Fd.

'These two red spots, like hearts [D 3] typify them, give the idea of carrying hearts on sleeves.'   D FC− Art.

∨ 'This red is like a parrot on a stick and the color is a parrot's too' [D 2].   D FC+ A.

Figure VIII

'Suggests the coloring of a flower and the general idea of a flower in nature, conventionalized.'   The spontaneous accent on 'coloring' would dictate a CF scoring, but the inquiry left no doubt that S was reacting first to form.   Hence, W FC+ Bt.

∨ 'A composite butterfly' [D 2].

∧ 'Two flags here [D 5], blue flags, not any flags I have known; two staffs here, and the flags are blowing out.'

'A boar colored pink' [D 1].   S refers only to coloring but experience regarding this detail is too broad to exclude form.   In the inquiry S further supported the F element in the scoring by noting that the detail more nearly resembled a 'cat' or 'rat.'

'A red rag in folds' [D 2].   The inquiry was inadequate.   Colored bits of cloth are occasionally seen here, with the form element predominating. Hence, D FC+ Cg.

'This looks like some sea animal [D 2], a jellyfish.' D FC− A.

Figure IX

'Chinese gods and they wear funny masks [D 3] with queer appendages, big ears, and funny noses, big stomachs [Dd 28], flowing skirts [D 1]; and their feet' [Dd 21]. D FC+ H, Rl P.

∧'Have you seen the colored moving pictures? This [D 5] reminds me of ... what do you call it in Paris? The eternal torch or light'—because of its 'color' and 'its soft shading' and because it is 'torchlike.' Oberholzer scored this FC. His reasoning was that it is a doubtful instance, a threshold example, but 'torch' is too undeniably the form of what is seen. Hence, D FC+ Art.

'Like a peacock' [D 1]. D FC− A.

Figure X

'A kindergarten child's effort—a conglomeration of shapes and colors.' S first mentions the *shapes*, evidence that form dominates.

∨ 'A flower, in the distance,' D 11 with both D 9, and D 10 as the 'pistil.' D FC+ Bt.

'Like the state of California, which is very often red on the maps' [D 9]. D FC+ Ge.

'Lovely girls with pretty summer dresses, fluffy and soft, as though they are headless.' Although in the inquiry S first noted the color, she laid about equal emphasis on color and form. *Human* detail is frequently seen in D 9 and is usually form-determined and most commonly feminine. Hence, D FC+ H.

'A brown ram running' [D 13]. No further information was obtained in the inquiry. Animal forms are common in this detail, more frequently without color. The safest scoring is D FC− A.

'This ... what can it be? [D 4] Not snakes, are bodies of snakes; but they come together with one head.' In the inquiry S gave precedence to color; the emphasis in her free association was entirely on form elements. D FC+ A.

'Like looking through a microscope at some tissue fluid of the body [W]; suggested not so much by the color as by the irregular outline.' S himself tells us that both color and form contributed, with form predominant. W FC+ An.

'A view of the bottom of the sea: crabs, sea urchins, and all kinds of different things.' The collections of *animals*, *plants*, and *insects* in this figure are as often CF as FC. *Butterfly* or *flower* collections are more frequently CF than FC but this cannot be taken for granted. In the present response S accented form. Hence, D FC+ Ls.

Not Color

Figure II

'I don't see any particular significance in the red.' Color naming and rejection.

'I have the impression that the red color is beneath the black and get a three-dimensional effect.' Description of blot structure, noting color.

'If it is an animal, the red part doesn't seem to have much purpose.' Criticism of color.

'I like the red; I like the splash at the bottom.' Color indications, with pleasant affect.

'Red and black . . . and a touch of brown. The red has a grayish black . . . and a scarlet.' Color naming and description, pure and simple.

∨ 'The red spots on the bottom resemble feet' [D 2]. Color here has only one function—that of identifying the details selected. This is a frequent kind of response in any of the color figures. None of these responses is scored as color-nuanced. The response here cited is scored D F− Hd.

∧ 'That will be about a butterfly [D 3] but the color is not right. It's only because of the shape.' Spontaneous criticism of color and rejection of it.

Figure III

'The red things up here look like lions with long tails' [D 2]. Color is named only to identify the detail; it has no force in determining the association. D F+ A.

'A butterfly in the center' [D 3]. In the inquiry S said that the *form* was the reason but added 'the fact is, the color attracted me.' She expressed thus what directed her attention to the detail and uncovered a color interest, but the color did not affect her association. D F+ A.

'The two red parts are like pictures I've seen of white mice' [D 2]. Note that the associational content is an animal of another color. S thus spontaneously tells us that the adjective 'red' is not the basis for the association expressed; it merely identifies the detail.

'The red color keeps forcing itself on you.' Color named, with unpleasant reaction.

'Just dabs of ink there . . . red ink.' Description only, of colored details.

Figure VIII

'The colors don't seem to fit together, except the pink against the orange.' Unpleasant reaction to colors, with naming.

'The whole thing strikes me as having rather good color; the colors are rather nicely blended together.' S directs attention to color without naming and indicates favorable affect.

'The blue part here [D 5 with D 4] reminds me of the dissection of a skate.' Color used only to identify the detail. D F+ A, An.

'There is marked contrast between the upper part and the lower part, because the upper is of warm colors, and the lower part is of cool colors.' Indication and description.

∧ 'The colors are quite a relief after the dark ones.' Indication only, with some pleasant response.

'What do you want, the colors in these? . . . I see four distinct colors—orange and red, almost a raspberry. I should say, a blue.' Color naming.

'Well, to begin with, the colors. Brownish, yellow, red, the axis, light blue, baby blue, bright red, perhaps that's scarlet, green down here, iregular outline, certain portions have identical outlines that distinguish them.' Color naming par excellence. The record was produced by a young man recovering from hypomanic excitement. He followed this pattern of response also in figures IX and X.

Figure IX

'The colors blend into one another and become confused.' Color indication and description.

'Again I don't like the color scheme.' Antagonism to color.

'As though the green is above and overlays the brown.' Naming, with description of blot structure.

'More colors.' Simple indication. After a single association S added, 'I am more impressed by the colors than I am by the design.' Interest in color, without naming.

'The green is like the face of an Irishman with short upturned nose, with long upper lip, a heavy jowl.' The color identifies the detail.

'I can't specify anything there; a lot of different colors; orange, green, more like raspberry. I can't make anything of that.' Expression of inability, with naming.

Figure X

'The red things are leaning backward, seem to be opposing each other . . . people' [D 9]. Color used in identifying the detail. D M+ H. S

followed with 'the blue things [D 6] are standing on crags of rock.'   Another
D M+ H scoring.

'I don't know quite what to make of this blue thing' [D 1].   Expression
of inability.

'The colors are not in harmony.'   Description with adverse criticism.

'The brown figure [D 13] means nothing at all; I can think of no association.'   Naming with rejection and expression of inability.

CHAPTER X

THE VARIATIONS IN LIGHT: V, Y, T

This determinant is found in one of three variations: vista (V), flat gray (Y), texture (T). Rorschach identified vista in the posthumous paper,[28] his "chiaroscuro" response. The diffuse gray is described by Oberholzer in two publications (ref. 24, 1931; ref. 25, 1948). The most extensive and systematic exposition of the light-determined associations is Binder's.[11] The most minute breakdown of the varieties of shading determinants is Klopfer's,[16, 17] and it becomes a dispersal which Bohm[12] criticizes. Klopfer was the first to identify the texture association.[16, 17]

Vista is the percept, among these light-determined ones, concerning which we know the most. In it the variations in shading give a three-dimensional effect, as of something seen in perspective. The only content categories scorable as vista associations are: the distant, usually landscapes, sometimes aerial views, occasionally astronomical percepts (lunar landscapes), and the heights in landscapes; architecture, usually as heights, less often as being distant; insularity, usually land in water, but sometimes water surrounded by land (lakes); depths, usually water, but also caves; reflections, usually in water, sometimes in mirrors.

Not all such responses are vista-determined, however. S's language must refer to distance, height, depth, or reflection, and the insularity must be described in terms of a differential perspective between the object and its adjacent area, e.g., figure V, W: 'island with water around it'; figure IX, Dds 29 and D 1: 'here is a lake, in the middle of a woods.' Or in figure VI, with the card on the side, the center black detail [D 5] 'a river running through a gorge, here are the mountains.'

The psychologic significance of V lies in uncovering the important character trait of inferiority feelings. Dynamic theory (Adlerian[1, 2]) can be adduced which rationalizes the relation between this trait and a vista response.

The flat gray responses are those in which the light values as such recall the thing seen. Thus: 'an animal skin all laid out, mottled like skins are' (figure IV) scored W FY+; 'a sombre mask, it's so dark, and it has the shape of grotesque masks,' for the entire of figure I, W YF+. 'Mist or fog, this gray spread out'—figure VI held on the side, and attending to the portions immediately adjacent to the center dark; Dd Y. *X-rays* are typical. We find also abstractions, *depression*, *fright*, projected by the massive grays (figures IV, VI). Most *smoke* and a few *cloud* associations

109

belong here. Occasionally the gray is used for its color value—'a black leopard' (figure IV, D 7). In all these the shading, as an element in the black-white series, is the essential factor in evoking the association. Thus, it closely parallels the force of color in determining certain associations. But, clinically, they represent a personality trend diametrically opposite to the elation with which color is connected. The grays, especially the massive ones, go with an unhappy mood.

Not infrequently, both V and Y must be scored for the same response, as a fusion of determinants: e.g., figure IX, card on the side, within the white space, the center portion [a part of D 5], 'a distant horizon, on the edge of a lake, mountains or a town, a haze over it,' scored VF.Y; in figure VII, the lower hinge detail [D 6], 'a house between two mountains, smoke curling up from above it,' and the inquiry accents the shading for the 'smoke,' as having set going the association; scored Y.FV.

A problem is frequently presented by the response of relief maps, which may be either V or Y. When S gives any indication in the free association or the inquiry that he interprets the differential shadings as though projecting the "height" of the relief map, the scoring is V; if not, Y. Then, too, many geographical associations are simply form-determined, as, for example, 'North and South America' for figure VII, the two upper sections of either lateral detail [D 2, card inverted]. Also, islands, lakes, and peninsulas as *maps* are not to be confused with the vista responses in which the percept is a *landscape*. As a map, it is the contours that are the determinants and the scoring is F. Sometimes a Y or a C determinant may enter in but this is only because S recalls some map detail out of his geography books, e.g., for figure X the large pink mass [D 9] 'California' and, as the inquiry shows, because of its length and because in S's geography book California is in red. In another example, in figure I the dots off of the lower lateral Dd 23 are 'a coastline, a map with islands and the white is the water,' scored FY, in which the Y is for the 'white.'

White as Y. The "white" associations present another special problem as to what goes on perceptually. Until some research is reported demonstrating that it belongs among the color determinants, where some writers place it, I can only feel warranted in looking on it as at one extreme of the light-dark continuum. Hence, scored Y.

The texture determinant, T. The sense modality in which the texturally determined association has its origin is touch. It reports an experience in which the skin feels directly. It is most common as something 'soft' in relation to fur associations; also with food topics; and occasionally with a more primitive theme, 'mess,' or explicitly 'feces.' 'Hard' associations are less frequent. The motifs in these are occasionally fabrics, e.g., in figure VIII the center blue [D 5] as 'silk,' or for figure VII, any of the details,

as 'rocks' or 'stones.'   The mere perceiving of 'fur rug,' 'ice-cream,' 'silk,'
and least of all 'rock,' does not warrant a T scoring.   If S verbalizes the
adjective "soft" or "hard" the response is so scored.   But the determinant
may be implicit in the language, such as to figure IV, W, 'a bear rug, . . .
I could almost put my hand on it,' is FT, and may be TF if so established
in the inquiry.   Most of the texture responses are FT, and only occasionally TF.   An example of the latter, for figure V, W, 'could be a toupée
with a little added on top,' and in the inquiry, 'very heavy hair.'   The T
responses unmodulated by form are extremely rare.   Two examples: figure
II, the lower red [D 3] 'something burst open, bloody flesh, soft, mucus,'
scored C.T; figure V, W, 'a satiny surface, a piece of satin cloth,' and in
the inquiry 'because of the shadows and the consistency.'   Scored Y.T.

Psychologically, this determinant is a clue to an affect hunger, at the
core of which is an erotic need, one persisting from the patient's earliest
developmental years.

Examples follow of V, Y, T associations.   As may be anticipated, figures
IV, V, VI are the chief source of Y responses, with figures I and VII next
in order.   But even the color figures occasionally yield such a reaction.
The V response is more evenly distributed.   It will be noted again that all
F in FV, FY, FT, as also VF, YF, TF, is plus or minus, depending on the
judgment made of the form element.

VISTA RESPONSE: V

Figure I

'The impression of a mountain pass; both sides [D 2] are mountains with
a pass or bridge [D 3] in between.   It is a narrow pass.   It looks very
sombre, all gray, and straight up and down.'   D VF+ Ls.

'The openness at the top [Dds 32] is as the top of a canyon or mountains,
with large boulders sticking up' [D 1, Dd 22].   *Mountains, valleys,* and
hills have been found to be V; the rule may be considered general, but
questioning is always essential.   The response is scored twice: Dds F Ls
for 'openness' and D FV− Ls for 'mountains' as related to the canyon.

In the response following, S directly verbalizes the evidence for vista.
'A feeling of mountains [Dd generally in D 1]; I can't quite define . . . I
like mountains . . . there is a feeling of masses'; and he explains, 'the darker
portions are darker or deeper areas.'   Dd VF+ Ls.

'These two marks [Dd 22] are something like a mountain'; S saw a
'mountain once' when with her parents 'and the curves were like this.'
Dd FV− Ls.

∨ 'This looks like a crater' [lower half of D 4]; as though 'looking down
a crater; it has that shape and shading.'   D FV− Ls.

$\wedge$ 'As if looking down off a mountain . . . a landscape in which there are lakes and light reflected from the lakes' [W, with Dds 26 as the 'lakes.'] Ws VF.Y+ Ls.

Figure II

'A promenade [Ds 5 and Dds 29], walking up through a flight of stairs, to a building [D 4]; and this on either side is a lot of architectural work.' Scored Ds FV+ Ar.

'Mountains, and hills in the back, very indistinct' [Dd in D 1, near D 4]. Dd VF Ls.

'The white in the middle has depth [Ds 5] because of these gray things' [D 1]. In the inquiry S added, 'The shadow gives it perspective.' A rare instance of pure vista abstraction without form element. The free association language is itself clear as to the V element and in the inquiry S added the supporting proof in her own words. D V Ab, depth.

$\vee$ 'Just the entrance to a cave' [Ds 5]. Cave entrances have been found to be V regularly enough to warrant giving them this classification generally, unless there is good proof to the contrary. Ds FV+ Ls.

'Reminds me of a lock canal, dredged out here [Ds 5]; the Panama Canal, from quite a distance . . . it is really a lake rather than part of the canal—seen from a distance, hence it looks small.' Ds VF+ Ls.

$>$ 'Looks like a person on a piece of ice, with image reflected in the ice.' Ws FV+ H Ls.

Figure III

'Mountainous terrain' [D 11]. See in connection with Figure I concerning 'mountains' as generally V. The scoring will be FV or VF depending, as usual, on evidence in S's language.

$>$ 'Getting the idea of this as a peak [Dd 21], you would get up considerable speed if you were speeding down,' i.e., along the edge of Dd 21 to D 6. Scored Dd VF Ls Rc.

$\vee$ 'A peninsula . . . land [D 5] surrounded by water; the white part would be deep water'; D 10 is 'low' (land) because it is a lighter shade. Scored Ds FV− Ls. The emphasis on 'deep water' points to the strong influence of the V factor. Experience with similar responses has shown that VF rather than FV leads to more valid interpretation.

$\wedge$ 'A tree . . . and this looks like a precipice [Dds 24] or a ravine; like two trees, and water running in the middle of it.' D 6 are seen as the 'leaves' of a 'tree' all bunched; the light variations of D 8 are the 'ripples' in the 'ravine.' Ds FV+ Ls: question of Ds FV.Y+ Ls.

$\wedge$ 'A bridge . . . like a Chinese garden. It is a Chinese rock garden,' with the tiny horizontal gray Dd as 'bridge'; the 'rocks' [D 6] are formed by the light values.   D FV— Ls.

∨ 'Like some auto lane running into a farm [Dds 24], with a barn directly in front [center Dd in D 8] and shrubbery'—the black exclusive of D 5— 'on each side of the lane.'   In the inquiry, S added that it was a 'lane' because of 'the light cast against the darker shadows on the shrubbery.' It is scored Ds FV.Y+ Ls.

Figure IV

'The outside of a cave, the white representing the inside . . . which is of course the reverse of what it ought to be in color.'   Dds 24 and Dds 29 are the 'inside' of the cave—but S would expect that to be 'dark,' hence 'reversed in color.'   Ws VF+ Ls.   Compare this response with the "depth" in Figure II above.   There is a question here too of pure V; i.e., Ws V Ls.   Present S's discrimination of 'outside . . . inside' leads to in- ference of a contour (form) percept.   The association illustrates the role which E's judgment must, in instances, play.   Yet the present response and the "depth" in the other do serve as frames of reference for each other: nothing in the latter suggests form.

> 'The whole thing is a reflection in the lake . . . of this; or vice versa,' i.e., one side is a reflection of the other.   Reflections in water, as depth reactions, are three-dimensional percepts.   It is safe to classify these as V, as a general rule.   S, in his free association, returned to the present re- sponse with 'it represents a woodsy scene . . . a dark woodsy scene.'   W FV.Y+ Ls.

'These could be shoals, looking down on land, if you were looking from a considerable distance . . . the land visible through the water.'   D 7 is 'land'; D 2, 'land covered by water'; and the surrounding white is 'water.' Ds VF.Y Ls.

'The first thing I think of is a fountain [D 5], the water flowing up here and falling off from each side,' lateral portion exclusive of D 2 and D 4. *Water* and *fountain* present special problems, since they are as likely to be pure Y or pure C as V.   In this example S himself accented chiaroscuro: 'flowing up and falling off.'   D FV+ Ls.   Compare 'fountain' in figure VI as YF.

∨ 'A tower [D 1], the front of a church, a steeple up at the top . . . seen just from the front of it.'   This is a perception of a height away from S. Hence, D FV+ Ar.

Figure V

'As if I'm up in the air and I see a landscape down below; and this [white around figure] would be water, and land there [figure itself] and water around, having docks coming out; I can visualize that.' S added, in the inquiry, 'It's a bird's view of an island.' Ws VF+ Ls.

'Looks like an inlet [Dds 29] and it suggests a bay' because of the black-white contrast. Dds FV Ls.

'Well ... could be a relief map ... the top view, photographed from above,' with Dds 27 and Dds 29 as 'deep inlets for harbors.' Scored Ws VF+ Ge, Ls.

∧ 'Then there's a line down the middle that looks like a ravine between high wooded hills [D 4]; as if looking down from the top.' D VF+ Ls.

Figure VI

'Looking down on a road [D 5] cut through a highway of some sort; excavated land on either side; like a driveway, as if you were seeing it from quite a height.' D VF+ Ls.

'An aerial map, with a road running down the middle' [W]; like 'a valley coming up.' W FV+ Ls.

> 'This might be an imperfectly dug channel,' D 5, because of the chiaroscuro effect, with D 4 as the 'top of the bank,' while 'the water is at the bottom.' D FV+ Ls.

'A map in relief' [D 1]. S sees 'peninsulas, with the darker portions as in relief,' and 'the raised' parts are 'mountains.' When the relief element is as clearly stated as here, I score V. Scored D FV+ Ge.

The *aerial* perspective and the *channeled-out passage* are common V in figure VI, with variations only in detail. Sometimes the two themes appear in one response: 'an airplane view of a river [D 12]; steep sides [D 4]; a canyon' [D 1]. D FV+ Ls. In another, S saw, in an aerial photograph, D 12 as 'a railroad line, so thin because the plane is so high'. Scored D VF Tr, Ls.

< 'A cliff sitting back on a plain ... trees towering out over one end of it ... and a tree hanging over,' D 4; the lighter Dd, adjacent to D 5, are the 'plain' and the darker, outer half of D 5 is the 'cliff,' with D 9 as 'trees' and Dd 25 as the 'tree hanging.' D VF+ Ls.

Figure VII

'A gate, beyond which there's a long grove of trees,' D 6; the lighter Dd are the 'gate' and the darker the 'grove.' D FV+ Ls.

'Relief maps,' details indiscriminately, because (in the inquiry) of 'the light and shadings and the dimensional quality of the shadings.' Here S simplifies things for us by speaking of the dimensional aspect. D FV+ Ge, Ls.

'Like a dam, a man-made installation [D 6]; a dam or a road, looked at from a great height.' Scored D VF+ Ls. This association elaborated on a previous one in which S saw 'a map of Japanese island installations —harbors, etc.' Ds FV+ Ge, Ls.

'A mountain, like . . . some place way off' [Dd 25]. Dd VF Ls.

'There's water, running through a creek [D 6], at the bottom.' D FV+ Ls.

Figure VIII

'This is a castle on top of a hill,' chiefly D 4, with Dd 24 as the 'castle such as the Germans have.' Scored D FV+ Ar, Ls.

'A tiger looking at his own reflection in a lagoon.' Card ∧; usually in this kind of scene it is >. Scored, as all reflections, except when the contrary is clearly shown, D FV+ Ls ('tiger' was separately scored).

∨ 'A snow-covered mountain in the distance,' Dd 23 and adjacent Dd; S can 'see the red portion of the clay sticking through the snow.' Since this CF element is added in the inquiry, it does not affect the scoring of the primary perspective response, Dd FV− Ls.

∧ 'A high hill [D 4] with some kind of point on it, almost a triangle but it isn't.' In the inquiry, 'because it has the shape of a hill'—verbalizing much emphasis on form. But the spontaneous accent on height confirms statistical experience, which points to V. D FV+ Ls.

< 'This looks like an animal there, standing from one side of the peak to the other [D 5 and D 7] sort of hanging in the air.' The animal is separately scored; the *peaks* are scored D FV+ Ls.

Figure IX

'Depth right here [Dds 22] as if looking down into a cavern.' Scored Dds V Ls Ab, depth. See note on depth as abstraction under figure II.

'Various coral maps; the shore line with mountain up at the shore [inner edge of D 3] as in South America; the mountains shade back [and because] portions are darker, it is a relief map.' The map association is well submerged under the perspective content. Ds FV+ Ls.

'Mountains,' D 3; a moment later, S saw D 5 as 'water.' 'Mountains' could be set down as FV as a matter of rule. But even the feebleminded S of this record confirmed the judgment when he said that he 'had often seen water coming down mountains near Staten Island.' *Mountains* is scored D FV+ Ls.

∨ 'A house on a hill.' Dd like a 'nose' in the lower edge of D 1 is the 'house,' D 1 the 'hill; it is vague and in the distance.' Dd VF Ls.

Figure X

'These long red things [D 9] represent like a chain of mountains . . . or like a cloud; it's darker in one place than in another . . . it's irregular.' D FV.Y+ Ls.

Similar to this, also for D 9, is, $\vee$ 'this looks like a mountain,' supported in the inquiry by 'the way it rises.' D FV+ Ls.

$>$ After seeing several tiny Dd on the projections of D 1 as sundry figures, 'man,' 'horse,' S continued, 'They seem to be standing at the edges of a promontory.' The questioning was not adequate; the response is scored V on the basis of experience generally with height perceptions. Hence, Dd FV Ls.

A frequent vista reaction utilizes the portion of D 9 adjacent to D 6 (latter seen as *humans*) as 'a cliff.' (D or Dd FV; sometimes VF.)

'Looks like some huge canal system, looks like the Panama Canal, a channel going through a system of locks, going through,' Dds 30, with D 10, D 6, and D 3 as 'locks.' Experience with canals, especially where both white space and blot details are utilized, leaves no doubt concerning the perspective factor. The best scoring is Ds FV+ Ls.

This figure is potent in eliciting *religion* associations with FV elements —more commonly in the psychoses, but also among healthy subjects, usually in cases of individuals of very high intelligence. Thus, 'this is just a plain deep pit at the bottom without much chance of getting out.' In the inquiry S explained that D 9 are 'forces outside working above and beyond an organized religion,' and continued with 'it is as though falling.' Scored D M.FV— Ls.

A young schizophrenic, seriously disoriented, saw 'the devil [D 10] and the pit up instead of down' [Dds 30]. After six intervening associations, he saw D 4 alone as 'the devil ... the bottomless pit, going down'; in the next association D 8 were 'two devils ... keep on going down to the bottom.' The mental status of such patients makes the inquiry difficult and not always reliable. Structurally, *abysses*, *pits*, and other depths are V when we can get introspection, and we follow this rule. Scoring here is Dds V Rl.

LIGHT VALUES: Y

Figure I

'And it's a sky [D 2], a strange grayness, not real sky, just a picture of a sky.' Light values alone determine this response. D Y Na.

$<$ 'Parts of this remind me of pictures I've seen of the heavens, and nebulae,' lower half of D 2, because of the dark and light parts; 'are crater masses, shadows, like the mountains on the moon.' D Y As.

'Like an x-ray of the bone structure or some histological affair' [W, because of the shading]. A frequent kind of associational content usually determined by both form and light qualities. Variations are:

'Like ribs, chest, an x-ray,' W FY+ An.

'It might be the x-ray of the pelvic region of a woman,' upper half, excluding D 8. D YF— An

'A biological specimen, x-ray of a crab, lobster, insect.' W FY— A

'From here up, it could be the silhouette of an animal'—the area comprising D 5 and D 8. S explained in the inquiry, 'It's an outline formed by a shadow, and it all runs together; it's complete as black and white,' and added that he saw 'only the outline, not the features.' Silhouettes are forms that are sharpened by certain light and dark values. The problem in them is whether form or gray predominates. The scoring here is D YF+ A.

'The lower half of a human figure, from the rear [D 3]; it is the bottom of the torso, hips, calves, heels, silhouetted against a screen.' This human figure is very frequently seen because of form; as a *silhouette*, it is influenced also by light. D FY+ H P.

'An obvious impression . . . it could be a relief map,' D 2, because of the 'shadings and the irregular surface; the dots give an island feeling.' D FY+ Ge. Emphasis here is too much on shading and too little on height or depth perception.

'Sort of a partial bat [W]; the blackness represents the wings and coloring of a bat.' Scored W YF+ A P.

Figure II

After seeing 'two women, with their hands against each other,' S continued, 'Looks like the hands are tied together with a ribbon, a black ribbon' [D 4]. Form and shading both present. Scored D YF— Pr.

'Like a dog's head, the position of a dog, with his nose [D 1]; two dogs, except this red [D 3]; it's like a black poodle dog.' Accent on form. D FY+.

\/ 'They all look like tree trunks [D 1], because it is black, and the form.' Light value dominates. D YF— Bt.

/\ 'A dark curtain' [D 1]. Scored D FY— Hh. The question of the relative dominance of F and Y was not adequately settled in the inquiry; *curtains* has as a rule been found to be form-determined.

'It might be a monument of marble; not marble . . . but stone, granite' [W]. 'It is not marble,' S explained, 'because of the shadows; marble would be smoother.' This was the response of a superior adult, who was, however, naïve in regard to the purpose of the questioning. His spontaneous evidence is therefore the more interesting. Note that he himself offers 'shadows' as a determinant and that he excludes 'marble' on a tactual basis: it would be 'smoother.' To this extent he also excludes the 'shadows' as a basis for this tactual image. Scored W YF+ Art. Most interesting, psychologically, is the fact that tactual experience is being activated, even if rejected as determinant. That is, this important modality is being aroused by the test. Whether we score, and what, becomes of less import here than the evidence adduced of a sensitive person whose sense of touch is readily excited.

'I wonder what sort of paint brush would make strokes like this' [D 1]. *Strokes* is a form percept but in the inquiry S accented the 'black.' D YF+ Art.

'Silhouette of a camel's mouth' [Dd 31]. See note concerning *silhouettes* under figure I. Dd FY+ Ad.

Figure III

'This black gray [D 11] . . . a section of a photograph in the sky.' It is possible that form contributed to this response. D Y Art, Sc.

∨ 'These remind me of big trees [D 4] with shadows,' i.e., the gray Dd within D 8. Scored twice: D F+ for 'trees'; Dd FY for 'shadows.'

Figure IV

'The first thing that comes to my head is the darkness and only because it is black.' W Y Ab, darkness.

'All this shade and shadow here, I don't know why it reminds me of a desert formation, but that doesn't seem to fit'—indicating the darker details—'and the lighter ones are the light shining through.' D Y Ls.

X-ray responses do not always have a form element. Thus 'the shading is very pleasing'—indicating the lateral portions exclusive of D 4 and D 2; 'it smoothes off from dark to light, the shading in the upper part is more like an x-ray; it has blotches'—referring to the upper portions generally. D Y An.

'This is a filament, like wings of a bug, like a mosquito, but bigger; a fly' [D 3]; because it is 'transparent, and [because of] its vein patterns.' D FY+ A.

∨ 'This haze is like smoke . . . from wood; it is rising, nebulous' [D 2]. D YF+ Fi.

∧ 'A map again [W] with surrounding water on either side.' In *map* when contrast with the white as *water* is verbalized, the Y element is scored, unless S clearly excludes it. Hence, Ws FY+ Ge.

'They look like clouds, dark clouds' [D 2]. Emphasis on 'dark clouds' dictates the scoring D YF+ Cl.

'This thing up here [D 5] suggests a very tall veiled figure with a black cloth . . . the hands here [gray Dd in middle of D 5] and the face is up top . . . it isn't all veiled [Dd 25]; it is sticking out and these definitely are feet' [Dd 26]. *Veiled* responses are almost always Y. Scored here D FY+ H.

The *fur* association with good evidence for the Y element is not particularly common in any of the figures. An example is: $\vee$ 'Like fur, of an animal, hanging up to dry,' [W] because of 'differences in color; and tops of fur are hanging over' [D 4]. W YF+ A P.

Figure V

$<$ 'Again it's dark, a dark picture . . . the ink . . . the darkness of it.' The word 'picture' suggests form but no further evidence of this was obtained. Scored W Y Ab, darkness.

$\vee$ 'It minds me . . . well, I had a cat, and it minds me of my cat; the color, this'—indicating details indefinitely—'because my cat was black, too.' D Y A.

$\wedge$ 'A butterfly . . . a black butterfly . . . typical of depression, or of blueness; symbolic of depression.' This could have been scored W YF+ A P. But the mood that S abstracts from the figure is so much a reaction to the black as such that it necessitates two scoring formulas, thus: W F+ A P; W Y Ab, mood.

'If I would get the suggestion of darkness, or a dark room, I suppose I'd suppress it, because it doesn't seem like a dark room.' The scoring is D Y Ab, darkness.

'A piece of burned cloth; because it is black, and irregular.' W YF+ Object.

'I can make out something that looks like a real face [D 6], blond hair'— the lighter Dd at the right edge of the 'head . . . protruding cheek bones.' S described other facial Dd and added, 'Somebody drew a pencil or eye line here' all in the free association. 'Blond hair' and 'pencil lines' were gray-determined. 'Face' is separately scored, and the present response is recorded as Dd FY.

Figure VI

'Cloud formations here,' the area embracing D 9 and Dd 29; clouds in the wind—'it is as though there is a beating downward.' Both form and light, but S heavily emphasized the light. D YF Cl.

$>$ 'Like some queer form of a ship,' either lateral half; 'it is nebulous, cloudy.' D FY+ Tr.

$\wedge$ 'That's a chest . . . an x-ray of the chest' [D 1]. D FY− An.

$\wedge$ 'Whenever pictures have black and gray, the impression I get is of an x-ray; it might be an esophagus or an x-ray of a woman' [D 2]. D YF+ An.

$\vee$ 'The thing as a whole might be the silhouette of a tree, a grotesque-looking tree; it's too symmetrical; here might be the roots.' A silhouette response in which the accent is on form rather than on light (cf. note under figure I on *silhouette*). D FY+ Bt, Art.

Figure VI

'It is, again, dark ... very dreary-looking.' W Y Ab, darkness.

'This looks like bad focusing under a microscope' [Dd in D 4] because of the 'mottling.' Dd Y Sc.

'Smoke, from a train,' the thin light gray Dd in the center of D 12. 'Train' had been separately scored. 'Smoke' is scored Dd Y Fi.

∧ 'From here up, a fountain [D 8], water going up and returning ... from the shading.' S adds in the inquiry, 'Light comes through the gray of the slopes [D 6] and gives a feeling of water, up and down.' D YF+ Ls. (See note on *fountain* as V under fig. IV.)

< 'Might be a scattering of leaves on the ground that have lain long enough to lose their color' [W]. The dull gray is emphasized. W YF− Bt.

Figure VII

'Cloudy' [W], because of the 'shading' only, 'not the shape: like stormy clouds.' Scored W Y Cl.

∨ 'That's whipped cream on top' [D 11] because of its 'color and the shape.' D YF−.

∧ 'Geopolitics,' because of the shape and the gray. W FY+ Ab.

'A map,' D 2, with especial emphasis on D 5 and Dd 21 as 'peninsulas' and the 'shaded edge as coastline.' D FY+ Ge.

The *two ladies*, almost invariably form-determined, sometimes have another aspect because of the light quality. Thus, 'two elderly women, their faces seem squashed ... as if they had their teeth out; the dark shadings on the face make them look as if their faces are dirty, or else light is coming from the back.' D FY+ H P.

Clouds, in any of its variations, is in most instances FY, in almost as many cases F, somewhat less frequently V, and in rare instances pure Y. It is as commonly W as D (D 1 or D 2).

'You can imagine two snow dogs down at the bottom [each D 10]; they are made out of snow.' D FY+ A. Inquiry was inadequate. '*Snow dogs*' strongly argues for YF, but these "dogs" are frequently seen in this detail and are always form-determined. On an empiric basis the scoring is FY, with a question of YF.

Figure VIII

'Like beautiful satin [D 5] with its folds and creases; it has a sort of sheen to it.' Only the variation in chroma was the basis of the response. It gave the effect of *sheen*. A good, even if rare instance of light quality, as the only determinant in a color detail.

'What's left [D 3] after the jackals got through ... sharp edges of bone ... spinal column.' Patient accented the whiteness, with form. D YF+

An. 'A sweet pea ... flowers'; the shading variation is 'not too important, but it helps.' W FY+ Bt.

Figure IX

'This too suggests snow. The top of this,' i.e., of Ds 8, 'suggests snow.' An all white response, Ds Y Na. A similar association, also for Ds 8, was 'this could be a snow mountain in here just because it is white.' The possibility of multiple determinants, vista and white, scored V.Y, needs to be considered. But S's indication of white is unhesitating. Hence, Ds Y Na, Ls.

< 'A flying cloud or something' [D 3]. The shading variation helped determine the 'cloud' association. D FY− Cl.

Figure X

'A couple of dogs, some kind of dogs, with face up there; a very faint silhouette' [D 2]. D FY+ A P. See note concerning *silhouette* under figure I.

'Well, this is a little goblin of some kind [Dd 27] with his shadow behind him' [Dd 28]; or it could be 'wings; it is the lighter half [of D 1] and it had to be something,' hence 'shadow.' A true shading reaction to a colored detail. Two scorings: Dd F+ H; Dd YF Na.

'Might be a jellyfish, only a jellyfish is bigger' [D 2]. The inner darker portion, Dd 33, is the 'nucleus, being darker.' The shape of D 2 as a whole also helped to determine the response. D FY+ A.

'Two faces [D 8] looking at one another face to face ... colored people.' A simple gray determinant, but many subjects see D 8 and D 7 as brown and give responses in which brown is a factor. In such instances the scoring would be D FC and not, as here, D FY.

TEXTURE DETERMINANTS

Figure I

'Cloud formation' [D 2], but in the inquiry patient elaborated on the 'fleecy texture.' Possibly a TF, but owing to the word "formation" in the free association, scored D FT+ Cl.

Figure II

'Wood,' looks like wood, because of the 'texture and the grain.' D T Oj.

'A brooch [Ds 5] against black velvet [D 2]; diamond, sapphire against black velvet.' The rare 'velvet' associations, when inquiry evidence is available, has been a 'feel,' and hence T association. In absence of evidence to the contrary, I would score this percept Ds Y.FT− Pr.

Figure III

< 'Messy substance; [>] or furry; it's hard to say which' [D 11 with D 4]. S elaborated: 'It is as if dripping; it hangs,' because of the form. D TF— Na.

Figure IV

'The dark has the resemblance of a skin of an animal [W]. It's like very warm . . . or cool . . . warm.' It is 'cool' because 'dark' and 'warm because that is how the skin would make a person feel if it were around them.' The *warm* is explicitly related to the *feel* experience; hence texture. These responses were produced by a young woman going through a schizophrenic episode. The accents on the shading dictate a scoring of TF (rather than FT). Hence, W TF+ A P.

'The sides here are dripping' [D 4]. The detail is 'thick, like dirty grease from a bike.' D FT— Object.

Figure V

'Tongs [D 3] pulling a gelatinous, or tarred, mass [Dd adjacent to D 3] sticking to the bottom, embedded in the mass.' Scored Y for 'tarred' and T for 'gelatinous.' Thus, D F+ Im for tongs; Dd T.Y Oj for the rest of the content.

Figure VI

'The whole thing . . . a tissue stain, nuclei of cells . . .' because of the 'variation in density,' i.e., scored density W T Sc.

'An animal skin jacket, sleeves . . . stretched out flat.' Clear accent on form, but in the inquiry, 'has the texture of the skin.' W FT+ Cg.

Figure VII

'This is ice; really quite cold-looking picture'—indicating D 8; 'cold' because of the gray. A probable T; but we need inquiry evidence from many more persons, for the comparatively rare *ice* associations. As 'cold' i.e., a feeling, which obtains also for *snow*, scored D T Ab, cold.

'A very pretty cloud effect . . . sky . . . beautiful, fleecy clouds' [W]; it is 'soft, fleecy, and diffused.' The tactual factor is accented; but clouds are so universally a light-determined association. The scoring: W T.Y Cl.

After seeing D 2 (∨) as 'two dancing girls with only leg [D 5] showing,' S continued: 'The leg seems to be covered with fleecy fur . . . a wintry effect . . . suggests a cold atmosphere.' Scored D T Ab, cold.

'Here again I find a very smooth wash; it reminds you of the wash of a water color [D 4]; here it seems very smooth.' A tactual element complicates a gray without form. Scored D Y.T Art.

Figure VIII

'A loaf of rye bread [D 7] split in half, and two open faces showing,' because of the form and 'it has a feeling of crust.'   D FT— Fd.

'Flesh or hair' [D 4 or D 5].   Inquiry not adequate from this very disturbed patient.   On basis of known determinants for both these themes, scored D T Hd.

Figure IX

'A soap-stone formation' [D 1]; in the inquiry, 'the feel—soapy—greasy —and rubs off on the hands.'   The accent on the feel element is too convincing in the inquiry, enough to outweigh the term 'formation' in the free association.   Scored D TF+ Hh.

Figure X

'Roast chicken' [D 7].   The form primarily, but also with the 'dry' texture, as if cooked.   D FT+ Fd.

'A shaggy little animal, woodchuck perhaps' [D 13].   D TF+ A.

'A piece of ham' [D 9], owing in part to color, but also to the 'feel.'   D C.T Fd.

Apparent Light Reactions: Not Y, V, or T

As in regard to the color responses, S may show interest in the darks or grays without using them as determinants.   The shading may simply identify the details' location.   Example: "these little black things are bear cubs," in Figure III, the lower roundish masses [D 4]; scored F, since S was here using the adjective 'black' only to point out the detail she selected; she did not see a *black* bear cub.   S may note the fact of shading, describe it, or he may react with strong feeling, usually unpleasing.   None of these is scored.   They are given weight in arriving at the interpretation, similar to what we do with such reactions to any of the color stimuli.

Other examples:

Figure I

After seeing 'a skeleton . . . part of the body,' S verbalizes, 'No, it wasn't a skeleton . . . I've studied something about this in college . . . it's black.' An elaboration, with Y naming, but without influence of the light quality on the response.

'Pagoda,' 'Japanese temple,' or other *oriental structure* is frequent in this figure (∨).   The inner spaces are windows or other architectural apertures only because of form.   The scoring is Ws or Ds F+.

Figure II

'And this whole formation [Dd 22 and Dd 23] a coast, like Greece . . .
very broken up, indented; or along the Carolina coast.'   Not all geography
associations are gray-determined.   Many use form only, as here.   Dd F+
Ge.

Figure III

'These two black [D 1] are cartoons,' and S proceeds to elaborate the
usual human response, scored D F+ H P.   Black simply identifies the
detail.   S's next response was, 'And this black portion [D 8] is that part of
the skeleton, the sacroiliac.'   D F+ An.

Figure IV

∨ 'The two less darkened figures in the upper corner [D 2]; one looks
like a barking dog; he is in a position as though to bark; more or less happy;
running along.'   S notes the differential in the light values but only to
identify the details.   D F+ A.

'On this side [Dd 22, left] like the features of a Viking, large shaggy eye-
brows, hairy head, large too.'   *Hair* details are sometimes erroneously
scored Y when there is actually not enough evidence that they are other
than F; the variations of light quality fashion the lines that make possible
the singling out the 'hair' and usually other fine details, e.g., 'shaggy eye-
brows.'   Scored Dd F+ Hd.

'This looks like a dried skin, an animal skin [W]; you know, those tiger
skins hanging on the wall, and the leather skin in a tannery, after they're
hanging up to dry.'   This 'animal skin' is representative of the great majority of percepts of *skins, furs, shaggy beasts*, and like content.   Some fur
responses are based on light quality but many are form-dictated.   They
are scored W F+.

Figure VI

∧ 'Pictures of germs that I've seen in the microscope'—the area from
Dd 25 to D 9 inclusive—'looking in the microscope, not any particular
germs.'   Questioning excluded shading.   Dd F− A, Sc.

'That's all just blurred . . . smeared, I should say.'   Description of blot
without associational content.

'A barber pole, with faintly etched stripings' [D 9].   This looks like a
simple gray response, but there is no proof that the light values are essential
to the 'stripings.'   *Stripes* also have form and this determinant has support here in the word 'etched.'   Dd F− Vo.

'This might be a light [D 8] with the light and the rays up here [D 7 and
D 5] and this is the background.'   *Burning lights, fire*, and *smoke* in the

noncolor figures are as a rule black-white reactions. In the present response, S unequivocally rested on 'form only.' She is a professional person whose evidence is dependable. D F+ Fi.

Figure VII

'Looks like a map of the United States,' D 2; the Dd connecting D 1 and D 3 is 'Central America, with the Panama Canal; and it is North and South America.' Geographic associations are frequent here—occasionally gray-determined, more commonly form only. D F− Ge.

Figure VIII

Not V. Numerous *rocks* associations occur for D4, 5, 6, 7, or 2 in relation to the animal stepping or climbing. Except when distance or depth is verbalized, these are not V. They are really by-associations made necessary by the animal, and scored F.

Figure IX

Not V. 'And there's a hole' [Ds 8]. Response of a 9-year-old S, no evidence of any three-dimensional perception. It is chiefly descriptive, with just enough indication of a real percept, i.e., a *hole* to warrant scoring. Hence, Ds F+ Ls. S saw also Ds 5 in figure II as 'a round hole' and Dds 29 in figure X as 'a big hole,' like one he had seen in the movies.

Chapter XI

MIXED FEELINGS

As has been seen in many of the examples in the preceding pages, a multiple determinant is found in numerous associations. In these blends, S is using any two of the affective determinants; in some instances, more than two. Most frequent are the interpenetrations of M with one of the C nuances.

In attempting to score them the first horn of the dilemma is whether (a) to score twice. This results in loading the record with too many responses, with more structural material (W, D, Dd), sometimes with more F, and frequently with more associational content, than is warranted. The other possibility is (b) to score only once—either C, M, Y, etc., and omit the other score. But the other happens to be as weighty in determining the association in question as the one we are entering. Which is to be omitted, and why the one rather than the other? More importantly, the omission of so significant a determinant leaves us with an inaccurate Rorschach picture of the individual.

The solution has been to enter both, as a multiple determinant. My scorings in these are M.FC, or CF.V, or M.C., etc. For purposes of arriving at the Experience Balance (EB) and Experience Actual (EA), each M is rated, as usual, at 1.00, and the C nuances as they would be if they stood alone, i.e., C, 1.5; CF, 1.00; FC, 0.5. These values are then added in with any other C scorings in the record, while all the M are simply counted.

In commenting on the coincidence of M and C in the same responses, Rorschach states this circumstance to be rare. This is inconsistent with later experience. He correctly notes that these associations are found in highly endowed subjects and in elated states. But in naming only catatonic schizophrenics as the clinical group in which they occur, he is reporting from a then limited experience. Actually they are produced by all except "simple" schizophrenics; in most neuroses, although not in certain hysterias characterized by mental impoverishment; in hypomanic conditions, but not in depressions; never in mental deficiency; and rarely in conditions due to brain pathology, although here too certain patients produce very florid associations including some M.CF or other blended reactions.

The blends are found in any combinations of C, Y, V, T, M, with one another. Some are naturally extremely rare. Examples follow.

Figure II

'Two Santa Clauses playing peas porridge hot.' They are 'Santa Clauses' because of the coloring. W M.CF+.

'Like two people [D 1] playing patty cakes [D 4] with large hats' [D 2]. They are wearing 'black coats,' are a little of 'magicians' because of the 'hat,' might be 'sitting,' are 'wearing red stockings.' Not only M and FC are present, but also a light reaction—'black coats.' Full scoring would demand M.FC.Y. But this is loading the scoring formula with too much. It is better practice to enter the two most important determinants and note the extra nuance in the margin of the scoring sheet. W M.FC+.

'The only thing . . . a silhouette of a couple of dancing bears, or a ballet dancer's composition of dancing bears.' The *silhouette* is a shading reaction. The scoring W M.Y+ A accounts for the movement and the light.

Any detail may be combined with the colored ones. For example: ∨ 'Hah! Close one eye and see something different; a white figure [Ds 5] with red feet [D 2] and red head [D 3]. It is a dancing figure, a Russian dancer sort of squat.' Ds M.FC−.

The lower red detail [D 3] is 'a table decoration in red, with candles sticking out . . . it's bright, Christmas.' CF.Y−. The lower red [D 3] 'sunset on a mountain . . . dark red, hilly, distant." CF.V+.

'That water is clear' [Dds 29] because it is 'smooth.' Only the white dictated this association. The term 'smooth' in the inquiry indicated that the percept utilized tactual imagery in part. The term 'clear,' however, accents the light factor. This response thus belongs among these blends as Dds Y.T Na.

Figure III

A sample in this figure that blends an elaborate movement response with all the color details in rich fantasy productions: 'This looks like two men in evenings clothes taking their hats off to each other [D 1] or else it might be a box in the opera, and there are the portieres' [D 2] because of their 'color' and 'form, and this is the lady's chair [D 3] and the men are going in to say hello to her; the red stuff is the lady's cloak thrown over the back of the chair'—hence the color of it blending with the form. A good illustration for the scoring W M.CF+ H P, original, and a healthy projection out of the mature young woman who produced it.

'A red devil; he has red fire coming out of his mouth.' D M.CF+ H. The plus in this scoring refers to the M; the fire would be CF− and a note to this effect needs to be made marginally.

'If this were a person [D 9] it would be as though she were looking at herself in the mirror . . . a trick mirror.' The unanswered question here is whether mirror reflections are depth perception, i.e., vista, or flat shadows, i.e., light. The movement response is clear. The scoring is D M.V or D M.Y.

Figure V

'These little things [both D 2] look like the heads of people . . . as you look from a distance, as though they're going over a hill.' Here S verbalizes both movement and distance perception in the free association. Yet it is a single association derived from only one stimulus area. D M.V+.

Figure VI

'An airplane shot of a railroad train or a railroad track' [W]. The light factor was accented in the inquiry in explaining the photograph. But these distance perspectives always are vista reactions. W VF.Y+ Ls.

Figure VII

$\vee$ 'Like a sun setting . . . with clouds in the background' [D 11]; the 'lighter' is the 'clouds' and the 'sun' is 'darker.' The light reaction thus determines the objects seen and a vista is built out of the differential in the shadings. D V.Y Ls Na. $\vee$ 'Like two girls dancing [D 2]; they seem to be graceful . . . hands outstretched.' S describes the dance in more detail and concludes, 'They look like blondes.' D M.Y+.

Figure VIII

$\vee$ 'A reflection in the lake,' excluding only D 1 from the entirety; 'it is only a reflected scene' because of the 'color' and the 'ripples.' S gives evidence as to the color, and *reflections* of landscapes are vista as a general finding. D C.V Ls. 'Stalagtites in caves, molded by water and the wind . . . they hang down and the color is softly shaded.' FC.Y−.

Figure IX

$<$ 'That's like Santa Claus climbing up a chimney [D 3] as if he's carrying something and as though he is wearing a red suit.' D M.FC+.

$\vee$ 'A contour map,' the area comprising Dd 22, and the portion adjoining D 1, because of the 'color' and the 'way it merges, and also the road.' The *merging* and the *road* are due to shading. Dd C.Y Ls.

$<$ 'Of course, this looks like a colored landscape . . . modernistic, impressionistic . . . a reflection as usual'; either lateral half could be the scene. D CF.V+.

'A mountain in part overcast by clouds, land seen as through a haze' [Ds 8]. Ds V.Y.

Figure X

'Two pretty good ghosts in blue [D 6]; they're hanging on to a cliff' [D 9]. D M.FC+ for the 'ghosts.'

Abstractions of feelings. To figure V, reacting to the entire card, the patient associated, 'This whole thing looks warm, feels warm.' The full scoring is W M.T Ab: warmth. This "warmth" example illustrates still another blending of determinants. In it the particular feeling experience—whether of the quality signified by C, Y, V, or T—generates also an innerly lived emotion. In these the M is abstracted out of the association to the color. Thus, the "warmth" set going by the "feel" association. Another example, internalizing both the C and Y tones and necessitating a triple determinant scoring: "How someones feels when they are mad . . . really angry—characterized by red, and the black is gloom and depression settling over. The red, just sort of unhappy. When you are angry, you draw it in red. After anger passes, you are miserable, then black, gloom." Full scoring: W M.C.Y Ab. I try to avoid such amalgam of scoring, but the intensity of the emotions packed in this association, its deep introverting, and the interacting of the three experiences cannot be recorded except by M.C.Y, all as a unit.

Whether we are justified in scoring such associations as M can be questioned. They fulfill only one of Rorschach's two basic requirements for M. This is that "it is something which is lived" (ref. 27, pp. 25ff; and cf. p. 94f.). It is not a percept of someone in action. One could argue that a kinesthetic experience is present in these, as a tension involving the muscles and skeleton of the patient, and the content does, of course, verbalize a human emotion and thus would be grouped among certain M responses described above (pp. 84f.). The further, and more substantial, support for the probability that such responses are M is that by so scoring, and interpreting, we are better able to etch out the clinical picture in the patients so associating.

These abstractions differ from the blends, but blends they are since it is certain that it is C, or T, or Y, or V, as the case may be, which sets these associations going, with rapid blending into M. All these concentrate some very intensely felt experiences, saturated as they are with introverted feelings (M), with pressure toward externalizing (C), or with sensed pain in them (Y, V, T). They are the mixed feelings of men and women—their excitements and agitations, their despairs and exaltations—inner experiences which the greater poets can so vividly and accurately portray.

Chapter XII

FORM, GOOD AND POOR: F+, F−

The F+ response—Rorschach's *gute Formen*—is a cornerstone of his experiment. Its usefulness in appraising the S's ability to perceive accurately, and hence to know realities, gives F+ this importance. The realities include the social values; they are "good form" in the social sense. It follows that a normative and operational practice in scoring F+ is of the essence in clinical use of the test.

Concerning the evaluation of form quality, Rorschach says: "In order to eliminate subjective appraisal so far as possible, statistical methods were necessary. The norm and base were those form responses that were most frequently given by a fairly large number (about 100) of subjects in good mental health" (ref. 27, 23ff.).

This rule sounds satisfactory. But practice and experience have shown it to be illusory. The fact is that no fairly large number of persons in good or any other mental condition give any considerable set of responses "most frequently."

The problems that exist in establishing an F+ standard I have discussed elsewhere.[7] The list of F+, F− published at that time has now undergone some ten years of testing. New scorings have been established in this time and some of the old ones have been made more valid by altering from plus to minus, or vice versa. A very important assist was given us in the overall revision by some two hundred psychologists using the test. We had addressed a request to approximately 1800 persons, including the members of the Clinical Division of the American Psychological Association, asking them for samples of Rorschach test responses that troubled them regarding F+ or F− scoring. Essentially all of the approximately two hundred replies from over the breadth of the land included responses which were useful additions to the lists. We are naturally deeply grateful to those psychologists who so aided in broadening the base for our normative F+ table.

Other form scorings are available, of course. There are the published test protocols by Rorschach,[27, 28] Oberholzer,[24, 25] Bohm,[12] Loosli-Usteri,[19] Schachter,[30] Hertz,[15] and the files of the Swiss *Zeitschrift*.[35] Small's compendium[32] has been very helpful. However, all these still prove inadequate, and every Rorschach test worker finds himself pondering daily over associations never given before and for which he has no exemplar.

The rule I follow is that if the *form* of the new association follows the form of any published F+, score F+; if the form follows that of a published

F−, score F−. For some associations, experience is so universal and conclusive that they can by now be scored F+ with absolute confidence. Such are the P responses (chapter XIII). In addition, some other responses can be scored F+ with nearly as much confidence: e.g., the 'bird' for figures I and V entire; in figure III, with the card inverted, what is now the upper middle detail [D 4], 'tree;' the 'totem pole' for the upper section of figure VI; the 'deer's head' or 'alligator's head' for the grayish orange detail in figure IX where the green and orange merge [D 2]; any 'Alice in Wonderland scene' for figure X as a whole. At the other extreme are the obvious F− responses, those that clearly deviate in form from the known percepts for the W or the D: e.g., W for figure I, 'x-ray of a tooth'; in figure VIII, the center blue [D 5], 'a tree swaying in the breeze.' In between, the degrees of certainty dwindle, and in too many associations the decision is arbitrary. A large element of subjectivity enters, as Rorschach himself noted—too large.

The Swiss have had a practice of scoring doubtful associations as F± or F∓ depending on the examiner's judgment as to whether the form is more plus than minus, or the other way. In the scoring summary the F± are counted as plus and the F∓ are counted among the F−. This practice thus evades the issue in the scoring and resolves it in the summarizing. It amounts to being the usual six of one and half-dozen of the other, a solution which does not provide the standards needed for the scoring itself.

Occasionally responses are given that can only be scored F, i.e., neither F+ nor F−. S is attending in these instances to details so rare that no normative data can be available for them, but the number of such responses is too small ever to vitiate the total F+ per cent in any one record. Then, too, the very small size of the selected Dd as well as their rarity are of a kind characterizing the approach of the excessively cautious (obsessive neurotic) or the fragmented (schizophrenic) intelligence. The total reaction patterns in these records are very clear from the other test variables and the minute Dd only confirm the found pattern.

F+ per cent for an entire test is obtained by the simple formula used by Rorschach: $\dfrac{F+}{(F+) + (F-)}$. The obtained per cent is as valid—that is, it is no better and no worse—as the individual F+ and F− scorings. This formula is applied only to those scorings in which the F is unaffected by any of the other test scoring categories; i.e., FY, FV, CF, M.FC and the others are not counted in obtaining the F+ per cent. The proposition has been advanced that F+ per cent can be more informative by using in the formula all the scorings in which there is a plus or a minus sign, including the FC+ and FC−, FV+ and FV−, and the others. Schafer[31] proposes this as the "extended F+" score. Another formula used by some workers is F+/R.

I tried both of these ways of arriving at F+ per cent, as well as some others that are possible, in my early years with the test (before 1932), and my experience always showed that Rorschach's formula could be validated best. In the light of the alternative proposals, however, the question is necessarily an open one. *Ad hoc* testing of Rorschach's formula against these others is needed to give the definitive answer.

Instructions for the Use of Table 10

Manner of listing responses. A response is usually a noun, but many responses also have an adjective modifier, or modifiers, important to the meaning. The general rule governing the listings in Table 10 is that the key word of the response is listed first and hence determines its position in the alphabetical listing. For example, almost all parts of objects, humans and animals are listed first, as "leg, horse's" and "crown, king's". The noun of a response is usually listed before its modifiers, e.g., "map, topographic." But there are exceptions to this rule. The listing "flying fish" refers to a specific species, in contrast to "fish, flying" which would indicate that an ordinary fish is seen as in flight. Occasionally the modifier is actually the key word while the noun is nonspecific or relatively trivial, as in "Christmas tree decoration" or "totem pole," in which case the modifier is listed first. Since there is sometimes a question as to which word has primacy, the user of the table may note inconsistencies in the manner of listing. If a response cannot be located by following the rules, it must be assumed that the rule has been broken and the response looked up again.

A parenthetical expression following a response may be an embellishment which does not change the scoring. Or it is explanatory, either about the area selected, or about the content.

Singular and plural responses. Because of the symmetry of Rorschach blots, many detail areas have an identical twin, like D 8 in figure I; or D 1 in figure VII. Respondents frequently generalize a single percept to include both twins, as "two . . . ." Of course, the form quality scoring of the plural response is the same as for the singular. The scoring for the response "two monkeys" to *both* D 2 of figure III is identical with that for the response "monkey" to *one* of the D 2 areas. These are listed in the singular in the table. When a single percept requires both of the twin areas, as "archway" to the Dd 25 of figure IX, this fact is indicated in the listing, i.e., "archway (both Dd 25)." In some instances, the scoring is the same whether the response to the area is singular or plural. Such responses are followed by (s) in the table.

Some details are composed of two identical, noncontiguous areas, e.g., Dds 30 of figure I, or D 8 of figure X. Other details have two identical, contiguous, but easily separable parts, as D 6 of figure II, or D 6 of figure

X. If the response is listed in the singular, it refers to the entire detail area, such as "brassiere" to the D 6 of figure X. A response listed in the plural usually means that the percept actually applies to each of the details, as "birds" to the D 6 of figure X. The form quality scoring for the response "bird" to either one of the D 6 would then be identical with that of the plural response to both details.

Cross-references. In some instances, a detail area and its identical twin constitute another detail area. For example, the two D 1's of figure II make up D 6. A plural response, "two . . ." is not listed under D 6, but the singular of the response is found under D 1. The reverse is also possible. If a response cannot be located under the one heading, it would therefore be prudent to check under the other. A series of such cross-reference indications will be found in the table.

Some details are composed of two or more dissimilar details. For example, D 9 on figure IX is D 5 joined with D 6. It is sometimes possible to score a new response inferentially, basing the judgment on a scoring for an allied detail. For example, the whole response "bat" to figure I is scored plus; the F response "bat wing" to the D 2 is not listed but, by inference, would also be scored plus. This method must be used judiciously. It is always possible, in view of the empirical basis of form quality rating, that inference from one percept to another will lead to a specious scoring.

The general response category. The nature of reality is arrived at consensually. Good form in a Rorschach response is determined in the same way. However, analysis of large numbers of responses suggests that a few blots or parts of blots have a particular stimulus "pull," a tendency to elicit a particular, *identifiable class of responses.* For example, the D 9 of figure III is frequently perceived as one of a variety of human figures, but it is rarely seen as any other mammalian form by normal individuals.

The blots are generally too amorphous to furnish more than a handful of general class or categories. Those which currently appear feasible are listed in Table 10. These provide a source whereby form quality ratings for many original, unlisted responses can be obtained. The rule is again simple: all responses which more obviously follow the plus responses are scored plus; those which resemble the general minus category are scored minus.

A word is in order concerning the use, in children, of this normative list, which has been derived mainly from adults' Rorschach test associations. To be sure, a child's perception of reality is not the same as that of adults. Yet, separate criteria for scoring children's records would not only be unparsimonious but difficult to establish definitively. It is much simpler and scientifically as valid to use a single standard for all respondents and to determine the F+ per cent expected for various age groups using these standards. Experience has shown, for example, that the normal adult will ob-

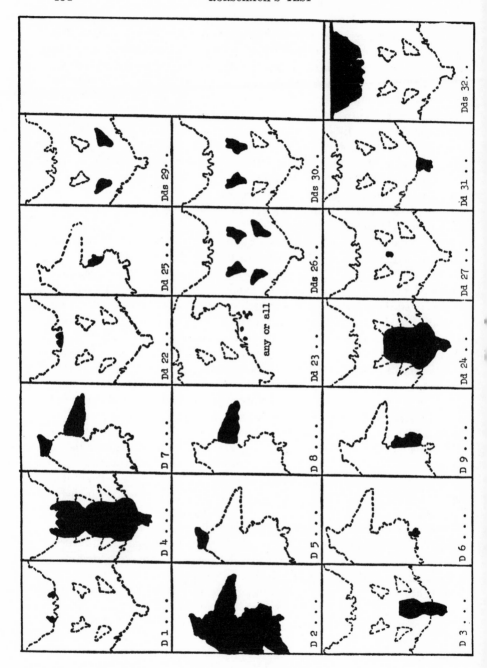

tain an F+ per cent of from 75 to 85, while children, scored by the same standards, will fall in the range 50–70 per cent.   In short, we use the same norms for scoring form quality for any individual, but we expect a different degree of accuracy depending on the age of the subject.

TABLE 10.—*List of F+ and F−*
Responses for all Figures

Figure I

W

(*See also D 2*)

General plus categories:

face (animal, human or inanimate); and
  winged objects (animate or inanimate,
  except a few insects)
− abdomen
− amoeba
+ angel
+ animal, marine
+ animal, prehistoric
− animal, split open
− bats, two
− bear
+ beetle
+ bench ∨
+ biologic cross-section
− blood, spilled
− blouse
− body, human
+ bone, skeletal
+ brain, cross-section
+ bronze (Chinese), cross-section ∨
− butterflies, two (divided horizontally)
− canoe, outrigger
+ cap, auto radiator
+ carving, stone ∨
+ castle ∨
− cat
+ cave
− chest ∨ (An.)
+ children
+ Chinese art
− Chinese letter
+ Christmas tree decoration
+ clouds
− clown
+ coat of arms

− cocoon
+ coral formation
+ crab
+ crawfish
+ crown ∧ ∨
+ crustacean
+ dancer
− dancer ∨
+ design
− dinosaur
− dirt on floor
− dish, fancy
+ dragon
− dragonfly
− explosion, atom bomb
+ figurehead
− fireplace
− fish
− flower
− fly
+ flying squirrel
− football player ∨
+ forest
+ fossil in stone
+ fountain with angels
− frog
+ girls
− governor on motor
+ hat ∨ ∧
  head: (no facial features)
    − animal
    − bull
    − moose
    − rabbit
    − ram
+ helmet ∧ ∨
− hill
+ insect
+ insignia, medical
+ island

+ jack-o-lantern ∨ ∧
+ kite
− lake
+ landscape and reflection <
+ leaf
+ lion, winged, in fountain ∨
+ lobster
− man with legs apart ∨
+ map, topographic ∨ ∧
− marine growth
+ mask (Ws) ∨ ∧
+ monster, fairy tale, four-eyed
+ monument
+ moth
+ mountains
+ mythologic characters
+ nightmare figure
− orange peel
+ ornament, including personal
+ pagoda, Japanese
+ pattern, lace
+ pelvis
+ photograph
− picture
− planet
+ pumpkin, Halloween
+ rock formation
− rocketship
− rug, fur
− saddle
+ scarab
+ sea animal
− sea shell
+ sedan chair
− sheep
− ship
− shrimp
+ skeleton, bird
− skeleton, outline of
+ sketch, charcoal
− skin, animal
+ skull (W or Ws) ∨
+ sky, clouded
− snowflake
− spider
+ spinal cord, cross-section
− sponge
+ stencil
− swamp
+ top, spinning

+ totem pole form
− train, front
− tree
− tree bark
+ tunnel
+ turban
− turtle
− United States
+ urn, Japanese
+ vertebra, outline of
− wasp
+ witches, two
+ woman, winged
+ x-ray plate (nonspecific)
− x-ray plate (scored F− when the
    specific anatomy detail named
    would be F−, e.g., lungs)

W without D 7

+ animal, microscopic
+ beetle
+ butterfly
+ jack-o-lantern ∧ ∨
+ pumpkin, Halloween
+ sting-ray

W without D 8

− man, hands on hips ∨
+ pelvis

Upper half of blot

+ airplane
+ bat
+ bird
+ butterfly
+ emblem
+ head, fox
+ insignia
+ mountains

Lower half of blot

+ bat ∧ ∨
+ butterfly ∧ ∨
− collar, shirt
+ crown, with jewels ∨
− pelvis
− prow, ship's

D 1

General plus category:

animal extensors (horns, feelers, claws)

+ antennae
− boulders
− cactus plant
− collar, woman's dress
+ coral
+ crab
+ crustacean
+ feelers
+ fingers
− fish
− fork and spoon
+ hands
− heads, animal
+ heads, bird
+ heads, duck
+ heads, snake
− human figures
+ mandibles
+ mittens
+ pincers
− rocks
− roots, tree ∨
− sticks
− teeth
− tongues

D 1 with Dd 22

+ crab
− genitalia, female
+ head, deer's
+ insect
+ lobster
+ nest, bird, with birds

D 2

See also W

General plus category:

human figure (including winged)

+ angel
+ animal
− bat
− bear
+ bird
+ brontosaurus

− butterfly
− carcass, hanging
− chicken
+ cliff
+ cloud(s)
− country
− dog
− donkey
+ dove
− dragon
+ elephant (D 8 is ear)
+ face (outer edge of D 2 as profile, D 8 long nose)
+ gargoyle
+ Gibraltar
− Great Britain
+ griffon
+ head, Pinnocchio
− head, swordfish
+ island
− lungs
+ map
+ mountain, or part of
+ Pegasus
− pig
− profile, dog
+ profile, witch
− rack, newspaper
+ rock
− sea horse
− skin, bear
+ sky
− stones, prehistoric
+ stork
+ trees
− water, bodies of
+ wings
− wolf, dancing

D 3

General plus category:

human figure

+ aqueduct of Sylvius
+ bell
+ body, baby
− body, human ∨
+ bowling pin ∨
+ chalice
+ legs

+ medulla
+ midbrain
− penis
+ scarab
− skeleton, human, lower half
− snake
+ spinal cord
+ statue of human
− submarine
+ vase
− x-ray machine

D 4

General plus category:

human figure or figures

General minus category:

infraprimate mammals

− alligator
− ant
− bat, wings folded
− bee
+ beetle
+ body (unspecified)
+ body, bird
+ body, insect
− bone
+ brain stem
+ Buddha
− caterpillar
+ cello
+ centipede
+ crab
− fish
+ flower pot
− fly (with Dds 26)
− frog
+ gorilla
+ gymnastic apparatus
− head, clown
+ humans, two
+ insect
+ lantern ∨
− lizard
+ lobster
− log
+ medulla
+ monument
− mountain
− owl

− pelvis
− rocket ∨
− sack of flour
+ scarab
+ scorpion
+ shield
− ship, front view
− skeleton
+ Sphinx
+ spider
+ suit
− tower
− tree
− turtle ∨
+ urn ∨ ∧
− vagina
− vampire
+ vase ∧ ∨
+ violin

D 4 without Dd 24

+ armor, suit of
− clip
+ crab
− crater
− face, deer
− face, monkey
− head, owl's
+ insect
+ lobster
− manta ray
− pelvis
+ people kissing
+ spider
− toad

D 5

General plus category:

human head

− bird, sitting
− chicken
+ comb, rooster
+ face, man's
+ face, wolf's
+ hat
  head:
+ bear
+ bird
+ dog

+ fox
− parrot
− horn
− horse
− house
− jaw, bear's
+ mountains
+ profile
− rabbit
− shoe

D 6

General plus category:

human head

− bell clapper
+ bust, of man
+ celery
+ crown
+ hay, bunch of
− head, dog
− human, whole
− leg
+ mushroom
+ shocks, of wheat
− tail, poodle
+ tree (usually ∨)

D 7

See also D 8

− Africa <
− animal (when accent is on D 8 as tail)
+ birds
+ dog
+ eagle
+ flying horse
  head:
  + bear
  + coyote
  + dog
  − duck
  + fox
− leaf
+ mountains <
− South America <
+ Sphinx
+ wing

D 8

See also D 7

General plus category:

wing (animate or inanimate)

− anvil
− arrow
− bird with beak
− blade, knife
+ cliff
− cloud
− dog
− face, human <
− face, animal
+ fin, shark
− flint
− funnel <
+ gargoyle
− ghost <
− head, alligator
+ head, dog or wolf
− head, Indian <
− horn
− insect
− isle, coral
+ mountain
+ mountain peak
+ nose, fox's
+ rock
+ seal (animal)
− thigh
− tree
− tree, fir <
− umbrella

D 9

+ cliffs, rock
+ clouds
+ dog <
+ face, dog
+ face, human
  head:
  − animal
  − buffalo <
  + cat
  + dog
  + human
  + lion
  + monkey

Dd 22

− breasts
+ boulders
− eggs
+ head, bumps on
+ head, split open
+ heads
+ hills
− humps, camel
+ labia
− mosquito bites
+ mountains
− rectum
− testicles
− trees

Dd 23

− dots
− flies
− insects
+ islands
− mosquitoes
+ notes, musical

Dd 24

− alligator
− beetle
+ bell
− bellows
+ cello
− chipmunk
+ crest (on shield)
− hourglass
− human figure ∨
+ insignia ∨
+ lantern, Japanese ∨
− people, two
− spinal column

Dd 25

+ animal
+ bushes
− cliff
+ face
+ gnome
+ head, old man's
− pig

Dds 26

See also Dds 29 and Dds 30

+ carvings
+ eyes, four
+ glaciers
+ mask details
+ puzzles, cutout
+ ventricles
  wings:
  + airplane
  + butterfly
  − fly

Dd 27

+ buckle, belt
+ central canal
− heart, human
− moon

Dds 29

− eyes ∨ ∧
− heads, human ∨ ∧
− mittens
+ pumpkin, Halloween, mouth of
− sails
− triangles
+ windows
+ wings, butterfly

Dds 30

− arms, doubled up
− brides
+ eyes ∧ ∨
− faces, animal
− ghosts
− gloves
− heads, rooster
− pelvis (with intervening dark area)
− rectangles
+ windows

Dd 31

− bird ∨
− exhaust, jet plane
− face ∨
+ feet
+ fiddle, bass, top
− hawk ∨
+ head, dog ∨

+ head, eagle, as emblem
− nose, goose <
− phallus
− rectum
− root, tree
− stick

− tail, animal
− vagina

Dds 32

+ canyon
− dish
+ road overpass ∨

Figure II

W

See also D 1 with D 2

General plus category:

human figures, two (∧ only)

General minus categories:

face; inframammalian animal (except butterfly and moth)

+ airplane, any (e.g., jet, with Ds 5 as plane, D 3 as exhaust, D 6 as smoke.)
+ anatomy, general
− anemone, sea
− bacteria
− bat
+ bears (in any movement)
− biologic, something
+ brain, cross-section
+ butterfly ∧ ∨
− cat
+ cave
+ Christmas tree ornament
− creature
+ designs
+ devils
− duelers ∨
− egg, fried
+ explosion
− firefly
+ flame and smoke
− football player kneeling (rear view)
− head, human, bloody with hole (top view)
− heart
− house
+ insignia
+ lava
− map
− mask
− meat, piece of
− men ∨

+ moth, fire
+ nervous system, central
− orchid
+ organism, primitive
+ painting
− pelvic girdle
− pot, flower
− rectum
+ ribs, x-ray of
+ rocket ship
+ spinal cord, section
+ statues
− sun in eclipse
− throat
− tooth
+ toys
− vagina
− vocal cords
+ volcano
− woman wearing fur coat

D 1

See also D 6

General plus category:

human figure (with or without D 2, but ∧ only)

+ animal ∧ >
− animal ∨
+ ape ∧
− ape ∨
− Australia
+ bear
− bird
+ bison <
− boat
− body, camel
+ body, animal
+ calf (D 31 as muzzle)
− calf (D 4 as muzzle)
− cat
− chest, human

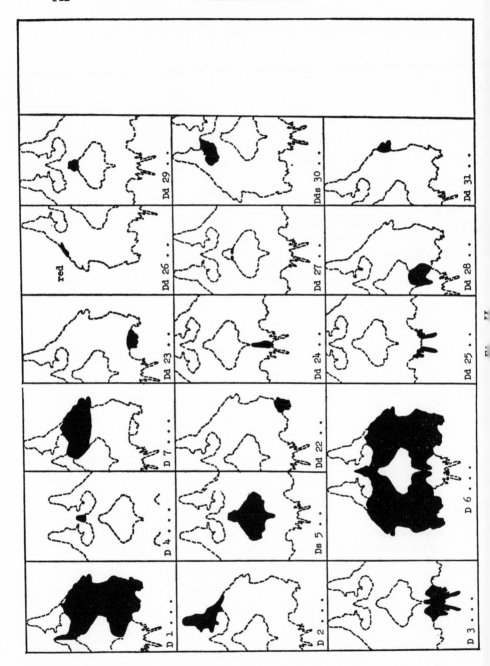

— clouds
— clown ∨
+ coat
+ cow
+ cub
+ dog <
— dog ∨
+ elephant
— embryo
— fish
— goose
— gorilla ∨
— grass
— guinea pig
— heart
— hippopotamus
— human, fighting, dancing ∨
— lamb ∨
— lamb (D 4 as muzzle)
+ lamb (Dd 31 as muzzle)
— lion
— map
+ monkey
+ mountain
+ pelt
+ pig
+ rabbit
+ rhinoceros <
+ ribs, showing through skin
+ rock, as mountain
— skeleton
+ skin, animal
— tree trunk
— turtle
+ wing

D 1 with D 2

See also W

— anteater <
— boar, wild
— camel <
+ carcass hanging by leg
— chicken
— duck
+ gorilla
— head, human (profile)
— rabbit
— rooster
— sheep

Outer edge D 1

+ face, weird
+ map contour

D 2

General plus categories:

headgear of any type; human figure (∧ only); human head or face

General minus categories:

animal head; anatomy

+ animal
— andiron
— anteater
— automobile
+ bird
— bison
+ blood
— bonfire
+ boot
— bug
— bugle
— bull >
+ butterfly
— candle, lighted
+ cat
— cells, body
+ centaur
— chicken
— chipmunk
+ creature, animated
+ devil
+ dog (and specific breeds)
— dove
+ dragon
— duck
— ear, human
— England
— face, camel < >
— face, horse < >
— finger <
— fingerprint
+ fire
— fish <
— flag
— flower
— flying horse
+ foot, human ∨

- foot, human
+ fox
- glove, boxing
- goat
- hand
+ hare
+ hippopotamus
- holster, gun
- hoof ∨
- human form ∨
+ Italy
- kidney
- knight, chess ∨
+ lantern, Japanese
+ lava
+ leg
- leg ∨
- lion
+ mask
- mitten
+ monster, ancient
- oxen (in yoke)
- penis
- piano, grand
- pillar
+ proboscis, shellfish
+ rabbit
- rat
+ seal ∧ ∨
- shell, clam
+ slide, microscope
+ snail
+ South America ∨
+ Sphinx
- squirrel
+ stocking, any kind ∨ > <
- tissue, body
- tongue
- tooth roots ∧ ∨
+ torch
- turkey
- worm

Dd projections of D 2

+ beak
- bird
+ cigarette
+ claw
- dove
+ finger
+ nose

+ tongue sticking out
- turtle

D 3

- anemone, sea
- bagpipes ∨
+ beetle
- bird
+ blood
+ bug
- bush
+ butterfly
+ buttocks
- chairs, two
- coral formation
- crab
- cradle, end view
- crawfish
- daddy longlegs
+ darning needle (insect) ∨
- devil
- easel
+ explosion
+ fire ∨ ∧
- fish ∨
- flower
+ genital organ, female, any
- girl with arms ∨
- hand, human
  head:
    - crab
    - devil
    - lobster
    + snail
- heart
+ insect
- jellyfish
- lobster
- lungs
- marine creature
- mask
- meat, piece of
+ menstrual flow
+ metal, molten
- minarets ∨
+ moth
- mouse
- pot, paint, with brushes ∨
+ rectum
- Sacred Heart
- sherbet

+ snow crystal
− stand, artist's
− stoves, two
+ sun, rising or setting ∨
+ torches with wicks
− udder, cow's
+ unicorn
− uterus
− water from faucet
− wine

D 4

Starred responses may include adjacent
dark areas

+ arrow
− beak, eagle
− bell
− bone
− bottle
− Buddha
− bud, flower
+ building
− candle
+ can opener
+ castle
− claw*
+ clippers
− clitoris
− clothespin
+ cornucopias
− Crucifixion
− curtain
+ dagger
+ delta, river ∨
+ dome, building
− drawbridge
+ drill
− face, lizard
− figures, human
− flashlight
− flowers*
− fetus
+ forceps
− glasses (vessel)
− gorillas, two
+ hands
− hat
  head:
 − bird
 + gargoyle
 − human

− headdress
− heart
− helmet, knight's
− hoof, horse's
− house
− ice cream cones, two
+ instrument, surgical
− jaw
− kidney
− knife*
− man
+ monument
− mountain
− mouse
− nose, goose
− package*
+ pen, point
− penis
+ pipe reamer
+ pliers
+ pyramid
− rabbit*
− rocket*
+ scissors
− seashell ∨
− shell, oyster
− shoe trees*
− shuttlecock*
− slippers
− snake, coiled
− snout, pig's
+ spearhead
− sword
− tail
+ temple
− Tibetan
+ tower
+ tree
− tree, palm
+ tree, pine
− unicorn
− uterus
− vagina
− veil
− wishbone

D 4 with Ds 5

− boat
+ castle and gate
+ channel
+ church

+ lamp
+ tornado funnel
− violin

Ds 5

General plus category:

building of any type

+ airplane, jet (may include D 3 and
     D 4)
+ basket, hanging
− bat
− beet
− bell
+ bellows
− boat ∨ ∧
− body, girl's, any part
+ bottle
+ bowl, for lamp
− butterfly
+ castle
− cat
+ cave, entrance ∨
+ chandelier
− Christmas tree
− cocoon
+ cover, pottery
− crown
− dancer, ballet
− dress, flared, old-fashioned
+ fissure, in rock
+ fountain ∨
+ gate
− ghost
+ goblet ∨
+ guided missile (may include D 3 and
     D 4)
− hat
− heart ∨
+ hole
+ inkwell
− island
− kite
+ lake
+ lamp
+ lantern, Japanese
+ light bulb, electric
− manta ray
− mask
− motor or engine
− mouth, open

+ pond
+ promenade
+ rocket
+ steeple, church
− sting-ray
− stomach
− throat
+ top (toy)
+ tunnel, entrance
− turnip ∨
− umbrella
− uterus
− vagina (may include D 6)
+ water, body of

D 6

See also D 1

+ airplane, wings
− animal, track of
− bat
− bear rug
− bird
− body, human, interior of
+ brain stem, cross-section
+ butterfly
+ cave, entrance
+ clouds
− collar, coat
+ fireplace
− flying squirrel
+ forest
− heart
− house
− inner tube
− insect, winged
− island
− lungs
+ moth
+ mountains
− New York State
+ pelvis
+ ribs, x-ray of
− rug
− soot
− United States

D 6 with Ds 5

+ cave opening
− crab shell
− doughnut

+ land, with pond
+ pelvic girdle
+ well platform

D 7

− Africa <
− bird
+ dog
  head:
  + animal
  + ape (muzzle at Dd 31)
  + dog
  + Dracula (face at Dd 31)
  + horse (muzzle at Dd 31)
  + Indian (face at Dd 31)
  + monkey
  − poodle ∨
  + sheep (muzzle at Dd 31)
  − turtle
  − whale
− hips (both D 7) ∨
− leg, human
− South America <

Dd 22

+ chicken ∨ ∧
+ bush ∨
+ face ∨
+ feet, bear's
+ foot, kangaroo
+ head, boy ∨
− head, dog
+ man, old ∨
+ profile, whistling ∨

Dd 23

− bush ∨
− frog ∨
+ head, old man
+ mountain ∨

Dd 24

+ anus
+ beacon on building ∨
− bowling pin
− candle
+ discharge system (An)
− dumbbell
− face
+ genitalia, female

− head, goat
− penis symbol <
− person with scarf
+ "sexual"
+ totem pole
+ vagina
− waterfall
− woman

Dd 25

+ antlers
+ candle sticks
− clubs
+ crystals
+ feelers, insect
+ horns, unicorn
+ icicles
+ legs, insect
− pens, fountain
− spears
− stalagmites
− sticks
+ sticks, candy
− swords
− table legs
− tail, lobster
− tusks, elephant
− veins
− whiskers

Dd 26

+ caterpillar
− seal
+ sunset
− tail ∧ >
− walrus

Dd 27

− bones
+ bridge
+ canal locks
− cigarettes
− claws

Dd 28

See D 3

Dds 29

+ dome [Ar]
+ flask

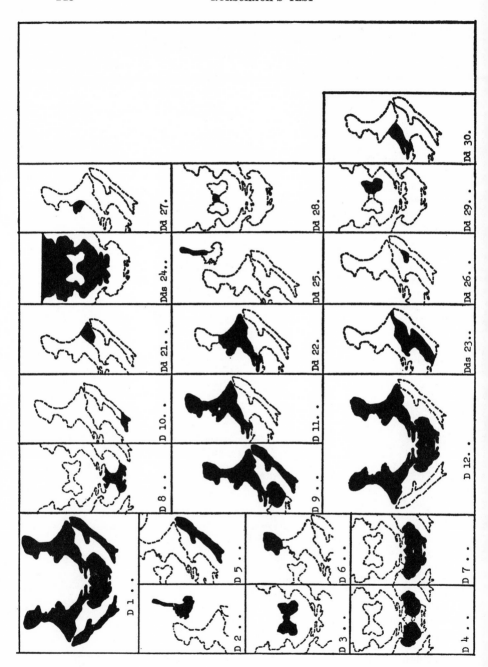

+ lake
− nose
+ pot

Dds 30

− chicken
− embryo
− eyes
− sea shell

Dd 31

+ beak, bird
− claw, lobster

+ crag, mountain
− ears, donkey
− ears, rabbit
head:
 − fish
 − rabbit
 + turtle
+ man, old, ∧ ∨
− mouth, camel
− mouth, fish
+ profile, animal
+ profile, human
− saddle seat

Figure III

W

See also D 1 and D 9

General minus categories:

face; anatomy

− ant ∨
+ arch ∨
− bug
− butterfly
− cat
− crab
+ design
+ figure, human ∨
+ fireplace with ornaments
− flower, blossom and leaves
+ fly ∨ (magnified)
+ frog ∨
+ fruit, bowl of
− gorilla
+ heraldry symbol
− human
− insect ∧ ∨
+ insect, magnified ∨
− knight (chess)
+ leader, orchestra ∨
− map
− owl ∨
+ pelvis
+ praying mantis ∨
+ puzzle, picture
− skeleton, human ∨
+ sketch, done in shadows
− spider
+ vase

D 1

See also D 9 and D 12

General plus category:

human figures, two

General minus categories:

face; animals, two (except fowl and anthropoids)

− ant
− animal
− bacteria
+ birds, large, resembling humans
+ bones (in x-ray)
− bug
+ chickens
+ cocks, fighting
− crown ∨
+ dolls
+ Donald Duck, two
− dragon
+ figure, human, arms up ∨
− figure, human, from waist down, squatting
− frog
− gorilla ∨
+ gorillas, two
+ hips
− insect ∧ ∨
− jawbone
− lobster
− map
− monkeys
− monster
+ ostriches

+ pelvis
− roots, tree
− skeleton
+ sketch
− skull ∧ ∨
− smoke
− spider ∧ ∨
− toad
− torso ∧ ∨
+ toy
− tree
− turtle
+ vase
− water, falling

D 2

General plus category:

human figure, including mythological, such as elf, gremlin, etc.

+ ameba
+ anemone, sea
+ animal ∧ ∨ > < (in any movement)
− ape
− artery and lung
+ bagpipe
− bananas
+ bird > ∧
+ blood splotch
+ branch and leaves
− butterfly
+ cat
− centipede
+ chicken < ∧
− club
+ cocoon
− crab
− dandelion
+ dejection ∨ (Ab)
+ devil
+ dipper, water
+ dog > ∨ ∧
− dragon
− eagle < ∧
+ embryo, human
+ esophagus and stomach
+ figure, human ∨
+ fire
+ firecracker
− fish

− flesh
− flower
+ flying creature
− fork
+ germ under microscope
+ gourd
− guitar
+ hat with string
+ head, horse
− heart (Dd 25 artery)
+ horse
− hook
− insect
− instrument, musical (or any specific one)
− intestines
− island
+ kidney, with ureter
− lightning flash
− lion
− lobster
− lung(s)
− meat, cut of
− microphone, hanging
+ microscopic life
+ monkey ∨ ∧ <
+ nerve process
− note, musical
− ostrich
− ovary
+ paramecium
+ parrot on pole ∧ ∨
+ pipe, smoking
+ plant bent by wind ∨
− pork chop
+ portiere
+ puppet
− question mark
− rabbit
− rat
− river and pond
+ rooster
+ sea horse
+ seaweed
− seed in garden
− shoe, hanging by lace
− snail
− snake rising from basket
− spider
+ stage decoration
− stick

+ stomach
+ tadpole
+ trapeze performer
+ tree ∨
− tree limb
+ turkey
− udder on cow
+ umbilical cord
− vase
− venison hanging from hook
+ witch, on broomstick ∨

D 3

− antlers
− apples
+ backbone, section of
− bird
− bivalve
+ blood
+ bone
+ bowknot
− brassiere
− breastbone
+ butterfly ∧ ∨
− chair, back of
− coccyx
− dam
− dancers, ballet
+ drapery
− dumbbell
− ear warmer(s)
− eye glasses
− figure(s), human
+ fire
− fly
+ gray matter of spinal cord
− gum of mouth
− heart(s)
+ hip bones
− hour glass <
− insect
− intestine
+ kidney
− lamb(s)
+ lung(s)
− mask
+ moth
− mustache
+ necktie
− nose, human

− nosepiece, spectacles
− notes, musical ∧ ∨
− oranges
− pants
+ pelvic bones
− protector, athletic
+ ribbon, any
− roof of mouth
− skeleton, parts of
− sky, red
+ spinal cord, piece of
− stage coaches
− testicles
− thorax
+ water wings
− werewolf
+ wings, butterfly
− wishbone

D 4

See also D 7

+ bags
+ balls, bowling
+ baskets
+ bear cubs ∨ ∧
− boots
+ boxing gloves
− buffalo(es)
− bust, woman's
− chickens
+ child(ren)
− cups
− dogs
− ear muffs
+ embryos
− eyes, any
+ faces, human
+ fans
− feet, human
− frogs
+ gourds, water
− hands
+ hats
  heads:
  − animal ∨
  + cannibal ∨
  − elephant
  + human ∨
  + skeleton
− hens

+ kettledrums
− kidneys
+ lamp, Chinese
− lungs
+ mittens
− mountains
+ muffs
+ porcupines
+ possums
+ pots
+ purses
− rats
+ rocks
+ sacks, any
+ shrubbery V
+ skulls, any ∧ V
− slippers, bedroom
+ stomachs, x-ray of
+ stones, round
− sunglasses
− testicles
+ trees V
− turtles

D 5

See also D 9

General plus category:

leg of large, hoofed, animal

− arm
+ arm V
− bird
+ claw, crustacean
+ club <
+ firewood V
+ fish
  foot:
  + human
  + ostrich
− frog
− gun
− hand ∧
+ hand V
− island
+ Italy V
  leg:
  − grasshopper
  + human
+ log

− Madagascar
− peninsula
− reef V
− river
− seaweed
+ shark <
+ skeleton, human, part of
− sleeve ∧
+ sleeve V
+ stick
− torpedo
− tree
+ tree limb ∧ V
+ wood, broken

D 6

See also D 9

General plus category:

head of bird or fowl

− acorn
− animal
− coconut
− eye
− football
  head:
  − animal
  − ant
  − bug
  + dog
  + skeleton
  + mask
  − monkey
− nostril
+ rock
− shell, clam

D 7

See also D 4

General plus category:

circular container, such as pail, pot, bowl

+ bivalve
+ body, lower part
− brain section
− bulldog
+ butterfly
+ cauldron, witch's

− crab
+ drum
+ entrance to park ∧ ∨
− eyeglasses
− face, human
+ fireplace
+ gate
− globe
− head, fly
− insect
− kidney(s)
− lung(s)
+ mask, modernistic
− motor, outboard
+ mushroom, atomic blast ∧ ∨
+ nest
+ painting, Japanese
+ pelvis
− record player
− rectum
+ sacroiliac
+ shadows
+ shrubbery
− spider
− spinal cord
+ stage property
+ stove
− torso, human
− turtles
− uterus
− vagina
− vertebra

D 8

− boat
+ bones
− brainstem, section of
− breastbone
+ brook
+ chest, human
− cloud(s)
+ crab ∧ ∨
− Crucifixion
+ doors, swinging ∨ ∧
− face
+ fireplace
+ firewood
− fountain
+ gate ∨ ∧
− genitalia, female

+ goblet ∨ (with or without Dds)
− hourglass
+ jack-o-lantern
+ lamp
+ landscape with inlets
− lungs
+ pelvis
+ precipice
− pubis
− pumpkin (with or without Dds)
+ reflection, land in water >
+ ribs
+ river, section of
+ shell, crab, frayed
+ skeleton
− vagina (with or without Dds)
+ vase ∨ (with or without Dds)
+ water (shore and creeks)
+ wood, splintered

D 9

See also W and D 1

General plus category:

human figure

General minus category:

animal, any (except fowl and anthropoids)

+ bird (large varieties)
+ cartoon character
+ chicken
− cloud(s)
+ design
+ doll
+ dummy
− monkey
+ monster
+ mountain with snow (with Dds 23) <
+ ostrich
− parrot
− root(s), tree
+ scarecrow
+ swampland >
− tree
− turtle
− woodpecker ∨

D 10

+ finger ∨
− finger ∧

− foot, frog
+ hand ∨
− hand ∧
+ hoof, any
+ shoe, high-heeled
− paw
− woman

D 11

− animal
− arms
+ bird ∨
− bird ∧
− bomb, atomic
− bulb (plant)
+ chicken
+ cliff(s), rocky ∨
− dog ∧ ∨
+ Donald Duck
− face, human
+ figure, human, legless
− hair, woman's ∨
− insect
− kangaroo
+ man ∧
+ rooster
+ seal ∨
− skeleton
− thigh, human
+ torso, human

D 12

See also D 1

+ archway ∨
− crab ∨
− figure, human
+ frog
+ landscape ∨
+ park
+ pelvic cavity
+ snow scene

Dd 21

+ beak, bird ∨
+ bird ∨ (any type)
− dog ∨
− head, any animal's ∨ ∧

Dd 22

+ airplane ∨
+ bird ∨

− chipmunk
− dancer, ballet
+ eagle ∨ > ∧
  head:
− animal ∧ ∨
− deer
− human ∧ ∨
+ mountain
− North America
+ rat
+ rodent
− saddle
+ turkey ∨

Dds 23

+ Adriatic Sea
+ design
+ eagle <
− ears
− dress, woman's
− head, dog
− machine part
+ water

Dds 24

+ bowl
+ chalice
+ Christmas tree
− face, cat
− face, human ∨
+ flower, conventionalized ∧ ∨
− lake
+ lamp, with glass chimney
+ mushroom ∨
+ road ∨
+ shirt front ∨
+ snow
+ stencil

Dd 25

See also D 2

+ esophagus
+ pole
+ queue (Chinese)
+ root, plant
+ rope
+ stick
+ string
+ tail, bird

− tail, lion
+ ureter

Dd 26

− leg, human
+ penis
+ skirt

Dd 27

+ breast
− cap, auto radiator
+ head, rodent V
− nose, dog

Dd 28

− bone
− door
− face
− tooth
− vagina

Dd 29

See also D 3

− bean

− breast
− chicken
− fetus
− figure, human
− peanut
− plate, dental
− tooth
− "U" <
− Valentine
− vase

Dd 30

− cloud(s)
− foot
+ hand
− penis

Projections from Dd 30

+ fingers
− head, bird V
− icicles
− knives

Figure IV

W

See also W minus D 1

General plus categories:
large, furry animal; human figure

+ airplane
− alligator
− ameba
+ anchor V
+ animal, four-legged (rear view)
+ animal, sea
− auto
+ baby
+ bat V ∧ (may be hanging)
+ battlements, castle
+ bell
− bird ∧ V
+ block, design of V
+ body, human, x-rayed
+ boots on a pole
− brain section
− bull V
+ burner, incense V
+ butterfly ∧ V
+ cactus
− candle and candlestick
+ carcass, animal

+ carpet
+ cave (Ws)
+ chandelier
+ clouds
+ clown
+ coat
+ column with winged figures
− coral, broken
− core V
− crab
+ creature, mythological
+ crest ∧ V (official seal)
+ design
+ developmental form
− dog
+ dragon, winged V ∧
− eagle
− elephant
+ elephants, two, back to back
+ embryo
+ escutcheon V
− face
+ fern
− fish
+ flower
+ flying squirrel
+ forest, reflected in lake <
+ fossil, of animal

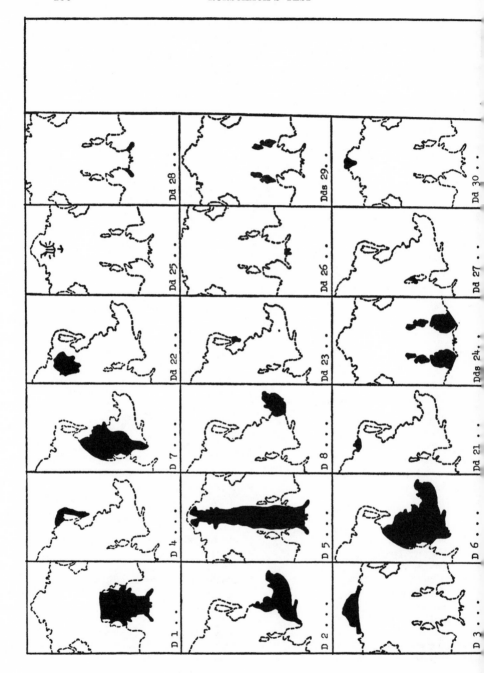

− frog
+ fungus
+ giant
− giraffe
+ gorilla
− governor on engine
+ hide
  head:
 − ant
 − fish
 + buffalo
 − dog ∨
 + ram
 − rocket
− horse
+ impression, sinister (Ab)
− insect, any ∨ ∧
+ insignia ∨
+ integration [Ab]
− intestines
+ iris (flower)
− island
+ jellyfish
+ kite, Japanese ∨
+ landscape, reflected < >
+ leaf, torn
+ lily
− lizard
− lobster
− lung
+ lyre ∨
+ man (D 2) on sleigh (D 7), ice reflected below >
+ man, headless
− man, standing on head (D 1 head)
+ map
+ mashed object
+ mollusk
+ monkey
+ moth
+ mountain
+ Niagara Falls (D 6 as mountains, D 5
  as water)
− octopus
+ orchid ∨ ∧
+ parachute uniform
+ pattern, art
− pelvis
+ phantom
− pig
+ plant

+ pond in woods, landscape reflected <
− 'possom ∨
+ robe, fur
+ rock formation
− root, tree
+ rug (fur)
+ sacrum
+ scarecrow, on post
+ seaweed
  skin ∨ ∧:
 + furry animal
 − frog
 + lion
 + tiger
+ sloth
+ smoke (clouds of)
− snail
− snowflake ∨
− spider
+ sponge, plant
− squab, plucked
+ squid
− starfish
+ statue
+ sting ray ∨
+ structure, Oriental
+ swamp ∨
+ temple, Chinese ∨
+ thistle
− tick (insect)
+ tree ∧ ∨
+ troll
− turtle
+ urn
− walnut kernel
+ wineskin
− worm, squashed
+ x-ray plate

W minus D 1

See also W

+ baby
+ bat
+ coat sleeves ∨
− frog
+ gorilla
− mouth, open <
+ pants, pair
− pendant
+ scarecrow

Lower half of blot

− animal ∨
\+ bat with wings ∨
\+ castle between two crags ∨
− fly, big ∨
\+ fountain with seals on side ∨
− pelvic bone
− pendant
\+ tail and two feet of animal

Upper half of blot

\+ animal
− bird
\+ butterfly
\+ cow with horns
\+ embryo design
\+ flower ∨ ∧
\+ fountain
 head:
  \+ animal
  \+ antelope
  − fox ∨
  − man
  \+ ram
  \+ reindeer
− spinal cord, section, with nerves
\+ skull, steer
\+ x-ray

D 1

General plus categories:

small, horned animal; head of large, horned animal

\+ animal
− arms, hanging
\+ bug
\+ cactus plant ∨
\+ candle ∨ ∧
− cart
\+ castle ∨
− cat
\+ caterpillar
− chair
\+ coccyx
\+ cow
\+ crab, hermit ∨
− crawfish
\+ crown, king ∨
\+ figure, Hindu ∨

− figure, human
− fish, without tail
\+ fountain
\+ fur, piece of
\+ ghost ∨
\+ goat
 head:
 − alligator
 \+ caterpillar
 − catfish
 − centipede
 − crocodile
 − dog
 \+ dragon
 − fish
 \+ fly (magnified)
 − horse
 \+ human ∨
 \+ insect
 − rat
 \+ snail
 − wolf
\+ helmet with radar device
\+ hydra
\+ hydrant, fire
\+ idol
\+ insect
− intestines, hanging
\+ lamp
\+ lighthouse ∨
− lobster
\+ medulla
− motorcycle
− neck, chicken
\+ owl ∨ ∧
\+ pelt
− penis
− sea horse
− seashell
\+ shrubbery
\+ skin, animal
− skirt
\+ smoke
\+ snail
− snake
\+ spine, section of
\+ squid
\+ stone
\+ stool
− stove, old

+ stump
+ tail
+ throne
+ totem pole
+ tower ∨
+ tree ∨
+ tree trunk
+ urn with legs
+ vase
+ vertebra
− worm

D 2

General plus categories:

*human figure; human head, face, or profile
(usually >)*

+ bear
− bird
− boat
− bone(s)
+ branch ∨
+ Cape Cod
+ cloud(s)
− cow
− deer ∨
+ dog > < ∧
− elk ∨
+ emblem
+ foot, human
− grass
  head:
  − camel <
  − horse <
  − lamb <
  − sea serpent <
  − seal <
  − turkey <
− jaw, moose
+ leg, animal
+ map
− Norway ∨
+ peninsula
− pig
− profile, moose
+ shoe
+ smoke
+ Sphinx >
+ totem pole >
+ wing, bat

D 3

− anus
− bird, wings out
+ bud, flower
+ butterfly ∧ ∨ > <
− buttocks
+ cabbage
− candle
− clam
+ collar, lace
+ crown
+ delta
+ fan
− face, bird
+ flower, any
− flying saucer
  head:
  + animal, mythical
  + bat
  + cat
  − fox
  + human
  + owl
  − rocket
  − walrus
+ helmet, ancient or oriental
+ insignia, air corps
− larynx
+ leaf(s)
+ lichen
− mollusk
− octopus
− rectum
− seashell
+ secretion, squid's
− skin, animal
− tail, fish
+ toupee
+ vagina
+ wings, insect
− whiskers, cat

D 4

− alligator
− animal
+ aorta
+ arm, human
− belt
− bird
− boy(s)

+ branch, tree
+ cap, stocking
− cat
+ claw, crab or lobster V
− crutch
− dripping (of liquid)
− ear, dog
− ear, elephant
+ eel
+ figure, human (bending over)
− finger
− fish
− flipper, seal
+ handle, pot ∧ V
+ hand
+ harpoon
+ head, bird (any with prominent
neck)
+ hook
+ horn, animal
− horse
+ icicle
− knife
− leg, human
+ lizard
− lock, oar
+ log
+ neck, long, of bird or animal
+ peninsula
− penis
+ root, tree V
− sickle
+ snake
− strap
− tail, animal
− tears, flowing
− tentacle (octopus)
− tongue, shoe
+ tree
+ trunk, elephant
− tube, fallopian
+ tusk, elephant
+ vine
− wing

D 5

− boar V
+ column
+ crater, volcano
− crawfish

+ devil, little V
+ figure, human
− fish
+ fountain
− husk, corn
− insect
+ neural groove
+ penis, dissection of
+ pole
+ post
+ river
+ rocket ∧ V
− sex organs, female
− shrimp
+ spinal column
+ stand, flower
+ statue
+ totem pole
+ tree, fir
+ tree trunk
+ vertebrae
+ x-ray

D 6

See also D 8

+ boot
+ face, bearded >
+ foot, big
+ figure, human V >
− fort
+ Italy
+ leg
− ram
− sea horse V
+ shoe
+ sky, stormy
+ smoke from volcano
+ trouser leg
+ wing, bat

Heel of (D 6) "boot"

− bone
+ handle
+ heel
− hat V
+ horn, animal V
+ lever
− mountain
+ stick V

D 7

General plus category:

human figure (∨ only)

+ Africa
+ animal, formalized
+ arch of trees (both D 7)
− bird
− chicken ∨
+ crag(s)
− elephant ∨
− figure, human ∧ > <
+ foot
− handle of jar
− lion
− mouse >
+ rock(s)
+ root
+ seal
+ sea lion ∧ ∨
+ South America
+ statue
+ tapir
− tree
− wolf

D 8

See also D 6

General plus categories:

human head (usually < >); *animal head*
  (usually < >)

+ camel
− Florida ∨
+ man, old
+ poodle

Dd 21

+ building, on hill
+ face, human < > ∨ ∧
+ figures, human, far off
+ gnome
   head:
   + grotesque
   + human
   − pig
+ landscape, distant
− squirrel

Dd 22

− breast(s)
   face or head:
   + dog
   − horse
   + human
+ profile, human
− teeth, animal

Dd 23

See also D 4

+ beak, bird
+ head, bird

Dds 24

   heads:
   + bird
   + dog
   + duck
− ladies with bustle
− tadpoles

Dd 25

+ face, human or any animal
+ head, human or any animal
− stomach, x-ray of

Dd 26

− claw
− clitoris
− ears
+ feet, human
− hands
+ heads, human ∨
− hooves
+ legs, human
− mountains ∨
− mouth
− pedals, piano
− penises
+ toes
− udder, cow

Dd 27

+ foot, animal
− foot, human
+ hoof, horse

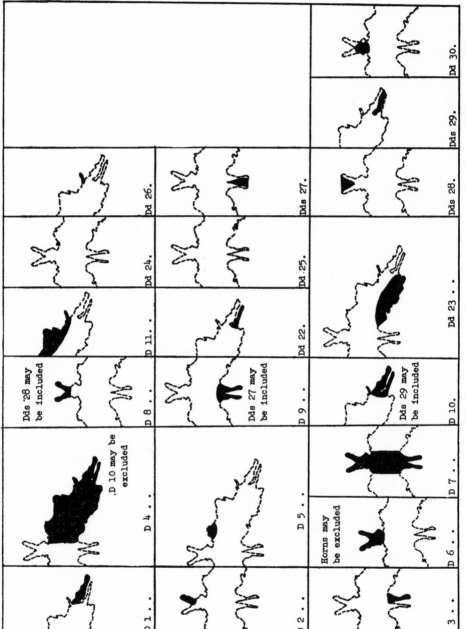

Figure V

Dd 28

See also D 1

− feet, human
− legs, animal
− penises
− tusks

Dd 30

− anus

− core, apple
+ flower
− heart
+ iris (flower)
+ lips, vagina
− penis
− pin
+ thalamus
− womb

Figure V

W

General minus category:

anatomy

+ airplane
+ angel
+ animals, run into each other
+ animal, squashed
+ bat ∧ ∨ > <
− bee
+ beetle
+ bird(s) ∧ ∨ > <
+ book ends
+ bridge
+ bug
− building(s)
+ butterfly ∧ ∨ > <
+ cape, fur
+ child in costume
+ cloth, black
+ clouds
− cockroach
+ crow
+ dancer
+ deer, split
+ devil, flying
− dragon
+ duck, taking off
+ eagle
+ felt
+ figures, human, lying back to back
   ∧ ∨
+ figure, human, winged
− fly
+ flying squirrel
− flower ∨
− fowl
− fungus
− germ

− grasshopper
− hands, skeleton ∨
− head, cow ∨
− head, bird <
+ hill with trees at shore line
+ insect, winged, spread out or flattened
− lake
+ land in water
+ landscape (aerial)
− leaf(s)
− map
− meat
− monster, two-headed
− mops >
− mosquito
+ moth ∧ ∨ > <
+ mountain
+ ostrich, with plumage
+ owl
+ peacock(s) ∨
− phallic symbol <
+ rabbit, with blanket, or flying
− raccoon
+ rams butting heads
− ray (fish)
+ ridge, mountain
+ robe, black ∨ ∧
− roller coaster
− sail
− skin(s), animal
− smoke reflected in water <
− spider
+ standard, Roman
− steak
+ stole, mink
− tent
+ tightrope performers ∨
− United States
− vagina

− vase
− wig (with or without extensions)
− windshield, fogged
+ wings, airplane
− woman, dancing ∨ >
+ woman, dancing ∧

D 1

See also D 10

General plus category:

leg, animal or human

+ bone
+ exhaust from airplane
− figure, human
− fish
− Florida
+ foot, animal
− head, horned, skeletal
− head, horse
+ Italy
+ muscle ∨
+ nose, alligator
− spear
− stream (mountain)

D 2

See also D 8

General plus category:

human figure

− bird
+ bone
− bottle
− chair
− chicken, fried
− comb, rooster
+ ear, donkey
+ ear, rabbit
+ elf
+ feeler, butterfly
− foot, human ∧
+ foot, human ∨
− finger
+ handle(s), sword
+ hat
− head, animal
+ head, human

+ horn
  leg ∧ ∨:
− animal
+ human
+ table
− mustache
− paw, cat
− penis
+ spout, water fountain
+ stocking, Christmas
− tree, part of
− worm

D 3

See also D 9

General plus categories:

leg, any type; head of bird

+ antenna
+ beak, eagle
− bell ∨
+ bone, animal
− carrot ∨
+ club
+ cone of rocket
− face, ostrich
+ feet
− finger
+ flower, petals ∨
− hand
+ match stick(s)
− root, tooth
− ski
+ snake ∨
+ stick, hockey
− stinger, bee
+ swan ∨
− teat, on dog
− worm

D 4

See also W

− animal, on its back
− banana
+ blanket, stretched out
− brush
+ bush(es)
+ carcass, animal
− cat

− caterpillar
− circle, half
+ cloud(s)
+ curtain
− dandelion, just burst <
+ drapery
+ driftwood
+ face, man, bearded
− face, pig
+ faces, two
+ figure, human (reclining)
+ goat (head at D 7)
+ hill
− horse
− kangaroo
+ landscape with clouds
− leg, animal
− lion
+ man with wooden leg
+ peacock ∨
+ plumes
+ profile, man, bearded
− skin, rabbit
+ smoke billows
− snails
− snowflake
− stump, tree
− swordfish
− table (D 3 supporting legs)
+ train of costume
− tree, part
+ wing

D 5

− bison
− breast
+ face, human
+ head, Satan's
+ hill
− lamb
+ stone

D 6

− chair ∨
+ devil
+ elves
+ face
+ figure, hooded ∨
+ figure, human ∨
  head:

− cow ∨
+ deer, with horns ∨
− dog
+ donkey
+ human
− insect
− mouse
− praying mantis
+ rabbit
− rat
− mountain top
+ mouth, fish, open ∧ <
+ scissors
+ sling shot
+ snail
+ wishbone

D 7

General plus category:

human figure

+ animal, on hind legs
− bug
− chicken
+ devil
− dog
+ donkey (front or rear view)
+ figure(s), human (two)
− fish ∨ >
− goat
− insects, two
+ rabbit ∧ > <
− skate (fish)

D 8

See also D 2

General plus category:

open mouth, any animal (usually >)

+ antennae, insect
+ bone(s)
− chair ∨
+ figure(s), human
− hoof, cloven ∨
+ horns
  legs:
  − animal
  − frog
  + human ∨
+ plant, open

+ scissors
+ seed, tree
+ slingshot
− tree with two trunks
+ vase

D 9

See also D 3

General plus category:

bifurcated tools or instruments

+ beak, bird's, open (with or without Dds 27)
− bells ∨
+ chopsticks
− dress, v-neck of
+ feet, animal
+ legs, animal
+ legs, human
+ mechanical device
− root, tooth
+ swans, two ∨
− tail, scorpion
+ tweezers
− vagina
− vase
+ wishbone

D 10

See also D 1 and Dd 22

− clouds
− coral
− fork
  head:
  + alligator
  + bird
  + crocodile
  − hog
+ legs, human
+ mouth, alligator or crocodile
+ nutcracker
− plants, sea
− snake, mouth open (with or without Dds 29)

D 11

Starred responses may include D 5

− animal, horned
− breast, woman's

+ crags*
+ face, monkey
− fingers
− head, animal
+ hills*
− hump, buffalo*
+ Indian chief
− lion
+ mask*
+ mountains*
− mouth, camel, open
+ nose
+ profile, human* ∧ <
− stethoscope
+ stone
+ wing

Dd 22

See also D 10

+ arrow
+ bayonet ∨
+ bone
+ cane
− finger
− fish
+ gun barrel
− head, crane
− head, ostrich
− limb, dead tree >
  leg:
  + animal
  − horse
  + wooden
+ serpent
+ spear
+ tail, animal
+ tail, horse

Dd 23

General plus category:

human face, head, or profile (either ∧ or ∨)

Dd 24

− breast
+ figure, human
− nipple

Dd 25

+ cannon $\vee$
− snout, pig

Dd 26

+ branch
− snake
− tongue
+ twig

Dds 27

− ear lobe
+ harbor
− morning glory, closed
− vagina

Dds 29

+ bay
+ inlet
− leg
− worm

Dd 30

+ dome (Ar)
+ face, owl
+ hat, derby
+ head, human
− human, sitting
− penis

Figure VI

W

See also D 1

Note: Starred responses may exclude
D 9 and/or D 6

General plus categories:

animal pelt or rug; stringed musical instrument

+ airplane >
− ameba
  animal:
  + being skinned
  + grotesque
  − sea
− Australia
+ badge
− bat
− bear
+ bears, two $\vee$
− bee
+ bell with handle*
− bird
+ blanket
+ blossom $\vee$
− body, human
+ bottle*
− bow and arrow <
− brain section
+ bug $\wedge$ $\vee$
+ building with beacon top
− butterfly
+ candle, dripping wax
+ cat (cut open or flattened)

− catfish
+ cathedral
+ cement, wet
+ chicken, opened up
+ Chinese decoration, hanging
+ church
+ cliff and water, with reflection >
+ club*
+ coat rack
− crayfish $\vee$
+ Christmas tree ornament
+ cross, covered
− crown
+ crumb plate $\vee$
+ desert
+ design
+ doll, rag $\vee$
+ door
− duck
+ dust brush $\wedge$ $\vee$
+ duster $\vee$
+ dust pan* $\vee$
+ eruption, volcano
+ explosion, any
− face, dog >
+ fan*
− figure, human $\wedge$ $\vee$
+ figures, human, leaning against post
    $\vee$
− fish < >
− flower
− fly
− flying squirrel
+ fountain

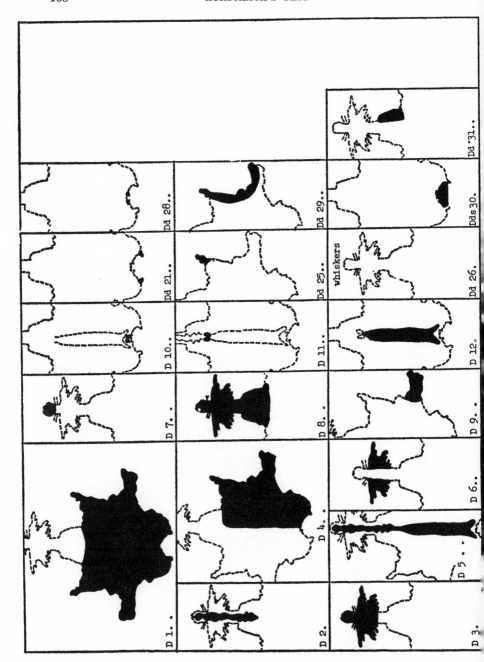

− fox
− fowl, hung up
− frog
− germ
+ goose, flying >
+ gorge in mountain
− hat
+ hinge
− head, dog
+ ice sheet, melted
− Indian
+ insect (squashed)
− insides, human
+ instrument, twirling
− island continent
− jellyfish
+ lamp, table
+ landscape, reflected >
+ lantern, Japanese
+ leaf, maple ∧ ∨
+ leather
− lion
+ map, topographic
+ mask, jester's
+ mirror, hand* ∨
− moth
− octopus
+ Oriental structure
+ painting, finger
+ pan, frying*
− pelt, bird's
+ penis and pubic hair ∨
+ picture, from airplane <
+ piston
+ plant, cactus ∨
+ rattle, baby or Indian* ∨
− ray, manta ∨
+ river between mountains
+ rug
− scorpion
+ sedan, Louis XIV style
+ shield ∨
− shrimp
− skin, fish
− skunk
− snowflake
+ snowman
− spider
− star, Jewish
+ statue

+ sweater coat
− tent
+ tiger
+ totem pole
− toupee
+ tree* ∨
+ turtle
+ wastebasket, with handle*
+ weathervane
− windpipe and lungs
+ woods > <
+ worm, squashed
+ x-ray

D 1

See also W and D 4

General plus categories:

animal skin or pelt; rug

− ameba
+ animal, cut open
+ apes, back to back (on hook) ∨
+ book, open
+ candleholder
− chest, x-ray of
+ cloud(s)
+ coat, spread out ∨ ∧
− cocoon
+ container
− creature, winged
+ door(s) (swinging) ∧ ∨
− ear muffs
− face, dog
− fish (opened up)
+ field
− flesh, piece of
+ grass patch
+ lake, with landscape >
+ land, piece of
+ landscape, and reflection > <
+ leaf, maple or oak
− lungs
+ map, topographic
+ mat
+ melon, inside of (excludes D 9)
− moth
+ mountains and river, aerial view
+ photograph, microscopic
+ picture, rural
− rectum

+ rock
+ sack
+ scoop of shovel
− seashell
− star
+ stone
− tail, animal
+ twins, Siamese V
− vagina

Lower half of D 1

+ buttocks
− face, bug
+ heads, human V

Midline

Note: Starred responses may include adjacent dark areas

− caterpillar*
+ crack in ground
+ highway
− incision
+ pipeline
+ shaft, mine
+ smoke left by rocket
+ spinal cord*
+ track, railroad
− worm*
+ zipper

D 2

See also D 5

− arms
+ beacon, traffic
+ candle
+ candlestick
− dancers, two
+ eel, electric
+ embryo
+ figure, human
+ esophagus (x-ray of)
− fish
− fly
+ god
− grasshopper
+ head, reptile
+ head and neck, insect
− knife
+ lamp, street

+ leg, furniture
+ mast
− neck, ostrich
− needle, darning
+ passage [An]
+ penis (erect)
+ phallic symbol
+ piston
+ pole, iron
+ rod, ebony
− rodent
+ shaft, rotating
+ snake
− spear
− submarine
− termite
+ thermometer
+ wood, turned V ∧

D 3

See also D 6 and D 8

General plus category:

winged insect

+ airplane
− animal
+ animal, winged
+ banner
− bat
+ beetle
+ bird
− cat
+ design
+ eagle
+ flower
− flying fish
− fish
  head:
  + cat
  + fox
  − insect
  + wolf
+ insect
+ insignia
− lizard
+ motif, military
− nervous system, embryonic
+ owl
+ penis, winged
+ pigeon

+ rocket
+ seaweed
− shawl
− spider
− snail
− snake
+ tadpole, winged
− throne
− tiger
+ totem pole
+ tree
+ wings
− witch doctor

D 4
See also D 1

General plus category:

human head or face ∨

− animal
+ ape ∨
+ Buddha
− bull, bucking >
− camera ∧ ∨
+ cloud(s)
+ dragon <
+ gorilla
  head:
  + dog, with pug nose ∨
  + lion ∨
  + wolf ∨
+ jungle <
+ king, wearing crown ∨
− lamb
+ landscape >
− legs
+ mask ∨
+ mountains ∧ ∨ > <
− pants, pair of
− pig ∨
+ rock ∨ ∧
+ steamboat (with funnel) > <
+ tank, army < >
+ tombstone >
− United States <
− whale <

D 5
See also D 2 and D 12

+ backbone
+ base, lamp

+ bone
+ canal
+ canal (An)
+ caterpillar
+ fissure in earth
− gate
+ gorge
+ knife
+ knife, handle of
− lady
+ lathe
+ lava stream
+ leg, furniture
+ mountain range
+ paddle, canoe
+ pen, fountain
+ penis
+ pipe
+ pole
+ projectile, path of
− rabbit
+ rack, hat
+ river
+ road
+ shaft, coal mine
+ snake
+ spine
+ stick
+ thermometer
+ totem pole
− tree ∧ ∨
+ trees < >
+ vagina
+ water, shooting up
+ wood, turned
+ worm
+ x-ray

D 6
See also D 3

General plus category:

wings, any type

− antlers
− arms
+ bird, any
+ branches
+ butterfly
+ cactus < ∧
+ corona, sun

+ duck
+ feathers
+ flames or fire
+ flowers
+ geese, flock of
+ gulls, flying
+ headdress, Indian
+ leaf(s)
+ light, rays of (sun)
+ mane, flowing
− membrane
+ moth
+ pelts, bunch of
− stalactites
+ trees < >
− vagina
+ weathervane
− whiskers, human

Projections from D 6

+ asparagus tips
+ beaks, birds, any
+ heads, turtles
− icicles
− opener, can
− pin, rolling
+ turtles
− wolfhounds

D 7

See also D 3

+ animal, microscopic
+ bug
+ creature, with whiskers
+ eyes, animal
− figure(s), human
+ fist
+ hands, clasped
+ handle, cane
  head or face:
  + bird
  + bug
  + cat
  + cobra
  + human
  + insect
  + owl
  + snake
  + turtle
− heads, bugs, two

+ mouth, animal
− nose, animal, any

D 8

See also D 3

− animal
− bell
+ bird, on tree stump
− bottle
+ bug, crawling from cocoon
− caterpillar
+ Crucifix
+ dragonfly
  figure, human
  + on pedestal
  + on hill top
+ flames and smoke
+ flower
+ fountain
+ gravestone
  head:
  − cat
  − catfish
  − wolf
+ insect
+ light, with rays emanating
+ lighthouse, on rock
− mountains
+ oil well
+ pedestal
− potato masher
+ scarecrow
+ seaweed
− spinal cord
+ spire, church
+ statuette
+ totem pole(s)
+ tree
− turtle

D 9

− boot >
+ castle >
+ figure, human >
+ foot, animal
− glass, drinking >
  head:
  − bird >
  − camel ∧ ∨
  + dog ∧ ∨

+ fox ∧ ∨
+ wolf ∧ ∨
+ leg, animal >
− nose, animal ∧ ∨
+ peninsula
− pole >
+ rock formation
+ sleeve
+ smoke >
+ smokestack >
− stalactite <
− stick, candy
+ tower >

D 10

Note: Starred responses may
include adjacent dark area

− claws*
+ eggs
+ eyes, insect
− flap, in throat
+ heads, human*
+ heads, insect*
+ insect(s)*
+ jewels
+ rear end, animal*
+ sacks
− spinal cord* section
+ testicles
− vagina

D 11

− ants
− beans
− birds
− boats
+ brain, ape or monkey
− bridge
− butterfly
+ eggs
− embryos
− flames
− flowers
+ jewels
− kidneys
+ lights, street
− lungs
− mice
+ molecule, splitting
− nuts

+ shell, clam, open
− testicles
− tonsils
− vagina
− "W"
− woodpeckers
− worms

D 12

See also D 5

− boat
+ candlestick
+ cocoon
− figure(s), human
+ guided missile
− hot dog, in bun
− needle, hypodermic
+ passageway
− penis
+ pole
− rectum
+ river
+ road
+ rocketship
+ shaft, mine
− spear
+ spinal column
+ trunk, tree
+ umbrella stand
− vagina, opening of

Dd 21

+ claws
+ feet, insect
+ hair, tufts ∨
− hands
+ heads, snake
+ heads, turkey
+ hooks
+ horns, cow
+ pincers, crab
+ talons, eagle
− teeth
+ tongs, ice

Dd 25

+ beads, strung
− cigarette lighter and flame
− chicken

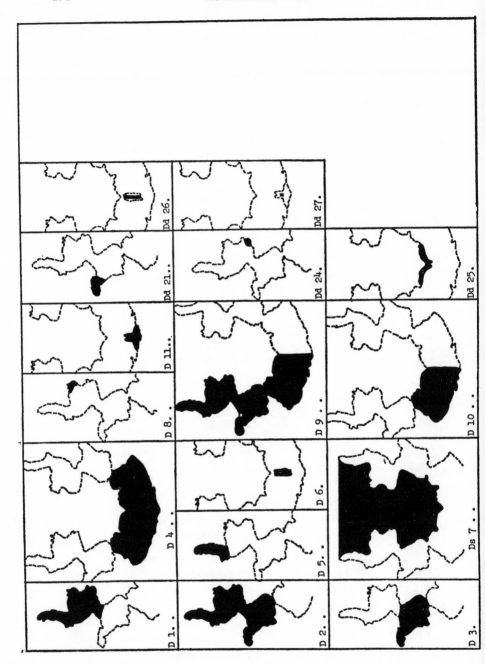

+ figure, human
+ Florida ∨
+ foot, human
− foot, pig
− hand
− head, dog
+ head, woman
+ mountain
+ paw, animal
− penis
+ prow, ship
+ shoe
− stalactite
+ toe
− wing(s)

Dd 26

+ antennae
− horns, animal
+ rays of light
+ whiskers, any

Dd 28

− breakwater

+ claws, crab
+ fangs
− feelers, fish
+ heads, birds ∨
+ jaws, snake
− knives
− labia minora
+ talons
− x-ray

Dd 29

+ head, human, with arms up
+ profile, human
+ shore line

Dds 30

+ gulf
+ insect pit
+ lamp
  mouth: (may include Dd 21)
− animal
− bird
− snake

Figure VII

W

See also D 9

General plus categories:

two human figures ∧ ∨; natural, topo-graphic entities based on a central space, such as canyon, harbor, lake.

− animal, cut apart
+ apes, two
+ archway ∨
− bed, end view ∨
− beefsteak
− bird
− blueprint
− body, human
− bone
+ bowl
− bracelet
+ bread, piece of, broken
+ bridge ∨
− bug
+ busts, two
+ canal and lock
+ candy, cotton

− cap, fur ∨
+ carving
+ cave mouth ∨
− chain
− chair ∨
− chops, pork
+ clouds
+ coat of arms
+ coast line
+ collar, for woman's dress ∨
− cover, bed
− crab
+ crown ∨
+ design, symmetrical
+ dogs, two (dressed as women)
+ dolls, two
+ driftwood
− figure, human ∨
− fly
+ food, fried, pieces of
− footprint
+ fountain
− fungus
+ furpiece
− frog

+ gate (fancy) ∨
+ ghosts, two
− grass plot with shrubs
− hairdo, long ∨
+ horseshoe
+ house, Japanese ∨
− insect ∨
+ islands, map of
+ lamp, kerosene
− legs, frog
+ map, pieces of
+ marine life
− mask
+ monument
− moth
+ mountains, above cloud
− mouth, insect ∧ >
+ necklace
− nutcracker
+ paper, torn
+ peel, orange
+ peninsula(s)
+ piecrust, out of shape
+ pile or pieces of (metal,
    candy, ice, etc.)
− pincers
− plants
− ponies, two
− potatoes, fried
+ puddle (mud)
+ puzzle, piece of
+ rabbits
− rag
+ reef, coral
+ rock(s)
+ scarf (fur) ∨
+ sculpture work
+ seacoast
− sheep, two
− shrubs
− skin, animal
− sleeves, kimono
+ smoke
+ snow, melting
+ spittoon
+ stadium
+ stone(s)
+ stool ∨
− stove, old fashioned
− table ∧ ∨
− trap

− tweezers
+ twins, Siamese
+ vase
− vise
− wig ∨
− womb, open
+ wreath

D 1

See also D 2 and D 9

General plus category:

human head or face (may be deformed)

+ ape
− breeches, riding, and boots
− camel ∨
+ cameo
− cat ∧ ∨
− Central America ∨ <
− chair
− chicken
+ cloud(s)
− coffee grinder, with lid
+ doll, crude
+ dwarf
− duck
− England
− excreta, human
− face, snarling (D 8 nose, Dds below
    D 8 mouth)
− fish
− Florida ∨
− France
+ goblin
− goose
+ gorgon
+ gnome
− hand, thumb up
    head:
  − alligator
  + animal
  + dog
  − donkey
  + elephant, with trunk ∨
  + monkey
  + rabbit
− horse ∨
+ Indian
− leg, table ∨
+ mask

− mountain
− pipe, smoker's <
− porcupine ∨
+ rabbit ∨
+ sculpture, modernistic
− skunk
− squirrel
+ statue
− stomach
− tiger
− turkey

D 2

See also W and D 9

Note: Most quadrupeds are seen <

General plus category:

human figure

+ ape
− ameba
+ angel
+ animal <
− arm
− calf
− cat ∨ ∧ <
− chair
− chicken
+ cloud(s)
− cow ∧ <
+ cracker(s), animal
+ dog (any) > ∧
− donkey <
+ dwarf
+ elephant, head and trunk >
− England
+ face, clown
− fish
− fox >
− hair, long ∧ ∨
+ hemisphere, Western ∨
− horse, reared up
+ island(s)
− kangaroo
+ lamb <
− lion <
+ map
+ mountain(s)
+ North and South America ∨
− pot, coffee
+ rabbit
+ sculpture

+ seaweed
− sheep <
− shrimp, fried ∧ ∨
− shrub
+ Spain and France
+ stone(s)
− thumb and fingers <
− tiger <
− tree, part of
− turkey
− United States
− "W" >

D 3

See also D 2

General plus categories:

human head or face (may be deformed);

animal head or face (except horned animals)

+ animal head
− Alaska
− beard
+ bear > ∧
− beehive <
− brooch
− buffalo
+ candy, cotton
− Central America
− cleaver, meat (Dd 21 as handle)
− cornucopia <
+ creature
− dinosaur
+ dwarf
+ figure, comic ∨
+ gargoyle
+ gnome
+ goblin
− ham
− head, buffalo
− head, goat
− horse
+ island
+ mask
− mug, shaving
− pig
+ Rock of Gibraltar
+ rock(s)
− sheep
− shirt on line

+ South America >
+ Spain

D 4

See also D 10

General minus category:

infrahuman mammal

+ apron, short
+ arch(way) ∨
− arms and shoulders
+ background for painting
+ bat
+ bird ∧ ∨
− boat
+ book, open
− bow
+ bowl
+ bridge
+ butterfly
− buttocks
− caterpillar
− chair
+ cloud(s)
+ collar
− couch
− crab
− cradle
− crown ∧ ∨
− fan
− fly
+ hill
+ hinge, open
+ hips
− horse, rocking
+ insect, winged ∧ ∨
+ land with canal
− map
+ mountain(s)
+ neckpiece
− pants (short)
+ paper, torn
+ pelvis
+ ribbon
+ rock(s)
+ shell, open
− shoes, big

− spinal cord
+ stone(s)
− teeter-totter
− tub
+ water color wash
+ wings
− x-ray

D 5

General plus category:

animal tail

− arrow
− castle
+ caterpillar
− claw, lobster
+ coiffure
− colon (An)
+ comb
− dog
+ feather
+ hair, sticking up
+ headdress
− horn, animal
− intestine(s)
− knife
− leg, any
+ leg ∨
− mantilla
− mountain
− phallic symbol
− pistol
− plant
+ plume
− potato, sweet
− reptile
− saw <
+ smoke
− snake
− stalactite
− sword
+ tassel (hat)
+ trunk, elephant
− volcano
− wig
− wing, bird
+ worm

D 6

See also Dd 26

General plus categories:

human figure ∧ ∨; flowing body of water between land areas

- \+ anus
- − blood vessel (drawing of)
- \+ bridge
- − cannon(s)
- − cap
- − casket
- − couch
- \+ dam
- \+ doll
- − fence
- − fly
- \+ gateway
- \+ guided missile(s)
- − hat
- \+ hinge
- \+ holder, cigarette
- − house ∧ ∨ <
- − insect(s)
- − mustache
- − penis, diagram of
- \+ post(s)
- \+ projectile(s)
- \+ river
- − roots (in ground)
- − spine
- − tree(s)
- \+ twig(s)
- \+ vagina
- \+ water
- − worm(s)
- \+ zipper

Ds 7

General plus category:.

natural, topograph entities based on a central space, such as lake, bay, canyon.

- \+ arrow (head) ∨
- − airplane
- − bell
- − body, human ∨
- \+ bottle, perfume

- \+ cave entrance
- \+ cloud, mushroom
- − dress, girl's
- − face, cat
- \+ fan
- − grass plot
- \+ head, human ∨
- − heart
- \+ helmet
- − keyhole
- \+ lamp ∨
- − mountain ∨
- − mouth, animal or human ∧ >
- \+ mushroom ∨
- \+ ocean
- \+ pagoda ∨
- − path
- \+ pool (swimming)
- \+ pot
- − river
- \+ shield
- − shovel
- \+ Sphinx
- − stomach
- \+ tent ∨
- − trap, fish
- − tree ∨
- \+ urn
- − uterus
- \+ vase
- − window

D 8

- − beak
- \+ cliffs
- \+ cock's comb
- − devil, with spear
- − face, human ∧ <
- \+ figures, human
- \+ forehead
- − hair
- \+ head, bird
- − head, squirrel
- \+ horns
- \+ icicles
- − monster
- − seashell
- \+ snail, horned
- \+ snout, seal

+ stalagmite(s)
+ splash of water
− teeth
− turtle
+ village on cliff

D 9

See also W

General plus category:

human figure (∧ or ∨)

+ animal, with human head
+ art, primitive
+ cloud(s)
+ dogs, two, kissing >
+ elephant > ∨
− horse >
− key
− lake
+ mountain
− pillows
+ rocks, piled or balanced
− sheep. >
− sideburn
+ stones
− tree

D 10

See also D 4

− animal, crouching
− building
− blood vessels, enlarged
− cat
− chair, rocking
− child (sleeping)
+ clouds ∨ ∧
− coccyx
+ crag
+ dog ∧ ∨ >
− fan
− football player
− hat, woman's
  head:
  + dog
  − horse ∨
  − human
  − lion > <
  − monkey
  − whale >
+ hill(s)

− knight (chess)
− lake
+ land
− lion > <
− mouse
+ pillow
− rabbit
− South America
− squirrel
+ support(s)
− tree trunk

D 11

General plus category:

building

+ archway ∨
− boat
+ eagle
+ entrance
+ figures, human, two
− head, goat (skeleton of) ∨
− ice cream, dish of, melting
+ insignia, winged ∨
− jello
− toadstool ∨
− stamen
− sun setting, with clouds ∨
− whipped cream
+ wings

Dd 21

− appendix
+ arm
− child >
− dragon
− face, witch >
− feather
+ finger
+ garment, piece of
+ hand
− head, animal
+ head, snake
+ horn
− island
− leg, animal or human
+ paw
− peninsula
− receiver, telephone
+ tail, dog

− teat, cow	+ lamp post
+ thumb	+ vagina
+ trunk, elephant	
− worm	Dd 27

Dd 26

See also D 6

− anus
− bullets
− teeth
+ post(s)

− body, human, cut in half
+ Christ on cross
+ figure, human

− whiskers
+ windows

Figure VIII

W

Note: Starred responses may exclude both D 1 without change in form quality scoring, though they should not then be scored as W. The general response categories also apply to these responses

General plus categories:

ornaments, such as emblem, badge, jewelry; gross human anatomy, such as "insides" or medical illustrations

General minus categories:

face, animal or human; insect

+ art, modern
+ astrological symbol
− bat
− basket
− bed
− biological illustration*
− bird
− bivalve*
+ boat (end view)*
+ bowl
+ bubble, irridescent
− butterfly* V ∧
− cabbage
− cage*
+ carousel
− cave*
+ chandelier ∧ V
+ Christmas tree (with presents)
+ coat of arms
+ color print
− crab (opened)*
+ crown
+ design

+ doorknocker ∧ V
+ drawing, scientific
− egg, Easter
− figure, human
− fish*
+ float, parade
+ flower (with leaf)* V
+ foliage*
− frog (dissected)*
− globe*
− head, peacock
+ headdress (ornate)
− heart
+ hill*
+ ice cream (brick of)
− intestines
+ iris V (flower)
− jellyfish*
+ kaleidoscope
+ landscape, mountainous* ∧ >
+ lantern, Japanese*
− map
− mask
+ monument
− moth* ∧ V
+ moss, sea
+ mountain (scene)* ∧ >
+ pagoda
+ Painted Desert
− paramecium
− pelvic cavity V
+ pyramid
+ quartz
− rainbow*
+ reefs, coral
+ rocket*
+ rocketship*
+ rocks*
− rubbish, pile of*

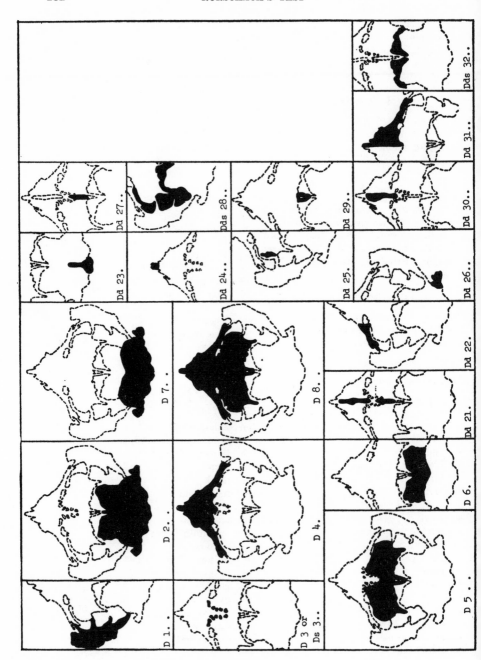

− scarf(s)
+ seal (crest)
+ seashell(s)
− shell, crab or lobster
+ shield
+ ship (with sails) (end view)*
+ sign, electric
+ skeleton, drawing of
− skull, animal*
+ stain [biology]
− stalactites
− statue
− stomach*
− torch ∨
− tree*
+ tropical scene
− turtle
+ underwater scene
− uterus
+ vase ∧ ∨
+ volcano (erupting) ∨*
+ x-ray (chest)*

D 1

General plus categories:

canine; feline; rodent

General minus category:

insect

+ animal
+ armadillo
+ art figure
+ badger
+ bear
+ beaver
− bird
− blood
− boar
− buffalo
− bull
− camel
− cloud(s)
− cow
− dinosaur
− dolphin
− dragon
− fallopian tube
+ ferret
− figure, human
− fish

− flower
− frog
+ Gila monster
− goat
+ gopher
+ groundhog
+ handle, bowl
− lamb
+ lizard
− lobster
− lung(s)
+ mink
+ mole
+ mongoose
+ otter
+ pig
− porpoise
+ possum
+ racoon
− ram
− reptile
+ salamander
− seal
− sheep
+ sloth
− shrimp
− tadpole
+ weasel
+ wolverine
+ woodchuck

D 2

See also D 6

General plus category:

any species of flower ∧ ∨

General minus category:

internal organ (An)

− animal (sea)
+ atomic bomb blast
− bat ∨
+ butterfly(s)
− buttocks
− chest (An)
+ cliff(s)
+ cloak ∧ ∨
− cloth, torn
+ coral
− crown ∨
− dog ∨

+ explosion
+ fire
− fur
  head:
  − antelopes, two ∨
  + cows, two ∨
  − dog <
  − lamb
  − lion <
+ ice cream
− insect
+ jacket, gaudy
+ jello
+ landscape
− leaf
+ moth
+ mountain(s)
− orange
− pelvis
+ petal, flower
+ quartz
+ rock(s) (colored)
− scarecrow
+ sculpture, cubist
+ slide(s), biology
+ smoke, colored
− spinal cord section, stained
− steak split in middle
+ stone(s) (precious)
+ suit, grotesque ∨
+ sunset(s)
+ tissue, body, stained
− vagina
− waist and hip area
+ waistcoat ∨
+ wings, butterfly

D 3 or Ds 3

General plus category:

bony anatomy

+ blouse, woman's
+ bones
− boat
− Buddha
− buoy
− cave
+ corset
+ costume, white, ruffled
− ducks, flight of <
  face:

− goat
− human
− tiger
− flowers
− funnel
− god, statue of
− head, goat
− lobster
− mask
+ medical insignia
− netting
− pagoda ∨
− scarab
− shears
+ skeleton
+ skull, steer
− teeth
− vines
− web

D 4

See also D 8

General plus category:

Arboreal botany responses

− abdomen
+ airplane
− animal (sea)
− antlers (deer) ∨
+ archway
− arrow (head)
− bat ∧ ∨
− beard ∨
− boomerang
− breast <
+ butterfly
+ cap, fur
+ castle on hill
− cell, microscopic
+ cliff(s)
− cloud
+ cover, bowl
− crab
+ crag
− crawfish
+ crown
− creature, prehistoric
− dinosaur(s)
− figure(s), human
− fish ∧ >

+ foliage
+ forest
− frog
− fur
+ hat
− head, antlered animal ∨
+ house
+ ice
− insect
− kite (fish)
− lobster(s)
+ mountain(s)
− octopus
− polyp
− pubis (with hair) ∨
− ray (fish)
+ rocket (nose of)
+ rock(s)
+ roof
+ roots, tree
− sail, ship
− scorpion
− ship
− silk
− skull
− spider
+ stump, tree
+ support (Ab)
+ temple
+ water, streaming down

D 5

+ accordion
− bat
− bird
− butterfly
− can, trash (cracked)
+ cliff(s)
+ cloth, (torn)
+ corset
− crown ∨
− fish (mouth Ds 3) <
+ flag(s)
− flower(s)
− fur
− hay
− head, tropical fish <
− house ∧ ∨
+ ice, cakes of
+ jacket, laced ∨

− lake
+ ledge
− leaf(s)
− lungs
− map
− moth
+ paper, torn
− pelvis
+ pillow
− ribs
+ rock(s)
+ sails, ship
− seashell
− shoulders, human
+ sky
− spider
+ trees
− trousers ∨
+ water

D 6

See also D 2

General plus categories:

flower; human head or face

+ apes
+ buffaloes (water)
+ butterfly ∧ ∨
− cats
+ cow(s)
+ design
− donkey
− frogs
  head or face:
  + animal
  + ape
  − bear
  + cattle
  − dog
  − frog
  + lamb(s)
  − lion
  − pig(s)
  − rodent
  − tiger(s)
+ ice cream
− larynx
− lungs
− moose
+ petals, flower

− potatoes
+ quartz
− rabbit(s)
+ rock formation
− sea lions
+ sheep
− toads
− tower <
− web

D 7

See also D 2

− bat
− bird
+ bloodhounds
+ blood stains
− bread, loaf
+ butterfly ∧ ∨
− buttocks
− cat(s)
+ coat, fur
+ crystal
− duck
− face, human
+ glass, cut
− hairdo ∨
− head, penguin ∨
− head, sheep ∨
+ hips
+ ice, orange
− leaves
− monster ∨
+ mountain
+ rock(s)
− sassafras
+ seashell
+ stone(s)
+ sun
− tent
− thighs
− tree
− turban
+ wings, butterfly

D 8

See also D 4

− anatomy, unspecified
+ bed, ornate, end view

− butterfly
+ church (inside of)
− fish
+ flower ∨
− head and body, gorilla
+ hill
− insect (water)
− lakes with land between
+ rocket
+ sailboat
− shell, crab
+ tree

Dd 21

See also Dd 27 and 30

+ bones, two, any
− esophagus
− figure, human
− gearshift lever
− mud streak
+ rocket
− smoke, rising
+ spinal column
+ spinal cord, insect

Dd 22

− alligator
+ arm and hand
+ branch, tree
− Central America <
− figure, human
+ hand
+ horn(s)
− paw, wolf
+ root(s), tree
+ wood, dead

Dd 23

− arms
− bladder
− bone
− canoe
+ club(s), golf
+ collar and ruffle
+ genitalia, female
− hourglass
+ pathway
+ mountain (snow-covered)

Dd 24

- − arrows
- − birds
- + feelers
- + figures, human, two
- + legs, human $\vee$
- − pincers
- + trees

Dd 25

- − dog, lying down
- − figure, human
- + fish
- + island
- − lake
- − otter
- + rocket
- + stone
- − submarine
- − tadpole

Dd 26

- − bird >
- − bottle, perfume <
- − cone, ice cream >
- + dog $\vee$
- − elephant $\vee$
- − figure, human, in chair <
  head: (usually <)
  - + animal $\wedge$ $\vee$ <
  - + bison $\vee$
  - + dog $\vee$
  - − duck
  - − horse $\wedge$ $\vee$
  - − human
  - − kangaroo
  - − sea horse
  - + sheep $\wedge$ $\vee$
  - − turtle
- − monkey <
- + rock (colored)
- − shell, conch
- + Sphinx <
- + turrett <
- − turtle

Dd 27

See also Dd 21

- − alligator
- + pen [writing]

- + pole (May)
- − snake
- + spear
- + stick
- − tear drop
- − worm

Dds 28

- − boy, wearing hat $\vee$
- − clouds $\wedge$ $\vee$
- + hen $\vee$
- + rooster $\vee$
- + water, bodies of $\wedge$ $\vee$

Dd 29

- + bell $\vee$
- + bottle, milk $\vee$
- − bridge
- − crutch, upper part
- + pendant
- − statue
- + stirrup $\vee$
- − tower $\vee$
- − vagina
- − wishbone

Dd 30

See also Dd 21

- + caterpillar
- + club (knobbed)
- + eel
- + flute
- + rocket
- + snake
- + spinal column (piece of)
- − swordfish
- + twig
- + worm

Dd 31

- − bird
- − devil
- − dog, mouth open
- − figure, human, reclining

Dds 32

- + bird
- + gull, sea
- + lamp (Aladdin's)

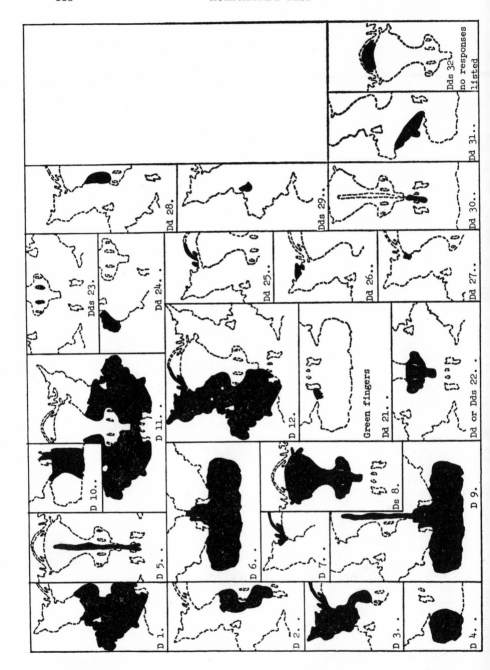

Figure IX

W

General plus category:

any species of flower

General minus categories:

face (animal or human); insect

− anatomy
+ art, modern
− bird
− bivalve, illustration of
− blood
− brain, cross-section of
− bug
− butterfly
+ candle, dripping wax
− cathedral $\vee$
+ cauldron, witch's
+ clothes, on a person (Ws) $\vee$
− clouds
+ coat of arms
− crab
+ decorative piece
+ design
+ eruption
+ fan $\vee$
+ figure, human $\vee$
+ fireworks
+ flames
+ flower arrangement
+ fountain
− fungus
+ garden, with fountain
+ hat, any $\wedge$ $\vee$
− head, cat's
− hill
+ Indian $\vee$
− island(s)
− jellyfish $\vee$ $\wedge$
+ lady, with parasol $\vee$
+ lamp
+ landscape $\wedge$ $<$
− leaf,
− lobster
+ map
+ mask, goblin
+ medical chart
− moth
+ movement (Ab)
+ ornament, glass

+ paint, smear of
+ painting, any $\wedge$ $<$ $>$
+ palette, artist's
+ philosophy of life (Ab)
+ pigeons, sitting below draperies $\vee$
+ plant, exotic, with red blossoms $\vee$
− rocket ship
+ rocks, colored
+ scenery $\wedge$ $\vee$ $<$ $>$
− sea life
− seashell $\vee$ $\wedge$
− shears, garden $<$
− skull
+ Spring
− sunrise
− throat $\vee$
− tissue, under microscope
− tree $\wedge$
+ tree $\vee$
+ vase
+ waterfall
+ whirling object with water shooting out
+ woman, gazing into mirror, and reflection
+ women
− x-ray

W minus D 6

− crab
− face, human
+ seaweed

D 1

See also D 11

General plus categories:

human figure; blunt-nosed animal, (muzzle at midline).

General minus category:

specific geography responses

− animal life, undersea
+ animal
+ ape (Dd 24 as head)
− baboon
− bear
− beryl
− bird(s)
− bottle(s)

+ buffalo
+ busts, human
− butterfly
− cactus
+ child on toy, riding <
− chipmunk
− circle
+ cloud
+ coat, woman's ∨
− dinosaur
− dog ∧ > ∨
− dragon ∧ >
− elephant
+ face, Irish (outer edge as profile)
− fan
− fish(es)
− flower sepals
+ foliage
+ forest
− frog
+ grass patch
− harp
− hat ∨
− head, hippopotamus (snout at Dd 24)
− head, hog (snout at Dd 24)
+ head, human (profile Dd 24)
− heart
− intestines
+ jacket
+ jade
+ land
+ lawn
− leaf
+ leaves, mass of
− lion ∨ ∧
− liver
− lungs ∨ ∧
+ map
− metal, rusted
+ monster
+ motorcycle rider >
+ nature scene
− peacock ∨
+ pig (muzzle at midline)
− pitcher, water
− plant
− porcupine
+ pottery, pieces of
+ profile
− rabbit ∧ >

− rock(s)
− sailboat
− seaweed
+ shrubbery
+ skirt(s)
+ smoke
− State (Ge.)
− thistle
− toadstool(s) ∨
− tree
− tree stump <
+ trees, massed in woods
− trenches
− turkey ∨
− valley
+ water, green
− willow ∨
− wing(s)

D 2

+ alligator
− bacteriology slide
− beak, rooster's >
− castle
+ crocodile
  face:
  + animal
  + dragon
  − on moon <
  − turtle
+ goat
  head:
  − bird
  + camel
  + cow
  + crocodile
  + deer
  + dog
  + elk <
  − fish
  − horse
  − monkey
  + moose
  + reindeer, with antlers
− man, prehistoric
− monkey
+ mountain(s)
+ rock(s), in landscape
− snake
− tree, broken <
− walrus

D 3

See also D 12

General plus category:

human figure (∧ only)

+ animal
− ape
+ bird ∧ ∨
− bison
+ blaze
+ blood smear
− body, butterfly
+ caricature
− carrot
− chicken
+ cliff
− clouds
+ clown
− club, cave man's
− cow
+ crab
+ creature, mythical
+ deer
− dirigible <
− dog
+ dragon
+ face, human
− fish
+ fire
+ flower cup (both D 3)
− foot, human
+ ghost
− gold, vein of
+ gremlin
  head:
  + devil, with horns
  − elephant
  + human
  + moose
+ hill ∧ <
− horn
− insect
− island
+ land, arid
+ lava
− leg, chicken, cooked ∧ ∨
+ lobster ∧ ∨
− lung(s)
− man ∨

+ map, relief, with mountain and fjords
+ mask
+ moose, running >
+ mountain(s)
− orchid
+ owl, on twig ∨
+ parrot ∨
+ petal, flower
+ plant, insect-catching (both D 3)
− praying mantis
− rat
+ rock <
+ sand beach
+ Scandinavia
− scorpion
− sea horse (with Dds)
− serpent, sea
− shrimp
+ skirt, orange (both D 3) ∨
+ smoke, trail of
− sun, going down <
− thistle, prickly part
− tiger
− tissue, body
− toadstool ∨
+ unicorn
− whale
+ wing, any
+ witch
− woods

See also D 6

General plus category:

human face or head

General minus category:

animal face or head

− apple
− bird
− blood
− buffalo ∧ ∨
+ bust <
+ caricature of man
− chicken
− dog
− elephant
− eye, ant
− fence
− fish

+ flower
+ head (any position)
− lungs
− meat
− pottery, clay
+ rock
− vase

D 5

General minus category:

animal, any genus

− arrow
+ backbone, human
+ bat, baseball
− body, insect
+ bone
+ brook
+ candle(stick)
+ cane
+ cascade
+ cooking spit
+ dagger
− esophagus
+ Eternal Light
+ fountain
− gun <
+ horizon, town, sky and shore >
− horn, animal
+ hose, water
+ lake, edge of >
+ lamp, floor (with Ds 8)
+ landscape >
+ nervous system, embryonic
+ obelisk
− peninsula
− penis
− rainbow
+ river
+ road
+ rocket
+ sceptre
+ smoke, rising
+ smokestack
+ stalactite
+ stem, flower
+ stem, mushroom (Dds 22 as mushroom)
+ stem, tree
+ sword
− tree

− trunk, elephant
+ tube
+ water colors, running together
   water:
   + current of
   + shooting up

D 6

See also D 4

− animal(s)
− ant, bottom view
− apples
+ babies, newborn ∧ >
− bag, punching
+ ballerinas, four
+ balloons
− basket
− bird
+ blossom(s)
− boat
+ bomb, atomic, cloud ∨
+ bonnet ∨
− buffaloes
− buttocks
+ candleholder
− caterpillar
+ cloud(s)
− cocoanuts
− collar, woman's ∨
− eagle
+ fire
+ flowers ∨ ∧
+ fountain, base of
− gums (mouth)
− heads, elephant, two ∧ < ∨
+ heads, human ∨ ∧
+ hoopskirts
− island
+ man >
− marshmallows
+ mushroom ∨
− ostrich ∨
+ petals, flower
− pigs
+ pillows
+ pots, flower
+ powder puffs
− radishes
− rectangles
− reservoir, water >

+ rock(s)
+ roses, pink
− section in microscope $\vee$
− shark, pink
+ sherbet, raspberry
+ shoulder pads, football $\vee$
+ shoulders, human $\vee$
− skin, burned
+ skirt
+ smoke
+ stain, berry
+ stone(s)
− toadstools, four
+ tornado
− vagina
+ vase, base of
− wings

D 4 plus D 10, i.e., half of D 6

See also D 4 and D 6

+ baby $\wedge$ >
+ bust of human
− chipmunk <
+ figure, human, sitting or squatting < $\wedge$
+ fetus

D 7

See also Dd 25

+ antlers
+ arm of statue
+ bones, connected
+ branch(es), tree
+ claw, crab or lobster
− dog
− eagle
− feeler(s), bug
− figure, human (in any movement)
+ finger nails
+ fire
+ gun(s)
+ hand(s)
+ horn(s), animal
+ horn (music)
+ leg, bird $\vee$ $\wedge$
− lightning
− map
+ root(s) $\vee$
+ sword(s)

+ telescope
+ tree(s) $\wedge$ $\vee$ >
+ vegetable growth
− wing(s)

Ds 8

General plus categories:

circular, glass object; body of water

− animal
− bell
+ bottle top
− buttocks
+ canyon
+ cave
+ chandelier
+ chasm $\vee$
− chest cavity
− church
− crab (with both Dd 25's)
+ design
+ dress
+ dummy, dressmaker's
− elephant $\vee$
− face, animal
+ fiddle
+ figure, human, female
+ garden vista $\wedge$ >
− globe, world
− head, creature $\vee$ $\wedge$
− holder, screwdriver
+ hole
+ hourglass
− kettle, tea
− keyhole
+ lamp
+ landscape, various types
− man, funny $\vee$
− masher, potato
− mask
− moon
+ picture, under water
+ shaker, salt $\vee$
− skull
+ sky
− skyscraper
− Sphinx
− uterus
+ vase $\wedge$ $\vee$
− veil $\vee$
+ ventilator on ship

+ violin
+ water

Ds 8 with both D 3

+ canyon
+ flower
+ mountains and canyon
+ skirt, open
+ volcano

D 9

+ atom bomb explosion
− barrel of wine
+ chandelier ∧ ∨
+ explosion ∨
+ fan
− figure, human
+ flower ∨
+ fountain
− hammer ∨
− island
+ lampshade ∨
+ mushrooms ∨
+ roses, bunch of
+ spindle, office
+ street light ∨
+ tree ∨
+ umbrella ∨

D 10

Note: human faces and heads are scored plus for this detail only when the response includes both D 10's and both D 4's, i.e., D 6. If D 10 or both D 10 are singled out, these responses are scored minus.

− animal
+ bird
− breast
+ buttock
+ head, elephant's ∨ (with D 5)
− lung
− map
− pear
+ penguin
+ poppy
+ rock
+ roots, tree, in burlap
+ ruffle, dress

+ tulip ∧ ∨
− vase

D 11
See also D 1

+ bat
− beard
+ butterfly
− cradle
− cup
+ pelvic area
− rock

D 12
See also D 3

− chicken
+ creature
− fungus
+ god, Chinese
+ landscape <
− toadstool
− tree ∨
+ workmanship on vase
− x-ray

Dd 21

+ claws
+ fingers
− guns, machine
+ hand(s)
− icicles
− keys, piano (with Dds)
− nerves of teeth
− spears
− teeth
+ toes

Dd 22 or Dds 22

+ bridge
− candles, four
+ cavern
+ columns
+ doors, swinging
− egg white, rotten
+ eyes, goblin, mask, or monster face: (may include adjacent dark areas)
    − animal
    + Halloween
    + human

− fish
+ garden, terraced
  head:
  − flatfish
  − fly
  − octopus
+ jack-o-lantern
− jellyfish
+ lace
+ lakes
+ mask (may include adjacent dark
  areas)
− mechanism, auto
− mushroom
− pelvis
+ pillars
+ ponds
− skull
+ tunnel
+ wall, castle

Dds 23

See also Dds 22

+ doors
+ excavations
+ eyes
+ holes for animal's home
+ holes shot through
+ hollows, two
− island
− moon, quarter
− mouth
− nostrils, horse
+ ponds
− shells, oyster
+ slits in material
+ windows

Dd 24

See also D 1

+ dog, Scotty
+ face, animal
− face, human
  head:
  + bear
  + camel
  + ram

Dd 25

See also D 7

+ archway (both Dd 25)
− bone, fish
+ bridge (both Dd 25)
+ claw(s), crab
+ dome, building (both Dd 25)
+ feeler(s)
+ finger(s)
− hook
− Italy, heel and foot of
+ lights, Northern
+ liquid, squirted
− nerves
+ smoke from gun
+ stick(s)
+ tentacle(s)
− whisker(s)

Dd 26

− boat
+ bugle
− dog
+ figure, human ∧ >
− foot, human
+ gun ∧ >
+ horn (music)
− nose
− saw

Dd 27

− angelfish
− animal
− bull
+ figure, human ∧ >
− head, dog
− penguin
− squirrel

Dd 28

− balloon
− blood splotch
+ breast
− dog
− head, animal
− moss
+ stomach
− tank, fuel, airplane <

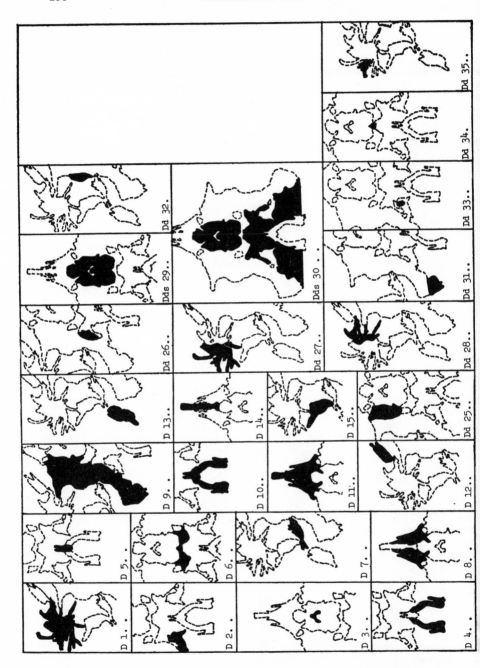

Dds 29

- − Africa ∨
- − bell
- + Caspian Sea
- − cat
- − face, lady
- − figure, human
- + lake
- − North America ∨
- − triangle
- + watershed

Dd 30

- − alligator
- + blood, drops of
- − caterpillar
- − intestine
- − penis
- − root, tree
- + bone

W

Note: Certain plural responses, i.e., "animals," or "fishes," contain equally strong elements of good and poor form quality, and hence must be scored both plus and minus. Such responses are indicated in the table by the symbol, ±. They should be distinguished from their parallel collective nouns, like "menagerie," and "aquarium," which are usually scored plus only. If the response includes many D indiscriminately, but not all of them, the scorings are D F+ and D F−

General plus category:

figured design or object based on a figured design, such as painting, tapestry. (Position of card is usually immaterial.)

- + algae
- + anatomic design
- ± animals (marine)
- + aquarium
- ± bacteria
- − balloon, burst
- + bandolier
- + biology slide

- + tallow, dripping
- + tears, dripping
- − vagina

Dd 31

See also D 1

- + cover, kitchen utensil >
- + face, animal
- + face, human
- − breast and nipple

Dds 32

Note: Responses to this area often include the long extension of both Dd 25's.

- + bridge, covered
- + ice cream cone
- + iris (of eye)

Figure X

- ± birds
- + botanic exhibit
- ± buds, flower
- − butterfly
- + chandelier
- − Chinese alphabet character
- − Christmas tree ∧ ∨
- ± clouds
- + coat of arms
- − cobwebs
- ± crabs
- + dance of life (Ab)
- + dream jumble
- − elephants, fairy tale
- + emblem
- − face, oriental
- + fair, country
- + fan ∨
- + festival
- + figures, weird
- ± figures, human
- + fireworks ∧ ∨
- ± fish (tropical)
- + flower(s) ∧ ∨
- − foods, different (on table)
- + fungus growth, microscopic
- + garden
- ± germs
- + glass, colored
- − headdress, fantastic

± insects, any type
− insides, human
+ islands
+ kaleidoscope scene
− leaves
− lizards
− map
− mask, Halloween
+ menagerie
+ mobile
+ music (Ab)
+ ocean bottom
+ orchid ∨
− pagoda
+ painting, modern
+ paints, splashed
+ palette, artist's
+ party, gay
+ plants
− pliers
+ postcard, picture
+ poster (illustrating Paris)
+ puzzle
+ rocks, colored
− salad
± seashells
± seaweed
− spiders
+ Spring [Ab]
+ stain, microscopic
+ temple, Oriental
+ tissue, under microscope
− tool, mechanical
− trees
+ tropical scene
+ undersea life
+ Walt Disney cartoon or scene
± worms
+ zoo

D 1

General plus categories:

microscopic or tiny object seen as magnified (position of card is immaterial); two or more human or mythical human figures, such as elves, goblins (position of card is immaterial)

+ ameba
  animal:
  + deep sea

+ grotesque
+ prehistoric
+ beetle
− bird, long-legged <
+ bouquet
+ branch
+ branches and stumps
+ bug, many-legged
− camel <
+ cell, nerve
− Chinese alphabet character <
− cloth, piece of
− cockroach
+ coral
+ crab(s)
− crow
+ crustacean(s)
− dragon(s)
− earring (with D 12)
− endive
+ fern, sea
− figure, human
− fish
− flea(s)
+ flower
+ germ
− head, deer <
+ ink, spilled
+ insect
− island
− jackass, braying
− jellyfish
+ landscape with trees
+ larkspur
+ leaf(s) (torn)
− lettuce
+ lobster (may include D 12 as claw)
− map
− mask
+ nerves
+ octopus
+ orchid
+ painting
+ pansy(s)
+ roots, mass of
+ scarab
+ scorpion
− seashell
+ seaweed
+ snowflake
+ spider(s)

+ starfish
− string, bunch of
− teapot(s)
+ water
+ web, spider
+ weed
+ witches (one may be on broom)
+ wood, dead

D 2

General plus categories:

bird, any species; dog, any breed; flower

General minus category:

human figure

+ ameba
− angel
− animal
− baby
− body, animal, baby inside
+ butterfly
+ cell with nucleus
− chair, easy <
− chicken
− clown
− coat of arms
− cricket
− deer
+ design
+ egg, fried or scrambled
− eye
− fish
− flesh
− frog
− goldfish
− head, rabbit
− jellyfish
+ lion
− monkey
+ petal, flower
− pitcher
+ pod, milkweed
+ poodle
− sea horse
+ seal
− shoe
+ stain, microscopic
+ sun
− witch on broomstick

D 3

+ airplane, jet
− antennae, insect ∨
− antenna, T. V. ∨
+ apricot
− bicycle
− bird
+ boomerang
− boxer, holding hands out
+ bud(s)
− bug
− buzzard
+ cherries
− circlet
− crab
+ design
+ diver, high ∨
− ear muffs
− figure, human
+ figure, human ∨
+ flowers on stem
+ governor of engine
− handle, to wind clock
+ instrument to measure wind speed
+ knocker, door
+ lavaliere
+ lights, electric
− lobster
+ marigold
− mouth, human ∧ ∨
− necklace ∨
− notes, musical
− ovaries, with fallopian tubes
+ parachutist
+ pawnbroker's symbol
+ pod, seed, maple
+ pollen grains ∨
+ prunes, two
− rubber band
− scissors
− scissors, handle of
+ seaweed
+ seeds
− spoons
+ stethoscope
− testicles
+ tongs, ice
+ twig
− "V" ∨
+ weathervane

+ wishbone
− "Y" ∨

D 4

See also D 10

Note: Singular responses refer to either lateral half of the detail; plural responses refer to the entire detail

General minus categories:

human figure ∧ ∨; *infrahuman mammal* ∧∨

− alligator
− animal
+ animal, mythologic
− Argentina ∧ ∨
− arms, human
− beard
− bug
− California ∧ ∨
+ caterpillar ∧ ∨
− chicken
− Chile ∧ ∨
− corncob
− cucumber
− dinosaur ∨
+ dragon
+ eel
− esophagus
− fan
− fish
− giraffe
− grass, blades of
+ head, dragon ∨
− head, human, grotesque
+ head, peacock ∨
− head and neck, swan or turkey
− hen, sitting
+ horns
− horse, toy
− insect
+ knight (chess)
− legs, human
− lobster
+ peacock
+ plant life, feathery ∨
− porpoise
+ prawn
+ saxophone
+ sea horse ∧ ∨

+ seaweed
− snail
+ snake
+ stamen ∨
− stem, flower
− swan
− swordfish
+ tail, lyrebird (whole detail)
+ tail, peacock
− tree
− turkey
− wings
+ worm

D 5

See also D 10

− acorn
+ angel ∧ ∨
− calf, with long ears
+ Christ on cross ∨
− clippers (hedge)
− clothespin
− Crucifix ∨
+ devil
− dog
face:
  + animal
  + creature
  − dragon fly
  − elk
+ figure, human, diving ∨
+ figure, human, with halo
− frog
+ gargoyle
− handle, nut cracker
head:
  + animal
  − ant
  + devil
  − donkey
  + figure, grotesque
  − giraffe
  − goat
  − grasshopper
  − human
  − Indian
  − insect
  − llama
+ rabbit
+ snail

− insect ∨
− key
− labia
− lobster
+ mask
− pliers
− starfish
+ swing, with person ∨
− vagina
− wrench

Projections of D 5 ("ears")

See also D 5

General plus category:

animal ears

− candles
− fingers
− icicles
+ legs ∨
− legs ∧
− teeth

D 6

+ angel(s)
+ animals
− apes
+ bagpipes
− bat(s)
+ birds(s) ∧ ∨
+ bluebird(s) ∧ ∨
− brassiere
− breasts
+ bridge
− bulbs, light
− cartilage (An)
+ chicken(s)
− cloud(s)
+ coral
+ dogs
+ dolls
+ dove(s)
+ duck(s)
− eagle(s)
− ear, inner (bones)
− eyeglasses
− faces, hook-nosed
+ figures, human:
  + shaking hands
  + performing on stage

− fishes
− flowers
− flying squirrel
+ ghosts
− girdle
+ gods, Roman
− gorillas
− hands
  heads:
  + animal ∧ ∨
  + dog ∧ ∨
  + elephant
+ hips
− insects
− insides, human
− kidneys
− lakes
− lungs
− masks, gas
− moose
− mountain(s)
− ostriches
− ovaries
+ pelvis
− pigs
− pipes, smoker's
− pitchers
− rocks
− seals
+ skeleton, human
− storks
− turkeys
− United States, two
− vise
− water

D 7

General plus category:

insect

General minus category:

birds and fowl

− alligator
+ animal, leaping
− bat
− cat
− clam
− cobweb
+ cocoon, on branch ∨
− cow

+ crab
+ crayfish
+ deer (leaping)
− dog
− embryo
− figure, human <
− fish
− frog
− Gila monster
− goblin V
− horse
+ kangaroo
− kidney and ureter
− leaf
− lion
− lobster
+ mouse < ∧ > V
− monster, little
+ moss, sea
+ nest in branches
+ pod, seed
+ rat
+ roots, bulbous (potato) ∧ <
− sea horse
− sea urchin >
− skull V
− spider
− squirrel
− stork
+ tree section, with roots and dirt
− turtle
− worm

D 8

See also D 11

Note: Responses refer to either lateral
half of the detail

General plus category:

*human figure, especially mythical (elf,
dwarf) or unusual*

+ animal (prehistoric)
− ant
− bat, wings folded
− bee
+ beetle
− buffalo
+ bug
− bull
− chicken

+ chipmunk
− crab
+ creature, weird
− deer
− dinosaur
− dog
+ dragon
+ face, grotesque V
− fish
+ flea
− flower
− fly
− frog
− goat
+ god, Egyptian
+ griffin
− head, grasshopper
+ head, human
− hen
− horse
+ insect
− kidney
− kitten
− leaf
− lion
− lizard
− lobster
+ Martian
+ mask
+ mouse, field
+ mold, furry
− monkey
− moss
− octopus
− ovary V
− parakeet
− parrot
− pheasant
+ plant
+ pollywog
− porcupine
− rabbit
+ rat
+ rodent
+ roots, tree
− sea leopard
− shrimp
− skeleton, piece of
− smoke
− spider
− squirrel

+ tadpole
− testicle
− turtle
+ unicorn
+ woodchuck

D 9

General plus category:

human figure (D 8 may be seen as head or hat)

General minus category:

anatomy

− ameboid mass
+ animal, fairy tale
− arch
− bacon
− bear
+ blood spot
− bone structure
− bug
+ California
+ caterpillar (magnified)
− Central America
− chicken
+ Christmas tree attachment
+ cliff
+ cloud(s)
+ coastline
+ coral, pink
+ curtains, stage, opened (both D 9)
+ design on coat (both D 9)
− dolphin
+ fire or flame
− Florida
− foot
+ gateway (both D 9)
− grub
− hair, red
− head, human [profile outer edge]
− insect, reared up
+ island
+ Italy
− jellyfish
+ map
− meat, cut of
+ monster, marine (prehistoric)
+ mountain(s)
+ mummy
− Netherlands

− ocean
+ petal, flower ∧ ∨
− planet
− pliers (both D 9)
− porpoise
+ rock
+ sea horse
− seashell
+ sea shore
+ suit, snow
− tissue, human
− trunk, tree
− ulcerated region
− worm

Both D 9 plus D 6

− butterfly
figures, human:
+ blowing bubbles
+ drinking from straw
+ holding hands
+ playing horn
+ smoking pipe
− skeleton

Both D 9 plus D 11 and Dds 30

+ "A"
+ bell (D 10 as clapper)
− butterfly
− face, any (may exclude D 11 or include D 10) ∧ ∨
+ flower ∧ ∨
+ funnel ∨
− necklace
− pelvis (may include D 6)
+ vase

D 10

See also D 4 and D 5

General plus category:

head of two-horned animal ∧ ∨

− amphibian, prehistoric
− animal, marine
− beard
− bird ∧ ∨
+ candleholder ∨
+ comb, old-fashioned ∨
− creature
− Cross

+ design
+ devil [D5 face]
− devilfish
− dog
+ door knocker $\lor$
+ doorway
+ drapery
− flower $\land$ $\lor$
+ fountain
− funnel $\lor$
− harness, horse's
− headdress
+ horns, animal $\lor$
− horseshoe
− insect
− light, electric, hanging $\lor$
+ lyre $\lor$
+ man, with halo and wings $\lor$
− marine scene
− monster, sea
+ music stand
− octopus
+ parachutist $\lor$
− pliers
− praying mantis
− rocketship
− saddle, with stirrups
− sea horse
+ seaweed
+ snake, with two bodies
− stamen $\lor$
− steeple
− tulip $\lor$
− tweezers
− "U" $\lor$
− "V" $\lor$
− vulture $\lor$
− wig
− wishbone
+ worm, on fish hook
+ wreath

D 11

See also D 8 and D 14

General plus category:

two figures in human-like action involv-
  ing a pole or tree, such as supporting,
  leaning against, dancing around
− airplane
− airplane, front end $<$ $\land$

− anteater
+ animals, supporting tube or tree
+ art piece, Oriental
− arteries
+ backbone and attached bones
+ bamboo stem, with roots
+ beavers, gnawing at tree
− bells, two
− body, human, part of
− broom
+ castle
− centipede
+ chandelier
− dagger
+ diving bell
+ Eiffel Tower
− fireplace
+ flower
+ funnel $\lor$
− hammer
+ headgear, Oriental
− implement, for tree pruning
+ insects, leaning against pole
− intestines
+ lamp, hanging
− map
+ marionettes, on string
+ mice, gnawing on stalk
+ mistletoe
− mirage
− nervous system
− pelvis
− pencil sharpener with pencil $<$
+ plant
+ rats, strung up on post
+ rocketship
+ roots, with tree
+ scarecrow
− shellfish $\lor$
− skull, steer
+ spine and pelvis
+ statue
+ stem, flower $\lor$ $\land$
+ stick, toy, with bells
+ stove, old-fashioned
+ trachea and lungs
+ transformers, on telephone pole
− tree
+ tree $\lor$
− universal, on automobile $\lor$

D 12

- − angel
- − animal
- − ax
- − bean
- − bird
- + bison
- − bomb
- − broom
- − bud
- − bug
- + bull
- − cat
- − caterpillar
- − claw
- − cloud
- − cocoon ∧
- − coral
- + cow
- − dog
- − fan
- + fish
- − frog
- − goat (mountain)
- − grasshopper
- − horseshoe
- − island
- + lamb
- + leaf
- − limb, tree
- − mouse
- − parrot
- + plant (sea)
- + plume
- − rat
- − rock
- + scarab
- − seed
- + sheep
- − snow bank
- − tree
- + unicorn
- + whale

D 13

General plus category:

dog, any breed ∧ ∨ <

- + animal
- + bear
- − beetle

- − bird
- + buffalo
- − bug
- − cat
- − caterpillar
- − chicken, roast
- − chip, potato
- + cloud
- − cocoon
- − duck ∨
- + face, dog
- − figure, human
- − fish
- − flower
- − honeycomb
- − insect
- + island
- + leaf
- − lemming
- − lion, lying down
- + mold
- + New Zealand
- + paint, daub of
- − pig
- − porpoise
- − potato
- − rabbit
- − rat
- − reindeer
- + rock
- − seashell
- − sheep
- − shell, oyster
- − skin, chicken, piece of
- + slug [insect]
- − snail
- − sponge
- − stomach
- − tonsil(s)
- − turkey, roast
- − whale
- − worm

D 14

See also D 11

- − arrow
- − artery
- + baton
- − bone
- + branch
- − bullet

+ candle
+ candleholder
+ cane
+ cannon >
+ chimney
− cigar
− dissection, piece of
+ face, African, ebony, carved
+ face, human, long and thin
   figure, human:
  + headless
  + tall and thin
  + wearing tall hat
− finger
+ flashlight
+ guided missile
+ gun (may include D 8)
+ hammer
− key
− knife (in sheath)
+ log
+ Maypole
− monkey
− necktie
− opener, bottle
+ pen
+ pencil
+ penis
+ pipe, piece of
− pistil, flower
+ post, lamp
+ rocket
− root
− snout
+ spinal cord, piece
+ stalk
+ statue
+ stovepipe
− stump, tree
+ test tube
+ thermometer
− throat, interior of
− tree
+ trunk, tree
− urethra
+ vase

D 15

+ ameba
− animal
− bag

− bean
+ bird
+ bud
− canary
+ cloud (across sunrise)
− drill, hand, power <
− fish
− Florida <
+ flower
− hat, Santa Claus
− head, rabbit
− insect
− island
− jellyfish
− key
− popcorn, kernel of
− rabbit
− rat <
+ rose
− rug
− seal
− seashell
− sheep
− South America <
− walrus <

Dd 25

See also D 9

Note: Responses may include all
of upper half of D 9

General plus category:

face or head of human or mythical human

− dog

Dd 26

+ face, funny
+ man, old
+ profile, human

Dd 27

See also D 1

+ clown on trapeze
+ figures, human
+ goblin
− head, wolf
+ horse
− sea horse
− vulture(s)

Dd 28

See also D 1

+ cat, sitting (reaching out)
+ head, horse
− head, fox
+ knights (chess)
+ monkey
− sea horse(s)

Dds 29

− bar, ice cream (D 14 stick) ∨
+ Buddha
+ chest protector (baseball)
− dog
+ face, human (front view)
+ faces, human (profiles outward)
+ fan (D 14 handle) ∨ ∧
− foliage
+ lantern (with D 14)
+ papoose
+ tennis racket (D 14 handle)
+ violin (D 14 neck)

Dds 30

− body, human, part of
+ canal and locks
+ canyon
+ pathway
− skeleton

Dd 31

− cat
+ face, human <
+ face, monkey <
+ head, animal <

Dd 33

+ acorn
− diamond
− dog
− eye
− handkerchief
+ head, baby
− head, dog
+ leaf, autumn
− orange
− tooth
+ walnut

Dd 34

− ball
− bathing suit, top, woman's
− boat
+ bone
− candleholder
+ connection, water-pipe
+ gate
− horns, animal
− muff
+ rock
− skull

Chapter XIII

POPULAR PERCEPTS: P

The responses scored P, being by definition the most popular, i.e., the most frequent, are *ipso facto* statistically based. It is also clear that all P must be plus. That is, they occur more frequently than any other F+ responses. The statistics whereby the present P list was derived are reported in the study of a normal adult sample.[7] The responses are all specific, and I do not depart from them; that is, I always score these associations P, and I score no others P. The frame of reference is unvarying. This is not to say that it can never change. A fresh statistical study in a group of normal adults representative of the middle groups in an American population can revise it. But until revised it is a standard.

Rorschach does not use the popular response concept in the *Psychodiagnostik*, but he does so in his posthumous paper[28] in his *Vulgärantwort*. Following are all P responses for the ten figures.

Figure I

Bat or *butterfly* for the W response. The variations are minor. *Moth* is P. The 'bat' may be 'bizarre,' and the 'butterfly' may have 'decaying wings.' The spaces may form part of what is seen: Ws F+ A P. In deviations such as 'bat-man' we still have P, since the basic form has been perceived.

No other winged figures are P: e.g., 'bird,' 'eagle,' 'double eagle,' 'crest,' are W F+. Nor is part of figure I as part 'bat' or part 'butterfly' rated as P—e.g., the upper half of the entirety as 'bat's wings' or even as 'bat' or D 2 as 'butterfly wing' are not P, and are likely to be Adx responses (212).

D 3 and D 4 as a *human form* are P. D 3 is usually a *woman*, frequently *nude* or *from the hips down*. Occasionally it is a *child*. Provided the human form is the nucleus of the percept, the response is P.

Figure II

W as *two humans*, usually but not necessarily M, is P. The variations in content are innumerable. The *people* may not be named, the content being a common human activity: e.g., 'peas porridge hot'; 'a game.' All are P.

In instances, only one lateral half is selected, with some *human form* as the content. This is still P, provided D 2 is included, as the *head* or some *headgear*. But D 1 alone as human form is not P.

D 1 as *dog*, or *bear* is P. No other animal is. The D 7 area of the detail must be the *head region* of the animal, whatever the position of the card. When D 2 forms part of the animal it is not P. The general term "animal" is *not* P.

D 3 as *butterfly* or *moth* is P.

Figure III

Again, the *two humans*, D 1, may be of any class; and representations of humans, e.g., *dolls, statues, caricatures.* Here too the associations may consist of only an activity—'a very violent dance.' All are P, provided (*a*) the basic *human* form has been perceived, and (*b*) D 5 is part of the human.

The response may be concerned with only one of the figures, i.e., D 9. Provided the foregoing conditions are met, it is P.

The card must be $\wedge$. The two *primitives* when the card is $\vee$ are not P.

D 3 *bow tie, ribbon,* or *butterfly,* or variations of these are P.

Figure IV

W as any variation of *animal skin*, i.e., *hide, pelt,* or *rug of animal skin,* is P. To these it is necessary to add the *human* dressed in *animal skin coat,* usually of raccoon, sometimes *bear, beaver,* or *wolf.* The P credit in these is for the *skin* forms, not the human, although the latter is very common. Also, 'animal,' when this is a massive, furry animal; including any of those whose 'pelt' is P; and including 'gorilla.' But the 'sea monsters,' and the similar percepts are not P. A human form in itself, including the large ones, i.e. 'giant,' is not P.

D 2 as 'human foot' or 'shoe'; D 6 as 'boot' or 'human leg' are P.

Figure V

W as *bat, butterfly, moth,* the most common responses in the test, may be considered the paradigm P. Variations must respect the basic forms. *Lunar moth* is P; 'bird' or any named bird is not.

In selections of D 1, any *human leg,* and many *animal legs,* are P. A variation such as 'drumstick' of the 'chicken's leg' is P. The basic form is a leg filled out by muscle development.

Figure VI

W or D 1 as *animal hide, pelt, skin,* or *rug* is scored as P. The variations are chiefly in respect to the specific animal named, but they may deviate to the extent of 'an animal carcass hung up' (i.e., after slaughter). All these responses are P, provided the basic *animal skin form* is perceived. The same rule applies in this figure to W and to D 1.

Figure VII

D 1 as *human heads* or *faces*, nearly always of *women*, are P. The response sometimes refers only to D 1; it may embrace D 2, as whole persons, or include W, each lateral half being a person, in some cases a *person on a rock*. The content may vary in being *busts* or *statues*. All these are P if the *human head form* is the nucleus of the response.

Figure VIII

D 1 as *animal*, or as certain kinds of animal, provide one of the most common responses in the test. They rank close to the *bat* or *butterfly* of figure V as the paradigm P. But the range of variations is wide. The specific groups scored P are: *bears*, including subgroups, as *cubs, polar*; *mice, rats*, the general term *rodent*, and specifically, *beavers, muskrats, squirrels*; and no others. The general term *animal* is always P, even when

TABLE 11.—*'P' Variation with 'R' Range*

	Variation in 'P'		
R	Low	Average	High
50–79	7–8	9–10	11–12
40–49	4–5	8	10–11
20–39	4–5	7	8–9
10–19	3	4–5	6–7

(See Ref. 22.)

modified, as, e.g., *heraldic*. The cats, including 'lion' and 'tiger,' and the dogs, or their relatives, such as 'wolf,' 'fox,' 'coyote,' 'lynx,' are not P.

In D 3 or Ds 3, the skeletal form is P. Most commonly the content is *ribs*, but it may be *bones, thorax, spinal column, fish backbone*. The white spaces are in some instances, but usually not, part of the percept. The basic element, *ribs*, is essential, for a scoring of P.

D 4 as *tree*, or as *bush* is now classified as P. But *woods*, any *massed trees*, or *mountain with trees on it*, are not P.

Figure IX

D 3 evokes very diverse thinking from the basic association of a *human figure*. Thus, 'Civil War veteran,' 'clown,' 'dwarf,' 'fireman,' 'ghost,' 'Santa Claus,' 'witch.' All these percepts are P.

In D 4, *head* or *face*, nearly always of a man, is P. Many subjects name the individual, usually a prominent person, e.g., Churchill, Roosevelt, or ascribe some vocation, e.g., 'a composer,' 'a general' (usually < >). But even when the card is ∧ or ∨, all these *heads* are P.

Figure X

D 1 as *crab, lobster* or *spider* is P. But *octopus* and other of the many-legged animals, e.g., 'centipede,' are not P. Occasionally, crustacean; or the scientific name of a *spider* genus will be given. All are P.

D 2 as *dog*, including special breeds, is P.

In D 5, the *rabbit's head* and the more common viariations, e.g., *bunny*, are P.

For the P norms found in our own investigations in adults[7, 23] and in children,[33] see Appendix 3. The question of norms in P is complicated by (a) the total productivity (R) of the test protocol, and (b) the limited total number of P: 21. An investigation by McCall and Doleys[22] has shown a relation between P and R. Table 11 shows the variations so derived and provides further help toward norms for P.

Chapter XIV

R, FLUCTUATIONS, L and x

Associational productivity: R. This refers simply to total number of scored associations for the test. When the associations are scored consecutively in the ten cards, the number of the last association is R. How accurate R is depends on how correct the scoring has been (see Chapter IV).

Fluctuations in productivity and in time per first response. Both of these are derived data, the one from the numbers of scored responses for each test card; the other from the times per first response in each test card. To measure fluctuation of productivity, subtract algebraically the number of scorings in each test card from that in the next. The sum of these differences divided by nine is fluctuation of productivity. When there is a rejection, subtract from the next test card to which the patient does associate: e.g., he produces two scorable responses in figure V, rejects figure VI, and gives four scorable responses to figure VII; this fluctuation, subtracting two from four, is two. To obtain the mean when there are rejections divide the sum of the differences by n − 1 (n being the number of test cards to which S associated with scorable content).

The rule operates exactly the same way for fluctuation of time per first response: it is (a) the sum of (b) the algebraic differences in (c) the time per first response of each card subtracted from (d) time in the next in which S produces scorable associations. This sum divided by n − 1 is the mean fluctuation for time per first response.

Lambda, or L. This is a derivative index, obtained as a ratio of all F to all non-F.* For lambda purposes F is defined as F+, F− and F. No scoring in which F blends with an affective variable, i.e., not CF, FC, YF, and the others; and not M, are F for purposes of the lambda index, or L. The formula for L will be found in Appendix 2. It is clear that a lambda index is only as sound as is the scoring of the F responses (F+, F−, F).

For the logic behind the lambda index, see the report for the normal adult sample.[7] The formula that I used there is: $\dfrac{(F+) + (F-) + (F)}{R}$.

By the newer formula, used in the present text, the found quotient states a ratio of all F to all that has anything in it that is non-F. In this way, lambda or L is a measure of the strictly form-determined associations which are unalloyed by any association scored as emotion-determined.

Hdx and Adx (Rorschach's Do). S sees Dd 22 of figure II as 'bear's

---

* This is equivalent to F per cent; see Klopfer and Kelley.[16, 17]

feet.' It is scored Dd F+ Adx. Most subjects, if they see a *bear* here, see all of D 1 as a *whole bear*. S in this case restricted her attention to only a portion of D 1 and saw only a part of the animal here commonly seen.

This is the x response. Its essence is: S sees a part of a *human* or *animal* where most healthy subjects, if they react with that content at all, see the *whole human* or *animal*. Other examples are:

In figure I, 'A bird's wings,' D 8: a healthy S would see the whole as a *bird*. Scored D F+ Adx.

In figure III, the markings within the D 6 that are commonly *heads* are singled out as 'like eyes and noses.' Scored Dd F+ Hdx.

In figure V, D 4, 'like wings stuck up.' A frequent x and a good example. If a *winged creature* is seen here, there is a mandate from statistical experience with healthy subjects to see the whole, usually *butterfly*, or whatever it may be. *Wings* are D F+ Adx. Another D F+ Adx in this figure is *antennae* for either D 2 or D 3.

Examples of Hdx are *leg* for D 5 of figure III, *arm* or *hand* for D 4 of figure IV. The x percept may be found in a Dd as well as in a D, and although usually plus, it may be F−. Thus, in figure IX, Dd 26 as 'a human nose' would be Dd F− Hdx.

It is important to note that the scoring is not x when the Ad or Hd response is the expected one. 'Cat's whiskers,' figure VI, Dd 26, or 'the human head,' figure VII, D 1, is not x. These are healthy reactions as Ad or Hd. In figure I, 'animal head' is common for D 5 and is not x. A little more doubt exists in regard to 'human head' for this detail. But this too is seen by healthy subjects separately from the rest of D 2; hence it is not x. There must be a mandate on the basis of the healthy response to see a whole human or whole animal. If in such instances S sees only a part, it is Hdx or Adx.

Rorschach knew this response but he called it Do or "oligophrenic detail" (ref. 27, p. 39). Another Swiss investigator, Loosli-Usteri,[19] was the first to point out that the response was frequently produced by anxious children who were not oligophrenic. She suggested therefore that it be identified as the constrictive reaction. Subsequent experience has confirmed her; and hence my designation x, for anxiety, as the dynamism behind this reaction. Also, the point at which x manifests itself characteristically is not in D or Dd but in the content. That is what S is modifying. It therefore seems most logical to attach the symbol to Ad or Hd. Thus Rorschach's Do is transformed into my Hdx or Adx.

Chapter XV

CHANCE POSITION: Po

A determinant rare in occurrence, but important diagnostically, is the position or Po factor. In it, the association is determined not by the qualities of form or color or by light variations or movement, but by the accident that the position of a feature in the given blot figure recalls or suggests a similar position that pertains to the association reported. Examples are here the best definition. In figure VIII, D 24 is 'the North Pole' because it is at the top. Scored D Po Ge. In figure VI, D 8 is a 'tree' and D 1 then becomes 'shrubbery and grass' because 'being at the base of the tree it would have to be shrubbery.' Scored D Po Bt. In figure VIII, D 6 are 'a man's kidneys' because 'that's where a man's kidneys are.' Scored D Po An. In figure I, S indicates the area about the middle of D 4 and reports that 'it looks like ribs' because 'that's the location of ribs.' In the inquiry S himself uncovers the lack of relation between his association and the stimulus when he says that he does not 'see the ribs'; he 'would have to have x-ray eyes to see them'; he only knows that that's where they are located.

In figure III, S sees D 1 as the usual 'two mannequins, playing with their hands at something' (D M+ H P) and D 3 is 'like a heart, because it's situated where their heart is.' D Po An.*

Figure VII, 'except for this (a D) I would say almost a section of a mountain of which the middle is where something has been dug in, put in, or which is there by nature.' He traces the contour, and, 'it's a section of a volcano with lava or stones [D 4] in the volcano,' and on further inquiry 'it has to be something that goes through. I could have said as well that it is a section of a volcano and in a volcano there is lava and that is why I see this as lava.' D Po Na.

After seeing D 3 of figure IX as Italy (D F— Ge), S continued, and Ds 8 'is the sea because I see blue and, (inquiry) 'because Italy is situated near the sea.' D C Po Ls.

Associating to D 11 of figure X, 'and isn't that like . . . I don't know . . . a heart like a human heart, because this [D 14] is 'the trachea, and so this is the heart.' D Po An. S then turned to D 9: 'and this must be the body,' because 'the heart is there and this is the body.' D Po Hd.

* For this and the following excellent samples of Po and of some doubtful not-Po associations I am indebted to a former student, Miss Maria Demeulemester, of Louvain, Belgium.

A child of twelve sees the center Dd line of figure I as 'the spinal column' because 'it is right in the middle.' She then sees Dds 24 of figure II as 'part of the spinal column' because 'it's in the middle and it has the form of a pair of pincers' (possibly Dd 25 was intended here). Again, in figure IV, she calls D 5 a spinal column, because 'it's in the middle.' The figure I and figure IV samples are not Po. Inquiry experience indicates that the language "in the middle" is more descriptive of a known reality than a choice determined due to location. Entirely healthy persons see these spinal columns, and so I score F. This experience does not hold for Dd 24 of figure II, and while it is a threshold example, position does appear to be one of the determinants. Score F Po−.

Other examples that are not Po: S describes a face in figure III and enumerates, 'nose, ears, eyes, mouth,' and about the chin he explains that 'it is where a chin is.' On further inquiry, S said he had really first had the idea of one face and the chin was merely one of the facial details. It was not so seen solely because of the accident that it is in a certain place on the test card, or in relation to something already seen by the patient. Therefore, not Po.

For D 1, figure VIII, S sees 'two little rats hanging against a tree,' because 'they hold themselves like this—on branches,' i.e., clinging to D 4. This is a very frequent relation, seen by the healthy; it is a proper organization of the test details and is not due to the accident of the position of either detail.

The general rule is: Score Po under either or both of the following two conditions:

(1) The sheer fact that the D or Dd is in its particular place on the test card, and provided that (a) this is the dominant, or only, reason why the patient so associates; and also (b) statistical experience does *not* point against Po, as for the 'spinal column' in figure I or the 'bears—tree' in figure VIII.

(2) The association is seen by the patient after and because of another association, e.g., 'trachea-heart' above. In these cases the new, i.e., the doubtful Po response, is not a usual property of the main association.

An F, M, or C response may participate with Po in determining the response. In figure VIII, S says, 'It makes me feel . . . the religious pictures of the great masters; I can't explain it; like in Michaelangelo; that lifting up one feels and can't express'—indicating only Dd 24, i.e., the topmost portion. No further information was obtainable from this disturbed woman. Scored D M.Po Ab, art. In figure IX the same patient, reacting to D 5, saw 'an uplifting, straight and tall . . . yet not very free.' Also scored D M.Po Ab, uplift. An example of a C.Po determinant is the percept in figure IX ($\vee$), D 1, 'bushes around the tree,' after D 9 had been seen as 'tree' and because D 1 were 'placed at the tree' and it is green.

Psychologically this determinant is an indicator of "accidental" thinking. That is, it results from thinking processes based on circumstantial elements in S's field of vision rather than on facts and logic followed in normal mentality. Rorschach considers Po entirely a schizophrenic phenomenon (ref. 27, p. 38). I have seen it also in other clinical groups, but it is most frequent among schizophrenics.

CHAPTER XVI

ASSOCIATIONAL CONTENT

The range of associational content projected by the Rorschach test figures has no boundaries. Anything may be seen and is seen. This is true in even a small group of records and the more so in an extensive one. Individualized twists, oddities, and sometimes bizarre constructions are forever turning up, so much so that no Rorschach test can be started without expectation of totally new content. Even simple records contain surprises. The originalities reach their qualitative and quantitative extremes on the one hand in adults of very high levels of intelligence and on the other in schizophrenia. The originality of superior adults becomes exaggerated, even by the standards for their group, when they are being psychoanalyzed.

For all this breadth, there is concentration in two principal categories. These are the percepts of *humans*, H, and *animals*, A, with *human detail*, Hd, and *animal detail*, Ad. Adding to these the *anatomy*, An, association, we encompass the majority of associations.

Among all the categories, those in which human beings are seen demand first attention in the interpretative analysis. A scoring of H tells that S has associated with a human form, in a human form. These responses may be most significant in what they tell us about the patient's percept of himself, and of persons of importance to him.

The specific humans include the usual man, woman, and child percepts and all terms whereby humans are identified, e.g., references to nationality, particular historical period, vocation, proper names of individuals. Of high importance, in projecting personal interest, are the more specialized human classifications: e.g., religious figures, such as 'angel,' 'devil,' these being scored H. Mythologic characters (including fairies, pixies and goblins) and some purely mental products (e.g., 'ghosts') are H when the form seen is human. Occasionally a response is H even though there is no naming of a human form, e.g., 'dance,' 'coitus.' Dolls are usually H. The simians, including anthropoid apes, are not H.

Hd records that S has associated with some part of a human, any external part. 'Headless man' or 'woman' always requires close inquiry, however. S may intend a decapitated body, which is scored Hd, but this is rarer than a whole human percept in which the 'headless' or 'without a head' phrase is a precision description. What the patient has perceived, as closer inquiry in these instances shows, is the integrated 'man,' 'boy,' 'woman,' or 'girl,' and he criticizes the form, 'head is missing.'

The animal, A, scoring attaches to all content referring to any species other than man: mammals, birds, fish, invertebrates, and insects. Still, some doubts may arise. For example, is 'clam shell' to be scored A? And how about 'ameba?'* Is it A or Sc (Science)? What about 'headless animal?' Is it A or Ad? The A category applies in scoring all zoological forms, but not the one-celled creatures. These tell of exposure to scientific education, if not actual vocation, and are scored Sc. The bivalves are Na (nature) whether the association is 'shell,' 'oyster,' 'clam.' But 'snail' is A. Animal carcasses, even though given as 'meat,' are A. When prepared for eating, e.g., 'a roasted chicken' or 'cooked lobster,' they are Fd (food).

Whether the animal is named by its scientific designation or by a child's word ('bunny'), it is still A. Specific breeds of dogs, named animals, and animals in art are A, although the latter are usually scored both A and Art. All simians are A.

All animal skins are A. In this I follow Oberholzer whose practice rests in the Rorschach logic that the animal forms were the ones primarily discerned. The animal percentage thus reflects the tendency toward a thought poverty in S's perceptions. 'Headless animal' is Ad. The Ad scoring otherwise applies to any external portion of an animal, however large or small: head, foot, claw, eye (but see concerning the An [Anatomy] scoring, below). For the animal per cent formula, see Appendix 2.

Anatomy content, An. This scoring pertains to any *internal* organ (lungs, esophagus, heart) or to an inner body portion (bone). The general rule for distinguishing An from Ad or Hd is that the latter refers to body parts that are externally visible, whether the person is dressed or nude. These are scored Hd or Ad. An is internal always, even though it lacks, in lay persons, anatomical accuracy. 'Teeth' are Hd or Ad, as is 'tongue.' The external sex organs are scored Hd, sex. The internal reproductive organs are An, sex. The An rubric takes in all 'x-ray' associations. The very technical x-ray and anatomical drawings perceived by physicians belong specifically in medical and scientific content, but I group them among the An and discount their significance as indicators of a pathologic concern with health. The 'injury' and 'wound' percepts, when not referred to a named outer or inner body portion, are simply entered in the patient's language in the scoring summary, e.g., 'wound,' 'cancerous tissue.' These associations are few even in extended experience and they are always clear as to diagnostic lead. When blood has been perceived, Bl is used.

The other content classifications used in this text, with their abbreviations, follow in alphabetical order.

Abstraction, Ab. Moods or emotions are the more common abstractions,

---

* In respect to 'ameba' my scoring departs from Oberholzer's, who scores A.

e.g., *depression, fright*. Sometimes it is a season of the year, because of connotation; e.g., green recalls *spring*.

Alphabet, Al. Responses like 'the letter *W*' or 'the numeral 7,' while rare, occur with sufficient frequency to warrant this grouping.

Antiquity, Aq. This denotes references to objects no longer in common use: 'hourglass,' 'suit of armor,' 'old coins.'

Architecture, Ar. All architectural associations belong here, also details in such percepts, as windows, arches. Some bridges present a problem, belonging rather to landscape responses, Ls (see below). Much of Ar overlaps on Art.

Art, Art. In addition to the more obvious art associations, this group includes seals and similar emblems, and commercial trademarks. Some caricatures belong here.

Astronomy, As. *Moon* and *stars* are the content in this group; it does not include sun because this is given as 'sunset' or 'sunrise' and thus always scored as landscape, Ls.

Anthropology, Ay. This classification is necessary for the "totem pole" which so many persons see in figure VI, D 3. But it is useful also for an occasional "aboriginal mask," and similar percepts.

Botany, Bt. All plant life is here grouped, including names of fruits and vegetables that are of primary interest as edibles. Occasionally the scientific name is given. In some instances the connection is with some festivity, e.g., 'Christmas tree,' and the general classification Bt is used with a second content symbol, e.g., Rc.

Clothing, Cg. This classification is usually clearly indicated. The departures are in respect to unusual kinds of clothing, reflecting particular personal interest, e.g., 'nun's habit.'

Clouds, Cl. Primarily this symbol refers to clouds as such. But several related associations are included, e.g., *storm, mist*.

Death, Dh. Responses here grouped are few and quickly recognized. Funeral associations are included.

Fire, Fi. A broad list of associations is comprised here: fire, smoke, burning candles, explosions—in fact, all products of combustion that are overtly visible.

Food, Fd. Prepared foods, of whatever kind, as sweets, desserts, etc., form this group. All meat is Fd, but slaughtered animals or those in butcher shops are A.

Geography, Ge. This classification comprises all specific place names and general terms for geographic details, e.g., *peninsula, strait*, when these are seen as though on maps. Occasionally the latter are true landscape percepts, Ls, and the distinction may be important.

Household, Hh. The interior of the household is represented in this group, i.e., *furniture, kitchen utensils*. Emphasis in some of the content is on the useful, in some on the ornamental.

Implement, Im. All tools, including aggressive ones, are here grouped (not musical instruments). This category is a valuable one in uncovering personal interests, sometimes at the intellectual level, sometimes deeper, of dynamic significance in producing the clinical picture.

Landscape, Ls. The varieties are many, and some associations are assigned here only with reservations—thus, *fountain* and certain *urban scenes* or *objects*. Ls now applies to all *seascapes*, e.g., *lighthouse* scenes, *harbors, ocean floor* scenes, and all others in which a large body of *water* is present.

Mineral, Mn. Two kinds of content are here grouped—precious metals or stones, and the coarser metals, e.g., *iron ore, quartz*, and similar materials obtained from the earth.

Music, Mu. This is a clear category for *musical instruments*, also *bells*.

Mythology, My. Dragons, gnomes, trolls belong here, as do all mythological creatures. Since the content is primarily H or A, My is likely to be a secondary content indicator.

Nature, Na. Responses like 'sky' and 'northern lights' belong here. They are of wider scope than landscape percepts and frequently are of much personal significance. But *seashell* is grouped here, rather than as A.

Personal, Pr. All objects of personal decorative use are Pr. Examples are 'fan,' 'perfume bottle,' 'bow tie.' It is a valuable grouping, leading in some patients to disclosure of important personal trends.

Recreation, Rc. Most of these percepts are children's games, but some are adult sport associations ('boxing'). Objects used in any of the games are also Rc, e.g., 'top.'

Religion, Rl. These responses are usually easily identified. Double content notation is frequent, with H primary, when the association names a person of religious significance, e.g., 'Mary,' 'Moses.' This grouping includes also religion associations of other cultures, e.g., 'Buddha.'

Rural, Ru. A useful classification, especially in our urban culture. It includes objects that are characteristic only of the rural scene, e.g., 'haystack,' 'barn.'

Science, Sc. Specimens, living or not, seen in scientific work, also the tools of science, belong here. The category is quickly identified, usually from the terminology.

Sex, Sex. All obvious names of sex organs are here included, also secondary sexual body parts, usually outer (e.g., 'breast'). Many anatomy responses are also Sex in content.

Travel, Tr. All means of travel, by land, sea, or air, and all parts of such travel media are here grouped. There is occasional overlapping on other content grouping, e.g., 'canoe,' Rc, or when an airplane is an instrument of war, and noted as 'war.'

Vocation, Vo. Some content is closely associated with a specific vocation: thus, 'plasterer's trowel,' 'wheelbarrow.' Overlapping on Im, e.g., 'stethoscope,' occurs, but these are specialized enough to uncover an interest valence.

DOUBLE CONTENT DESIGNATION

'An Assyrian lion' in figure X (D 2) would be scored D F+ A, Art. It is necessary to indicate the animal content for the purpose of the animal percentage in the summary, and also the especial interest in art. This kind of overlapping interest is very frequent. Ds 8 of figure IX may be seen as 'a lovely vase.' The inquiry shows that S is simultaneously contemplating an art object and something useful in the home. Therefore Ds F+ Hh, Art, records both interests. Other examples are:

'A lobster (fig. II, D 3) red, as if cooked,' scored D F− A, Fd.

In figure III, D 3 is seen as 'underpants hanging on a clothes line.' Scored D F− Cg, Sex.

In figure V, D 1 is 'the skeletal head of a horse' or 'a prehistoric monster.' Scored D F− An, Sc.

Content in the Rorschach test reveals the mental furniture in S. It is thus a source of knowledge concerning his interests, and through the avenue of these, in many instances, concerning his personal needs. The double notation helps in this inspection of interests. For purposes of the summary, however, only the first of these content scores is used; i.e., in the last-cited example above we use simply A as part of the count of animal responses; the score Art is just so much additional qualitative information.

CHAPTER XVII

SHOCK

With this chapter we are making a transition from basic processes to whole personality interpretation. What a shock finding tells depends always on what the whole person is. The finding can be known only from the basic data that are the province of this volume.

Shock reactions are in two modalities: the one is set off by the color stimuli and the other by the shadings. The identifying observations are both quantitative and qualitative.

The exposition that follows is lifted almost bodily from my previous descriptions of shock.[8] Certain other shock behaviors have meanwhile been described by Bohm[12] and by Loosli-Usteri,[20] and these are reported below.

COLOR SHOCK

This is observed, as the term indicates, in the test figures with chromatic details in them. The order of the figures as shock inducers, from most to least, both in frequency and in degree of severity, are II, IX, VIII, X, III; with little to choose between II and IX for first place (no statistical basis for this estimate; only an empiric judgment), and with VIII not far behind. While rare in X, it is severe when occurring. Figure III very seldom in itself induces shock; when found in this figure it is likely a delayed effect from figure II. The observable evidences of shock are: (1) strictly *quantitative*. Time per first response retarded. Scorable productivity significantly reduced. Organization activity, Z, diminished or lacking. Form accuracy, i.e., F+, reduced. Popular responses, P, lacking or delayed. Animal content increased. Emergence of x responses, or trends to. Hd percepts rather than H; Ad rather than A. Rejection of the figure without scorable association. Affective ratio for the shock figures measures less than 0.40. The lambda index in the shock figure shifts as compared with this measure for this S in the other test figures, becoming either very low or very high. Sequence shift toward the less controlled, i.e., from methodical to irregular, or from irregular to confused. Approach is thrown off balance in the direction of any of the three variables, W, D, Dd, at the cost of attention to either or both of the others; in many cases the attention is fettered to the Dd and other minutiae on the test figures.

(2) *Normative but not measurable.* Fantasy activity, M, in the shock figure either (a) increased in quantity and if so even more notably regressed in structure (M−, Dd M, M Hd, and especially M in A), with private

222

world, regressive, autistic content, or (b) reduced as compared with expectancy for the test record as a whole, or totally lacking. In the color-determined associations, domination by the regressive structures: FC−, CF and especially CF−, C. Deterioration in the thought content: pathologic anatomy, regressive sex percepts, anal. (3) *More qualitative observations.* Thought content is unique, individualized. Avoidance of, flight from, rejection of, color-determined associations, i.e., naming the colors, without scorable associations; forthright expression of displeasure ("This is ugly" "I don't like these colors"); and much talk around the colored details, sometimes undirected talk, without scorable content. Increased qualifying of the responses, apologetics, trends to reject particular associations or the entire test figure. Notably more turning of the shock cards in a restless manner; edging; gestures related to unpleasant affect; speech disturbances, e.g., hesitations, and near stutterings.

SHOCK AT THE DYSPHORIC AFFECTS. SHADING SHOCK

The order of effectiveness of the all-gray figures as shock inducers is: IV, VII, VI, I, V. The difference in degree of the disturbance induced is small as between IV, VII, VI, but they differ in respect to the personal focus of anxiety which each stirs up. Figure I infrequently sets shock going, but the upset can be a severe one. So far as figure V is concerned, I find myself revising my former conclusions, i.e., that apparent shock here manifested is a carry-over from IV. It is that sometimes. But V does activate disturbance on its own, and again the focus of anxiety which it probes is specific for it. The observable shading shock data in the main parallel, and differ only in small amount from, those described for shock at the lively affects.

Thus, (1) *strictly quantitative.* Retarded time per first responses; reduced productivity; Z diminished or totally lost; F+ reduced; P lacking or delayed; animal per cent heightened; Hd, Ad, and x responses; rejections; shifts in lambda; imbalance in Ap; deterioration in Seq.

(2) *Normative, not measurable.* M may (a) burgeon, with regressive structure and themes, or (b) sharply decline or be lost altogether. The shading and the vista determinants are naturally more frequent in the five all-dark figures. When one of these triggers the anxiety shock, it will be manifest in both deterioration of form accuracy and in heavier saturation by the shading quality: FY−, FV−; YF, and VF, and especially YF− and VF−; Y, and more rarely, V.

(3) *More qualitative observations.* The unique, pathologic, regressive themes. The qualifications, and these can be inordinately heavy, more so than in the color figures, with long circumlocutions and pathetic apologetics and self-devaluings or doubtings. The motor and language behaviors de-

scribed for color shock can be even more severe at shading shock; most drastic are some of the expressions of repulsion, especially for figures IV and VI.

SHOCK ANTI-SHOCK

In this defense against a trend to disruption, S's behaviors in the shock figures are: time per first response is markedly faster than in the other test cards; productivity significantly greater; heightened interest, in some S's, in symmetry; F+ heightened; M release greater than to be expected from the test pattern as whole but likely to be regressive in structure and autistic in content; phobic ideas. In all these, S is trying to counteract his anxiety by reacting in ways the very contrary to those toward which it impels him: a psychologic toxin-antitoxin.

Not all the shock tactics, in fact only a small number, are employed by any one S. Some are reaction formations (high R, high F+, fast time per first R); some are undoings (S describes symmetry); some are binding (phobic thinking). With this language, we are, however, overstepping the bounds of basic processes and entering the area of dynamics, which is beyond the scope of the present book.

The European writers Bohm[12] and Loosli-Usteri[20] describe what the one calls "white-shock" (*Weissschock*) and the other, "void shock" (*choc au vide*). Concerning white shock, Bohm says: "It consists of a peculiar ambivalent attitude of the subject to the space details; they have attraction for him and he occupies himself with them greatly, but he does not succeed in covering up with a response" (pp. 103–104). Loosli-Usteri credits the initial observation of "void shock" to Orr,[26] who at first reported it as occurring only in figure VII. In her own description of it, Loosli-Usteri sees it as a "stuporous reaction to a test card characterized by a large hole (*creux*), notably in figures VII and IX" (p. 24). The signs of stupor consist of "all the signs of disturbance which, when manifest at the color cards, are looked on as color shock or its equivalent" (ibid.). Her paper includes response samples from test records of 70 normal women. Bohm cites its occurrence in one of the protocols he reproduces in the German text. He also describes shock for the brown and the blue details of the test (p. 103).

All these phenomena are really special forms of anxiety or color shock. The case for "white" and "void" shock (both Bohm and Loosli-Usteri distinguish their observations each from the other's) appear strong enough to warrant inquiring into them as something *sui generis*; still a form of anxiety shock but in a class by itself and diagnostically significant. Here is an open opportunity for a definitive research effort.

Chapter XVIII

SUMMARY AND STRUCTURE

Below is a record of the scorings in one Rorschach test, together with the summary into which these scoring formulas are structured. From this summary the personality is patterned out. All the symbols in these records are by now familiar to the reader, but some of the operations involved are new.

The ten cards are identified by Roman numerals, the responses by Arabic numerals. The numbers for responses are cumulative, hence the final one shows the total number of responses, or R.

After each Roman numeral, in the parentheses, is stated the time required for the first response in that figure; e.g., it was 12 seconds in figure I, 22 seconds in figure II, and so on. The total time is stated after the last scoring formula (29' 57"). This is T.

Under some of the scoring formulas, numerals are set, such as 2.5 1.0, 4.0 etc. These are the organization values, Z, credited to those responses in which there has been organization activity (see chap. VI, also App. 4).

In the summary, the number of W, D, and Dd are added to form the first column. This includes variations of these, i.e., DW. The number of white spaces (Ds and Dds) is noted in parentheses after W, D, or Dd, depending on which of these included the space form. Just below this column are stated Z sum and Zf. The former is the sum of all the weighted Z values (Appendix 4); for all the responses; Zf is the simple count of the number of times that organization responses were scored. Ap and Seq are next recorded.

In the middle column are included all the factors stemming out of the inner living: M, C, Y, T, or V, and their variations or combinations, Po when it occurs, and F. The plus and minus signs with accompanying numerals in parentheses after FC, CF, FY, or other scores tell the number of times these were labeled minus in the separate scoring formulas. When it comes to interpretation, the relative quantities of these, e.g., FC+ and FC−, provide a valuable index to certain finer nuances in the personality. Under this column, I set the calculated EB and EA (see chapter IX, p. 100).

The third column is reserved entirely for content. The importance of H, Hd, A, Ad, and An dictates the listing of them in that order. After that, no rule obtains.

The last column contains certain numerical values. The calculation of some has been described in the text. All the formulas will be found in Appendix 2.

The white space total (s) is reported both as the absolute incidence and as a percentage. This is obtained simply by adding the total of space percepts in the parentheses after W, D, Dd. Here also P is recorded in terms of the absolute incidence. Below this column are stated the time and fluctuation findings.

SCORINGS

I. (12″)	1. W FY+ An	
		1.0
	2. W F+ A P	
		1.0
	3. D F+ Hd	
	4. D M+ H	
	5. D YF+ A	
II. (22″)	6. W M.Y+ A	
		4.0
	7. D CF+ Cg	
III. (2″)	8. D M+ H P	
		4.0
	9. D F+ A	
	10. D F+ A	
	11. Ds F− Hd	
	12. D F− Hd	
	13. Dd F+ Hd	
	14. Dd F+ Hd	
IV. (18″)	15. D F+ Hd	
	16. W F+ A	
		2.0
V. (2″)	17. W F+ A P	
		1.0

VI. (14″)	18. W F+ A	
		2.5
	19. Dd F− Hd	
	20. W F+ A P	
		2.0
VII. (11″)	21. D F+ Hd P	
		3.0
	22. D F+ Hd	
	23. D F+ Hd Rc	
VIII. (5″)	24. DW CF+ An	
	25. D F+ A P	
	26. Ds FY+ An	
IX. (12″)	27. D F+ A	
	28. D F− A	
	29. Ds F+ Mu	
X. (9″)	30. D CF+ A	
	31. D F+ A P	
	32. D FC+ A	
	33. D FY+ A	
	34. D F+ A	

Total time 29′ 57″
Summary
R 34

W	7	M	2	H	2	F+	83
DW	1	M.Y	1	Hd	10		
D	23 (s 3)	CF	3	A	17	A	50
Dd	3	FC	1	An	3		
	—	YF	1	Cg	1	P	7
	34	FY	3	Mu	1		
Z	20.5	F+	19		—	S	3
Z f	9	F−	4		34	S %	8.8
Ap	W D Dd		—			T/R	52.9
Seq	methodical		34			T/1R	10.7
		EB	3/3.5				
		EA	6.5				

It will be noted that the sums of the scoring symbols in the first, second, and third columns in each case add up to R, or the total number of responses. This follows from the fact that each response is scored once for each of these columns, i.e., with respect to (1) what is selected, (2) the determinant, and (3) the content. When double content is noted in the same response, as in response 23, D F+ Hd Rc, only the primary content, Hd in this instance, is entered in the summary. Thus, the total checks; at the same time, the additional interest can influence the personality evaluation.

With the completion of the summary, the task of observing the Rorschach test behaviors ends. Here the interpretation labor begins. E here ceases to be a recorder. He becomes a psychologist. How good he will be in grasping the psychological significance of his test data will be a function of three variables: how accurately and impersonally he has observed and recorded; how soundly he knows the Rorschach test concepts; and how deeply as well as broadly he knows human nature. The Rorschach test answers no questions. It is only ten ink blots. It is never better than the brain of the psychologist using it.

APPENDICES

APPENDIX 1

TABLE 12.—*Synopsis of Rorschach test scorings and the test behaviors to which they refer*

The Intellectual Sphere		The Affective Sphere	
R	scored productivity	M	percept as a movement
W	whole	C	undiluted color determinant
Z	synthesized percept	CF	color modulated by form
D	isolated detail percept	FC	form dominant over color
Dd	rare detail	Y	undiluted shading determinant
Ap	selective approach	YF	shading modulated by form
Seq	selective sequence	FY	form dominant over shading
F+ per	perceptual accuracy	V	undiluted vista determinant
cent		VF	vista modulated by form
A	animal content	FV	form dominant over vista
P	most popular percepts	T	undiluted texture determinant
L	intellect-dominated percept	TF	texture modulated by form
		FT	form dominant over texture
		F+	accurate percepts
T/R	average time for response	F—	inaccurate percepts
T/first R	average time for first response	F	accuracy not known
		Po	position-determined response
Fln R	fluctuation of productivity between cards		
Fln T/first R	fluctuation of time for first response		

228

APPENDIX 2

TABLE 13.—*Numerical values and formulas*

Ap, for R 32 is W, 6; D, 23; Dd 3.

Z sum: total of weighted Z scorings.

Z f: simple frequency of Z scorings.

C 1.5; CF 1.0; FC 0.5; C_{sum} = sum of all C values

M 1.0; EB = all M/C_{sum}; EA = sum $M + C_{sum}$

F+ per cent: $\dfrac{F+}{(F+) + (F-)}$

A per cent: $\dfrac{A + Ad}{R}$

P: absolute number of P

s per cent: $\dfrac{all \; s}{R}$

Af r: $\dfrac{R(VIII, IX, X)}{R(I - VII)}$

L: $\dfrac{(F+) + (F-) + (F)}{R - [(F+) + (F-) + (F)]}$

T/R: $\dfrac{\text{total free association time}}{R}$

T/first R: $\dfrac{\text{sum of time for first R}}{10 \text{ (or by } 10 - \text{ number of rejected cards)}}$

Fln R: $\dfrac{\text{sum (diffs R I, II, R II, III} \ldots \text{R IX, X)}}{9 \text{ (or by } 9 - \text{ number of rejects)}}$

Fln T/IR: $\dfrac{\text{sum (diffs R I, II} \ldots \text{R IX, X)}}{9 \text{ (or by } 9 - \text{ number of rejects)}}$

APPENDIX 3

NORMS

The means here listed are selected out of more extensive findings in various researches. The figures for the adults were obtained from a population sample (157) representative of the middle range of urban (Chicago) Americans. The statistics are not valid for persons of much higher intelligence endowment, say in the upper five per cent of our population. The children (155) similarly were out of middle to lower middle-class sectors, with those in the 14–17 year group including some from high schools in the above average population range. For fuller data, including some significant differences among the healthy, neurotic, and schizophrenic samples, the student must be referred to the respective publications.[9, 23]

TABLE 14

	Adults Means	Children All Means	Ages 6–9 Means	Ages 10–13 Means	Ages 14–17 Means
R	32.65	27.15	21.93	27.40	41.35
W	5.50	3.14	2.64	2.77	5.08
D	22.85	20.0	16.21	19.9	30.34
Dd	3.02	4.46	3.0	4.81	5.76
Z	22.48*	11.05	7.15	8.45	28.90
M	3.50	1.28	0.87	1.02	3.04
C sum	3.11	2.02	1.98	1.62	3.03
C	0.49	0.35	0.43	0.27	0.33
CF	1.44	0.81	0.74	0.47	1.92
FC	1.36	0.98	0.99	0.92	1.13
Y, YF, FY Total Number	1.96	1.08	0.84	0.58	2.92
FY	1.41	0.81	0.55	0.42	2.50
V, VF, FV Total Number	1.84	1.12	0.90	1.06	1.92
FV	1.04	1.08	0.87	1.0	1.87
Af r	range:0.40–0.60	0.57	0.53	0.59	0.60
H	4.02	2.03	1.68	1.86	3.50
Hd	1.78	3.74	2.30	3.16	4.16
An	1.55				
F+ per cent	79.25	70.05	67.17	73.69	70.95
A per cent	46.65	47.95	45.86	51.68	48.85
P, number	7.0	4.54	3.19	5.23	6.75
L, range† 1.50–2.50		†	†	†	†
s, number	1.90	1.14	0.75	1.19	2.08
s per cent	5.87	3.9	2.8	4.6	3.9
T/IR‡					
T/R, range	15″–30″				
FLN R	1.35	1.16	0.92	1.21	1.67
Fln T/IR	23.36	25.85	27.0	32.11	14.1

Footnotes for Table 14

* This is the mean for the weighted Z scores. Its near equivalent Z f range (frequency of Z responses) is 7–8 as can be seen from the Wilson and Blake[34] table.

† Lambda statistics were obtained by a formula which I no longer use. My 1.50–2.50 rule is an empiric one. For children it runs somewhat higher, in the 6–9 and the 10–13 year olds, a range of about 1.75–3.00. But it is moderately lower for the 14–17 ages, i.e., the full-blown adolescents; nearer 1.25–2.50.

‡ Average initial response is not a meaningful statistic for two reasons. One, it differs for the ten cards, the range of the means being 20.86–37.80.[7] Secondly, even more important for clinical purposes is that each patient's deviation in initial response time has meaning only from his own average as a frame of reference, not from that of a population sample.

APPENDIX 4

TABLE 15.—*Organization (Z) Values in the Ten Figures*

Figures	Type of Organization (Z)			
	W	Adjacent Detail	Distant Detail	Solid with White Ds, Dds
I	1.0	4.0	6.0	3.5
II	4.5	3.0	5.5	4.5
III	5.5	3.0	4.0	4.5
IV	2.0	4.0	3.5	5.0
V	1.0	2.5	5.0	4.0
VI	2.5	2.5	6.0	6.5
VII	2.5	1.0	3.0	4.0
VIII	4.5	3.0	3.0	4.0
IX	5.5	2.5	4.5	5.0
X	5.5	4.0	4.5	6.0

Refer also to pp. 51; 56; 57, for special kinds of Z occurring in figures III, VI, and VII.

APPENDIX 5
CONVERSION OF Z SUM INTO Zf
Best total weighted Z prediction when total number of Z responses is known†

Zf	Best Z prediction (to nearest .5)	Zf	Best Z prediction (to nearest .5)
1	‡	26	88.0
2	2.5	27	91.5
3	6.0	28	95.0
4	10.0	29	98.5
5	13.5	30	102.5
6	17.0	31	105.5
7	20.5	32	109.0
8	24.0	33	112.5
9	27.5	34	116.5
10	31.0	35	120.0
11	34.5	36	123.5
12	38.0	37	127.0
13	41.5	38	130.5
14	45.5	39	134.0
15	49.0	40	137.5
16	52.5	41	141.0
17	56.0	42	144.5
18	59.5	43	148.0
19	63.0	44	152.0
20	66.5	45	155.5
21	70.0	46	159.0
22	73.5	47	162.5
23	77.0	48	166.0
24	81.0	49	169.5
25	84.5	50	173.0

* After, Wilson, Glen P., and Blake, Robert R.: A methodological problem in Beck's organizational concept. *J. Consulting Psychol.* 14: 20–24, 1950.

† The standard error of an estimated Z score is 4.74.

‡ Regression line does not cross the x axis exactly at the origin.

BIBLIOGRAPHY

1. ADLER, A.: The problem of distance. *In* The Practice and Theory of Individual Psychology. New York, Harcourt, 1924.
2. ———: Compulsion neurosis. Int. J. Indiv. Psychol. **2:** 3–22, 1936; reprinted as pp. 79–90 of *Reflex to Intelligence*, (Eds., Beck, S. J., and Molish, H. B.) Glencoe, Illinois, Free Press, 1959.
3. BAUGHMAN, E. E.: A new method of Rorschach inquiry. J. Proj. Techniques **22:** 381–389, 1958.
4. ———: The effect of inquiry method on Rorschach color and shading scores. J. Proj. Techniques. **23:** 3–7, 1959.
5. BECK, S. J.: Configurational tendencies in Rorschach responses. Am. J. Psychol. **45:** 433–443, 1933.
6. ———: Rorschach's Test, Vol. II, A Variety of Personality Pictures. New York, Grune & Stratton, 1945.
7. ———, RABIN, A. I., THIESEN, W. G., MOLISH, H. B., AND THETFORD, W. N.: The normal personality as projected in the Rorschach test. J. Psychol. **30:** 241–298, 1950.
8. ———: Rorschach's Test, Vol. III, Advances in Interpretation. New York, Grune & Stratton, 1952.
9. ———: The six schizophrenias. Res. Monog. No. 6, Am. Orthopsychiat. Assn., New York, 1954.
10. ———: The Rorschach Experiment. New York, Grune & Stratton, 1960.
11. BINDER, H.: Die Helldunkeldeutungen im psychodiagnostischen Experiment von Rorschach. Zurich, Orell Füssli, 1932.
12. BOHM, E.: A Textbook in Rorschach Test Diagnosis. New York, Grune & Stratton, 1958.
13. FORD, M.: The Application of the Rorschach Test to Young Children. Minneapolis, Univ. of Minn. Press, 1946.
14. GOLDFARB, W.: Organization activity in the Rorschach examination. Am. J. Orthopsychiat. **15:** 525–528, 1945.
15. HERTZ, M. R.: Frequency tables for scoring responses to the Rorschach ink-blot test. Cleveland, Western Reserve University Press. 1951, ed. 3.
16. KLOPFER, B., AND KELLEY, D. M.: The Rorschach Technique. New York, World Bk. Co., 1942.
17. ———, Ed. Developments in the Rorschach Technique. Vol. I, 1954; Vol. II, 1956. Yonkers, World Book Co.
18. KROPP, R. B.: The Rorschach "Z" Score. J. Proj. Techniques **19:** 443–452, 1954.
19. LOOSLI-USTERI, M.: Le test de Rorschach appliqué à différents groupes d'enfants de 10–13 ans. Arch. de psychol. **22:** 51–106, 1929.
20. ———: A propos du choc au vide. Rorschachiana IV. Berne, Huber, 1953.
21. LÖPFE, A.: Über Rorschach'sche Formdeutversuche mit 10–13jährigen Knaben. Ztschr. f. ang. Psychol. **26:** 202–53, 1925.
22. McCALL, R. J., AND DOLEYS, E. J.: Popular responses on the Rorschach test in relation to the number of responses. J. Clin. Psychol. **11:** 300–302, 1955.
23. MOLISH, H. B.: The popular response in the Rorschach records of normals, neurotics and schizophrenics. Am. J. Orthopsychiat. **21:** 523–531, 1951.

24. OBERHOLZER, E.: *In* Dubois, C.: The People of Alor. Minneapolis, Univ. of Minn. Press, 1944.

25. ———: Zur Differentialdiagnose psychischer Folgezustände nach Schädeltraumen mittels des Rorschachschen Formdeutversuchs. Ztschr. f. d. ges. Neurol. u. Psychiat. **136**: 596–629, 1931.

26. ORR, M.: Le test de Rorschach et l'imago maternelle. Groupement francais de Rorschach. Paris, 1958.

27. RORSCHACH, H. Psychodiagnostik: Methodik und Ergebnisse eines Wahrnehmungsdiagnostischen Experiments (ed. 2). Bern, Huber, 1932. All references are to the English translation by Lemkau, P., and Kronenberg, B. New York, Grune & Stratton, 1942.

28. ———, AND OBERHOLZER, E.: Zur Auswertung des Formdeutversuchs. Ztschr. f. d. gesam. Neurol. u. Psychiat. **82**: 240–74, 1923. Republished in Rorschach, H.: Psychodiagnostik (see above), pp. 193–227 (Engl. transl., pp. 184–216).

29. SCHACHTEL, E. G.: Projection and its relation to character attitudes and creativity in kinesthetic responses: Contributions to an understanding of Rorschach's test, IV. Psychiatry **13**: 69–100, 1950.

30. SCHACHTER, M.: Contribution à l'étude du psychodiagnostic de Rorschach chez des jumeaux. Encephale. **41**: 23–44, 1952.

31. SCHAFER, R.: Psychoanalytic Interpretation in Rorschach Testing: Theory and application. New York, Grune & Stratton, 1954.

32. SMALL, L.: Rorschach Location and Scoring Manual. New York, Grune & Stratton, 1956.

33. THETFORD, W. N., MOLISH, H. B., AND BECK, S. J.: Developmental aspects of personality structure in normal children. J. Proj. Techniques **15**: 58–78, 1951.

34. WILSON, G. P., AND BLAKE, R. R.: A methodological problem in Beck's organizational concept. J. Cons. Psychol. **14**: 20–24, 1950.

35. Zeitschrift für Diagnostische Psychologie und Persönlichkeitsforschung. Bern, Hans Huber.

INDEX